p 199   The "3 Door" problem

p 229   SEND + MORE = MONEY

p 242   The only one where Marilyn was
          corrected by a reader

p 237   No. of ancestors

Ask Marilyn ®

Illustrations by Andy Rush

Marilyn vos Savant

♦ ♦ ♦

Ask Marilyn ®

The Best of "Ask Marilyn"® Letters Published in

PARADE

Magazine from *1986* to *1992*

and Many More Never Before Published

St. Martin's Press ♦ New York

Design by Judith A. Stagnitto

Word problem on pages 216–217 from *Scott, Foresman's Algebra,* © 1984 by Scott, Foresman and Company. Reprinted by permission of the publisher.

Library of Congress Cataloging-in-Publication Data

Vos Savant, Marilyn Mach.
      Ask Marilyn / Marilyn Vos Savant.
         p.   cm.
      ISBN 0-312-08136-7
      1. Questions and answers. I. Title.
    AG195.V66 1992
    031.02—dc20   92-25226
                                CIP

First Edition: October 1992
10 9 8 7 6 5 4 3 2 1

To
Walter Anderson,
who always tries to keep me out of trouble
but doesn't always succeed

Contents

$\blacklozenge$

Part Three: Nature at Work and at Play

The 3 - Door Problem — -199..200

Part Four: Thinking About Thinking

Part Five: Questions That Need No Answer!

CONTENTS

A Letter to Readers

Dear Readers:

Sometime last year, I bought a new pair of shoes, and it took me nearly a month to break them in. But then they became my favorites, so it's not surprising that I was pleased when I ran across a brand-new pair of the same shoes not long ago, and I carted them home with great satisfaction. What *was* surprising was that when I sat down at my dressing table and put them on for the first time, they fit perfectly. Reluctantly, I came to the conclusion that I hadn't broken in that first pair of shoes—I'd broken in my feet!

And that's the way it's been with the "Ask Marilyn" column that appears in the most widely read magazine in the United States—*Parade*, the Sunday magazine in more than 343 newspapers, which has a circulation of 36 million and a readership of 70 million, the largest in the world.

After reading an article about me that was being written by one of his writers, Walter Anderson, the editor of *PARADE*, contacted me. We met for lunch, where the two of us looked at each other warily. "How would you feel about taking a risk?" he asked me. Well, Walter's a big guy, an ex-marine, and I felt pretty sure that I was no match for him in the "risk" category, but I asked him what he had in mind. "We'd like you to answer a few questions for us in print. It would follow the article about you. What do you think?"

Compared to combat, it didn't sound like a risk at all, and I told him so, but he assured me that it was. "Our readers will let you know how they feel about your answers, and that's a judgment you'll have to accept, whether you like it or not."

That gave me pause. I see myself as objective as I can be, an "independent" with regard to both politics and religion, and only an "armchair" feminist. But what if they hated what I wrote? Or worse, what if they just didn't care? The prospect of knowing that answer kindled my interest. "I'd like to try it," I told him. "Passing up an opportunity to hear that verdict would be about as easy as throwing away your laboratory tests unopened."

He leaned back in his chair, ordered coffee, and smiled. Walter Anderson knew what to say to me, all right.

The article was published in *Parade*, and the next thing I knew, more than a thousand letters arrived in my office. Nearly all of them contained more questions, and "Ask Marilyn" was launched. I had one idea after another about how to handle the column, but millions of readers can exert considerable influence, and, as with those shoes I mentioned, we developed a very comfortable fit. (I'll tell you about the blisters later in the book.)

Over the next five years, I received tens of thousands of letters. I've heard from everyone from prisoners to priests, and I've been sent everything from baked goods to bibles. (One lovely, hand-knit sweater somehow became separated from its return address, and I *still* feel bad about not being able to acknowledge it.)

Sara Brzowsky, the unsung heroine behind this column and the editor who has personally handled it from the start, operates, like a physician, on the principle, "First of all, do no harm," and has become a genius at spotting ambiguities and weaknesses and nudging me into making improvements.

But most important to me, by far, are my readers. You have given the gift of life to this column and made "Ask Marilyn" into what you wanted—a reflection of what's best about America.

Sincerely,

Marilyn vos Savant

Marilyn vos Savant
New York City
May, 1992

Part One

The Pleasure and Pain

of Being Human

1.

Good and Evil

Dear Marilyn:
How do you tell the difference between good and evil?

L. Jaeger
Brooklyn, New York

Dear L.:
You give it power.

◆ ◆ ◆

Dear Marilyn:
Please define the nature of good and evil.

Larry Woods
Las Vegas, Nevada

Dear Larry:
It seems that good has become what we want, and evil has become what we don't want.

◆ ◆ ◆

The following answer was published, but I've since learned that I was wrong.

Dear Marilyn:
Is humankind basically evil or good?

Donald W. Douglass
Kingston, Washington

Dear Donald:

Well, I wouldn't go so far as to say we're evil, but I don't know of any *other* animals that kill for sport.

Apparently, there are plenty of other animals that do kill "for no good reason," but we've been reluctant to admit it.

◆ ◆ ◆

Dear Marilyn:

What is the greatest punishment for anybody?

George W. Howe
Fredericksburg, Virginia

Dear George:

Other than the penal system and excluding inhumane punishments, ostracism ranks among the most profound. One of the harshest of penalties is to be shunned by good people.

◆ ◆ ◆

Dear Marilyn:

Is "bad" the opposite of "good"? And is "not good" also the opposite of "good"? If both answers are yes, then does "bad" equal "not good"?

Sue Sheeley
Idaho Falls, Idaho

Dear Sue:

We can call "bad" an opposite of "good," but we can't call "not good" an opposite. After all, "black" may be an opposite of "white," but we can't call "not white" an opposite, can we? The whole rainbow of colors is "not white."

◆ ◆ ◆

Dear Marilyn:

Good things seem to require constant effort. And if no effort is used, I think it has become a compulsion. Conversely, I think "bad things" initially require less effort, and in the final analysis, no effort at all. My question is, "Is there such a thing as a good habit?"

Shawn McCraney
Mission Viejo, California

Dear Shawn:

I think so; we differ on this matter. You seem to feel that humankind is uncaring and lazy by nature, that goodness and enterprising behavior come about only as a result of great effort, and if little exertion seems required, we're more neurotic than humane or wise! Instead, I think that man and woman are highly social animals, very fond of living in community, and are therefore likely to be kind by disposition. I also think that shiftless people have a much harder life than industrious ones. Speaking for myself, I've always found it *easy* to hang up my clothes or to hug an ugly dog.

◆ ◆ ◆

Dear Marilyn:

Who is a perfect altruist?

Erika Krech
Mansfield, Ohio

Dear Erika:

I doubt that anyone can hold that title because of the great diversity of the value systems learned at an early age from the various religions. What one person perceives as compassionate—for example, providing drug addicts with clean needles at no charge to help keep them free of AIDS—is seen by another person as disgraceful behavior.

◆ ◆ ◆

Dear Marilyn:

Can you compare the survival value of loving behavior to that of aggressive competition?

Monte R. Hall
Klamath Falls, Oregon

Dear Monte:

I'd say that loving behavior contributes to the group at the expense of the individual. Competition contributes to the survival of the individual at the expense of the group. In the garden of life, some people are more like flowers, and other people are more like weeds.

2.

Human Nature

Dear Marilyn:
   How would you define "normal"? And "conventional"?

Robert D. Kauffman
Asheville, North Carolina

Dear Robert:
   "Normal" is wanting to be the president. "Conventional" is telling everyone how awful it would be.

♦ ♦ ♦

Dear Marilyn:
   How do you tell the difference between a kook and an eccentric person?

Julian Hammer
Carteret, New Jersey

Dear Julian:
   From what I read in the newspapers, a person with money gets the title of "eccentric" for the same behavior that gets a person without money the title of "crackpot."

♦ ♦ ♦

Dear Marilyn:
   What is human nature?

John A. Prata
Hudson, New York

Dear John:

I'd say that human nature describes how people would behave if there were no outside influences such as church or state. This is impossible to describe in such a short space, but self-interest would probably play a major role, and I don't see that as bad. I don't believe it's healthy for us to be taught to consider ourselves less worthy than other individuals.

◆ ◆ ◆

Dear Marilyn:

Why is it that mankind dedicates his whole lifetime to pleasing others rather than trying to please himself?

Susan Bibb
Havelock, North Carolina

Dear Susan:

Probably because he's been taught—by others! But this can be very ineffective. What we think would please others is unlikely to be what would actually please them. How many times, for example, have you received a gift from an associate that is just what you would have chosen for yourself? And what we think *should* please others is even *less* likely to satisfy. Hardly a person exists who would enjoy having his mother choose his wardrobe.

◆ ◆ ◆

Dear Marilyn:

Would we (or could we) change if we could see ourselves as others see us?

Jerry Lurie
Dothan, Alabama

Dear Jerry:

I think we certainly *could* change. After all, we routinely change for far lesser reasons than that. Whether we *would* change, though, might depend upon whether we actually dislike what we see or whether we just gain a new perspective on ourselves.

◆ ◆ ◆

Dear Marilyn:

Am I who *I* think I am? Or am I who everybody *else* thinks I am?

J. K.
Edgewood, Maryland

Dear Reader:

I suspect you're who *you* think you are, even if you never admit it to yourself or to anyone else. You may be in the worst position to judge, but you're in the best position to know.

◆ ◆ ◆

Dear Marilyn:

Please don't laugh at these questions; I've been trying to sort this out for fifty years. What is a pretty woman? What is a beautiful woman? What is a gorgeous woman?

Emily Spencer
Crown Point, Indiana

Dear Emily:

A pretty woman is one who turns the heads of the teenage boys as she walks by the bus stop. A beautiful woman is one who turns the heads of the men, too. But it takes a *gorgeous* woman to turn the heads of the *women* there.

◆ ◆ ◆

Dear Marilyn:

Aside from the fact that "beauty is in the eyes of the beholder," what makes a person photogenic or not? Why do some attractive people not photograph well when others' looks seem to be enhanced greatly?

Mike Morrow
Jacksonville, Florida

Dear Mike:

For still photographs, where this is most dramatic, I'd say that attractive people who don't photograph well frequently have attributes like poise, grace, and charm. But more ordinary people who *do* photograph well may lack those qualities and instead have comparatively good bone structure. The classic case, of course, is the woman who can be made to look gorgeous in a photograph, but who is unrecognized as anything special by her neighbors without the careful attention to makeup, lighting, and the like.

◆ ◆ ◆

Dear Marilyn:

I'm curious to know why some clearly gorgeous people are not conceited and why are some obviously unattractive people *are*.

Tricia Marrapodi
Tucson, Arizona

Dear Tricia:

Maybe these people don't consider looks to be that important. Unfortunately, this may be a minority view. I'm always dismayed to hear a man or woman express surprise when a good-looking member of the opposite sex turns out not to have any other positive qualities as though these attributes were somehow supposed to be related to looks. Whether a computer is cute has nothing to do with how it works; whether a stereo speaker looks adorable has nothing to do with how it sounds; whether a medicine is pretty has nothing to do with how it heals. A good-looking person is just an ordinary person wearing an attractive mask (and hoping to remain undiscovered).

◆ ◆ ◆

Dear Marilyn:

I guess I'm old-fashioned, but I cannot for the life of me understand why men wear earrings. Would you please be so kind as to explain it for me?

D. B.
San Diego, California

Dear Reader:

How can I? I've never figured out why *women* wear them!

◆ ◆ ◆

Dear Marilyn:

Is it true that you can't trust a man who wears a bow tie?

Julian Hammer
Carteret, New Jersey

Dear Julian:

If it is, women are in big trouble. Look at what every man wears on his wedding day!

◆ ◆ ◆

Dear Marilyn:

What is a way to determine whether someone's advice is sound?

John Sherman
Berrien Springs, Michigan

Dear John:

A person who gives sound advice is asked for advice more often than he or she offers it.

◆ ◆ ◆

Dear Marilyn:

If a person makes the statement, "I know I'm not supposed to tell you this," when he obviously can't *wait* to tell you, and then after telling you, he wants you to swear not to tell anyone what he told you, what would be your opinion of him or her?

Vivian Renetta Gifford
Fort Worth, Texas

Dear Vivian:

Pretty low—even lower than my opinion of the person who *listened.*

◆ ◆ ◆

Dear Marilyn:

What do you suppose is the most talked-about subject among the peoples of the world?

A. Bruner
Granbury, Texas

Dear A.:

Honestly, I think we talk more about *ourselves* than anything else!

◆ ◆ ◆

Dear Marilyn:

What do you do when you're a captive audience of people who talk incessantly? I have close friends whom I like very much, but I don't visit them or invite them over often because the ceaseless chatter is so nerve-wracking. Nothing seems to work.

Lawrence F. Terry
Baltimore, Maryland

Dear Lawrence:

Let me tell you what *I* do—I interrupt them constantly. This relieves them of the burden of talking continuously if they don't really want to do that, and it keeps them from getting their way if they *do.* And anyway, it's a good exercise in assertiveness.

◆ ◆ ◆

Dear Marilyn:

How does one go about improving one's self in the art of repartee, or is it innate?

Charmaine Griffith
Brooklyn, New York

Dear Charmaine:

I've never tried (or wanted) to dazzle the dinner guests with clever comebacks, but if did, I would practice by talking to lots of strangers—on the bus, standing in line, or sitting in the dentist's waiting room. Your friends will be too polite to give you accurate feedback, and strangers will represent a far wider range of people.

◆ ◆ ◆

Dear Marilyn:

Are people who hate being alone lacking in understanding?
                                        Gary P. Delaney
                                        Hilton Head Island, South Carolina

Dear Gary:

I'd say instead that they're lacking in self-respect.

◆ ◆ ◆

Dear Marilyn:

Do you believe a person would want to know when he or she will die?

                                                        Anonymous
                                                        New Jersey

Dear Reader:

I think so. Can you imagine receiving an envelope in the mail that you knew contained that information and *not* opening it? (Admittedly, you'd sit down first. But just think of the sheer *joy* of knowing. Why, you could take up *parachuting* if you wanted to!)

But paraplegics wrote in to point out that you could not take up parachuting unless you didn't fear what had happened to them.

◆ ◆ ◆

Dear Marilyn:

As each holiday season approaches, I am appalled at the nonsense people buy. What do *you* think about it? Every time I mention this to anyone, I get called "Scrooge."

                                                        Anonymous

Dear Reader:

Necessity used to be "the mother of invention," but now invention is becoming the mother of necessity.

◆ ◆ ◆

Dear Marilyn:

Why is it that if we have a project that would take six hours to complete, and we keep putting it off until close to the deadline, we are able to complete it in maybe only two hours?

Sharon Jones
Richmond, Virginia

Dear Sharon:

Because it's never too late to do a bad job.

◆ ◆ ◆

Dear Marilyn:

What is your definition of a fool?

Gerta Huck
Escondido, California

Dear Gerta:

A fool is someone whose pencil wears out before its eraser does.

◆ ◆ ◆

Dear Marilyn:

Are people usually more bright or less bright than they think?

Anonymous

Dear Reader:

More bright—far more than they would ever believe. Either people seldom realize how bright they really are, or in other instances, they put on a facade of confidence that they rarely feel. The bad news is that our first twenty years of intellectual passivity are difficult to put behind us, and most of us never rebound from our early teachings. However, the man or woman on the street, regardless of how he or she evaluates himself or herself, has a core of great intelligence that usually remains untapped unless he or she happens to run into someone who knows it's there and how to find it. The good news is that we each can be that "someone" for ourselves.

◆ ◆ ◆

Dear Marilyn:

Should a woman ever hide her intelligence?

Anonymous

Dear Reader:

A woman, like a man, should hide her intelligence only around her enemies.

◆ ◆ ◆

Dear Marilyn:

Do extremely intelligent people find regular people boring?

Karen Fleming
Akron, Ohio

Dear Karen:

I think many intelligent people find others more *threatening* than boring. This mainly occurs because that's the way the "intelligent" people so often find out that they're not quite as smart as they think they are.

◆ ◆ ◆

Dear Marilyn:

Does the fear of boredom increase proportionately with intelligence?

Gary Howell
San Diego, California

Dear Gary:

Yes. The more intelligent the person, the more you fear you will be bored by him or her.

◆ ◆ ◆

Dear Marilyn:

Who recuperates first, the person who does physical labor or the person who does mental work?

Anonymous
Schenectady, New York

Dear Reader:

I'd say it's the person who performs manual labor because our bodies are far more forgiving than our minds. Our muscles have long forgotten the marathon we ran last year, but our minds will always remember the feeling of finishing last. Or first.

By the way, I want to point out that the previous reader asked to remain anonymous. Now, why would that be? The question was totally innocuous. The number of people who sign the most inoffensive possible letters and request anonymity (or who don't sign their names at all) is a continual source of surprise to me. And they don't seem very likely to be shy, or they wouldn't have written in the first place, would they?

◆ ◆ ◆

Dear Marilyn:

Why are some people luckier than others?

R. E. Garms, Jr.
Tucson, Arizona

Dear R. E.:

More often than not, it's because they work harder.

◆ ◆ ◆

Dear Marilyn:

My friends all seem to luck into opportunities that I don't. Do you think it could be my fault?

Anonymous

Dear Reader:

If you never hear opportunity knock, maybe you're never at home.

◆ ◆ ◆

Dear Marilyn:

Our class was stumped by this question: Which is more dangerous— a clique or a gang? We debated it all period, but never came up with an answer.

Joel Kodicek
Chula Vista, California

Dear Joel:

I'd say a gang because "danger," to me, implies immediate threat, and the more negative aspects of a clique lie in the longer term. Believe me, if it's dark and I'm lost and tired, I will be far more unhappy to see a street gang round the corner than a bunch of snobs.

3.

Feelings

Dear Marilyn:
What is your definition of the difference between "human" and "humane"?

Lester Flatley
South Bend, Indiana

Dear Lester:
"Human" is not wanting to donate your organs after death; "humane" is agreeing to do it anyway.

◆ ◆ ◆

Dear Marilyn:
Please name the distinguishing characteristic that separates man from all other living things.

Charles Lippy
Gardners, Pennsylvania

Dear Charles:
There are many, but the one in my mind at the moment is this: man cries. This "little" distinguishing characteristic symbolizes the gulf of understanding that separates man from the other animals as much as the other animals are separated from plants.

◆ ◆ ◆

Dear Marilyn:

What is the difference between thinking and feeling?

Colleen Kelley
Spokane, Washington

Dear Colleen:

Feeling is what you get for thinking the way you do.

♦ ♦ ♦

Dear Marilyn:

Which comes first, a thought or a feeling?

Jeffrey Stacy
Greensboro, North Carolina

Dear Jeffrey:

Psychiatrists say that a thought comes first, but I once saw a fourteen-year-old boy react to Brooke Shields more like the way a dog reacts to a hambone.

But recent research has indicated that in certain situations, a feeling may indeed come first. For example, we may jerk away from the sight of a rope that unexpectedly drops down into our peripheral vision even though we see it's not a snake. It's as though the fear occurs before the rope has had a chance to fully register in our minds.

♦ ♦ ♦

Dear Marilyn:

I'd like to know what you think of dreams.

Waldemar R. Valen
Santa Rosa, California

Dear Waldemar:

I believe that dreams may well be a window to our emotions, but we haven't yet learned how to pull up the shade.

♦ ♦ ♦

Dear Marilyn:

Which is the stronger feeling: love or loyalty?

Elizabeth Klein
Richmond, Virginia

Dear Elizabeth:

Love. After all, I know of numerous dramatic places called "lovers' leaps," but not a single "loyalty leap." And contrast a "lovers' lane" with a "loyalty lane." What would people do there? Shake hands vigorously? And which do we treasure most, love letters or loyalty letters? (Unless you're the President, that is.)

◆ ◆ ◆

Dear Marilyn:
What is your own definition of love?

Bonita Velina Osborne
Detroit, Michigan

Dear Bonita:
One of my definitions is the feeling that makes you do the right thing for people regardless of who they are, whether they deserve it, and even if they'll never know it. A very simple form is the love of a boy for his pet toad; a more complex form is the love of a parent for her child. An even more abstract form, I believe, is the love of mankind, an attribute only rarely reached. Uncommon as it is, however, this is a quality I think we should consider a priority in anyone we choose as a leader.

But we must never forget how often love is foolish and misplaced, both comically and tragically. It may be more often than we'd like to think.

◆ ◆ ◆

Dear Marilyn:
The answer to this question may help me get my life together, so please think hard and try to answer it. I have a lot of love to give, yet no specific individual to give it to. What do I do with it? Also, what if there is no specific individual, ever?

Anonymous
Evansville, Indiana

Dear Reader:
If your heart isn't busy, let your head go to work: consider giving your love to the most deserving, but "neediest" individual you can find, whether at work, at school, or down the block—the person who deserves love the most but who has it the least. And don't stop with just one; give it to another and then another. But do me a favor, will you? Include a few unmarried members of the opposite sex.

◆ ◆ ◆

Dear Marilyn:

What's the difference between loving someone and being *in* love with someone?

J. C. Robillard
Port Allen, Louisiana

Dear J. C.:

If the telephone rings at three in the morning, the last voice you want to hear is that of a loved one. But when you're *in* love, that's the *first* voice you want to hear.

◆ ◆ ◆

Dear Marilyn:

As a group, the staff of the *Platte County Record Times* has come up with a question we need answered. Is love blind? And if so, why?

Donna B. Moore and Kent Sturman
Wheatland, Wyoming

Dear Donna and Kent:

Love isn't blind, but it could certainly use glasses. This, as your mother may already have told you, is a direct result of spending far too much time in the dark.

◆ ◆ ◆

Dear Marilyn:

Which is more painful—to lose someone you love by death or by divorce?

Ben Espinosa
San Diego, California

Dear Ben:

As bad as divorce can be, I think death is infinitely more painful. After all, if you were given a choice, guilt aside, of your loved one either leaving you or dying tonight, which would you choose? (Then again, maybe you'd be like the poet who said, "When he's late for dinner, and I know he must be either having an affair or lying dead in the street, I always hope he's dead.")

I received bitter letters in response, nearly all from women, and I thought I was beyond shock when I came upon the following reader's letter. (The emphases are hers.) "Divorce is infinitely more painful than the death of anyone except one's child.

"If he had died, my sons and I could have grieved and come through it. Instead, there is the constant pain of knowing he purposely left us. I live under the stigma of being a divorcée rather than receiving the sympathy accorded a widow.

"If he had died, we would have had his life insurance, retirement benefits, medical care, etc. Instead, here I am, living at a fraction of our previous standard of living, on the brink of bankruptcy, with no hope.

"My older son is so hurt by his father's betrayal, so bitter, so depressed, that he has totally given up on life. If he had died, none of this would be true. My younger son is failing ninth grade for the second time, and for no other cause except the divorce and his father's betrayal and abandonment. Again, if he had died, I am absolutely certain that this child could have continued to be the well-adjusted, happy little boy that he always was."

The above reader's ex-husband clearly took last place in her affections (she indicates she'd far rather a husband die than a child), even while providing husbandly and fatherly services that were obviously excellent or they wouldn't be missed so much. She even placed money and social acceptance before him, preferring that he die so she could have his money rather than live to use it on himself.

And then I read that her older son is so deeply embittered that he holds no hope for the future. This is pathological behavior and may well be caused by the reader's own bitterness, perhaps even as an unconscious mechanism of making the ex-husband suffer guilt, an effort to effectively prevent him from having his freedom. After all, can you imagine a healthy eighteen-year-old man having this reaction without influence? And this was bad enough without reading that she would prefer her ex-husband dead rather than have her younger son flunk the ninth grade!

After considering the matter carefully, I suggest that a woman capable of emotion this powerful would not have handled death with the equanimity she thinks.

Dear reader, you who wrote the above, please listen. You're deeply incensed by now, and I know that. I can feel the heat of your anger as I write these words. This will ruin your day, if not your week. And that's just the kind of emotion to which I'm referring. You're destroying both yourself and those around you. If only for the sake of your sons, make this the first day that you start to turn that heat down.

And if you ever stop hating me, I ask you to write again in another six months or so. I'd like to hear from you.

◆ ◆ ◆

Dear Marilyn:

If it is better to have loved and lost than never to have loved at all, then why do we have so much misery after losing a loved one?

Will Lee
Severn, Maryland

Dear Will:

We have the misery because it is better to have loved and *kept* than to have loved and *lost*.

◆ ◆ ◆

Dear Marilyn:

Which is worse to have—a broken heart or a broken spirit?

Ruth August
Lakewood, Colorado

Dear Ruth:

A broken spirit, by far. A good spirit can mend a broken heart, but a good heart can't mend a broken spirit.

◆ ◆ ◆

Dear Marilyn:

Which do you think best describes the opposite of love—hatred or indifference?

Marcia Smith
Sacramento, California

Dear Marcia:

Although I realize it's currently popular to say it's "indifference," I think it's "hate." In the interest of both the mental and physical health of all concerned, however, I strongly advocate the cultivation of indifference as an honorable alternative.

◆ ◆ ◆

Dear Marilyn:

Is it better to tell the truth and hurt someone or to lie and spare his or her feelings?

Kristin Meeker
Winston-Salem, North Carolina

Dear Kristin:

As for me, I'd rather hear bad truth than good lies because I can't fix something if I don't know it's broken.

◆ ◆ ◆

Dear Marilyn:
Which is better to hear first—the good news or the bad news?

Robyn Rutkowski
Swiftwater, Pennsylvania

Dear Robyn:
If good news makes your spirits rise the way bad news makes your spirits fall, I'd choose hearing the good news first. Your mood would ascend with the good news, then sink back to normal with the bad; the other way around, it would sink with the bad news, then ascend back to normal with the good. With the former, then, you've spent the time above normal; with the latter, you've spent it below.

◆ ◆ ◆

Dear Marilyn:
What would happen if all children were told tomorrow that there is no Santa Claus?

Kathy Hill
Clark, New Jersey

Dear Kathy:
Kindergartens would be as festive as a funeral, and there would be a junior crisis of confidence that we would richly deserve. After all, how would we react to a head of state who told us a similar fairy tale? If we want to give our smallest children gifts in celebration of our holidays, maybe we should just invent a custom in which the parents participate instead. After all, I don't know of a single child who wouldn't be even more thrilled to feel the spirit of Santa Claus in his own mom and dad.

Look at all that undeserved credit that Santa Claus gets! And then the ones who do deserve the credit get into trouble!

◆ ◆ ◆

Dear Marilyn:
Why does almost every human being feel peaceful when walking through the woods or seeing a lovely landscape?

Valerie Levack
Wallingford, Connecticut

Dear Valerie:
I'd say it's because our instincts have prepared us to feel comfortable

with nature, our native environment. We can and do learn to live with things like stereos, subways, and skyscrapers, but they are no more natural to us than an aquarium is to a goldfish.

◆ ◆ ◆

Dear Marilyn:

There are at least four things that are never satisfied. Can you name them?

Dorothy Cochrane
Putnam Valley, New York

Dear Dorothy:

A bad critic, an average baby, a good doctor, and a great artist.

◆ ◆ ◆

Dear Marilyn:

How does one go about making oneself happy?

J. Hoffmann
Troy, New York

Dear J.:

"Making" happiness implies a conscious effort, and one major area where you have a choice is your occupation, consisting not just of a title, but of an activity that "occupies" most of your day, most of your week, most of your life. For that reason, it may make more sense to choose what you actually enjoy *doing*, even if you're less than thrilled by its title, than to choose the title itself and find yourself spending most of your time performing tasks that you wouldn't especially want to do otherwise.

For example, unless you want to be strapped into a chair facing a window of nearly blinding brightness for hours at a time, most of it with little of interest to do and occasionally being scared silly, all the while responsible for the lives of hundreds of people, maybe you'd better not be a pilot.

◆ ◆ ◆

Dear Marilyn:

What is the meaning of "happy" when someone asks you, "Are you happy?"

Roy W. Hermalyn
River Edge, New Jersey

Dear Roy:

Judging just from the times that *I've* heard that question asked, both of myself and others, I'd say it usually refers to whether we feel the last major decision we made was the right one. People usually ask this question after an event like getting married or getting divorced or changing careers or giving birth to a baby. But I sometimes wonder about the motivations involved. Even when we answer, "Yes," they often follow it up with, "But are you *really* happy?" This makes me think that maybe they didn't like the *first* answer!

◆ ◆ ◆

Dear Marilyn:

Why is it so hard for some people to admit they're wrong?

Vivian Renetta Gifford
Fort Worth, Texas

Dear Vivian:

Earlier in life, when there is less self-confidence, admitting an error can cause the very real suspicion that perhaps there are other things about which we're wrong! It shakes one's faith in one's self, however misplaced. Later in life, however, errors become longer-standing, thereby compounding the problem. In other words, admitting an error that is only five minutes old usually has fewer consequences than admitting an error that is five years old or fifty years old. It is virtually intolerable, for example, to admit to yourself after thirty years that you entered the wrong occupation or married the wrong person. If life were endless, it wouldn't matter so much, but the thought of having been wrong for so long a part of a limited life may be unbearable. All of this goes to show that the sooner we admit our errors, the better, not just for the sake of the past, but for the sake of the future.

◆ ◆ ◆

Dear Marilyn:

What single thing do you believe is the best motivator of human beings?

Louise S. Lane
Richmond, Virginia

Dear Louise:

Probably love. Fear may be the most powerful motivator for defensive behavior, but love may well be the most powerful motivator for productive behavior. Fear arouses our primitive survival instincts, but I doubt that it could bring much inspiration to great artists, great scientists, or great thinkers.

♦ ♦ ♦

Dear Marilyn:

We can have mental pain or physical pain. Which, do you feel, can cause the most suffering?

Carol A. Miller
Bartlesville, Oklahoma

Dear Carol:

I suspect mental pain is worse. I would rather have physical pain and be happy than have no physical pain and be unhappy.

♦ ♦ ♦

Dear Marilyn:

I got rid of tension headaches, and it was easy. Just repeat this twice a day: "If it's not life or death, it's not worth worrying about." Don't you agree?

Steve Chaddock
Brooklyn, New York

Dear Steve:

Good for you! (But I sure wouldn't want you to be my attorney.)

♦ ♦ ♦

Dear Marilyn:

Is it true that your attitude can make you well? If so, how is it done?

Raymond L. Reynolds, Sr.
Huntsville, Alabama

Dear Raymond:

I believe that your attitude can make you better, if not well, but not in a mystical sense at all. When you're trying to accomplish something physical, you summon bodily resources into action without even being aware of it. For example, when you try to catch a ball, you don't think about moving specific muscles. You just try.

And that's what you should do when you're sick. While obeying all your physician's instructions, set your mind to "getting well" the way you set it to "catching a ball" and let your subconscious physiology go to work for you. You may not be able to do enough to completely overcome whatever forces may be against you, but good things can still happen. If you don't get well, you may still get better, and if you don't get better, you may still slow down the disease process. And if you can't even do that, you'll still be better off psychologically.

◆ ◆ ◆

Dear Marilyn:

People say to me, "You don't look 45 years old." As we age at different rates, what does 45 years of age look like?

Peggy Gould
Denver, Colorado

Dear Peggy:

A 45-year-old looks a lot like a 25-year-old who's been out all night. And feels just as good about having survived the experience.

4.

Relationships

Dear Marilyn:
  Is there any advantage at all in having an enemy instead of a friend?
                                                                Anonymous

Dear Reader:
  Well, he'll be more predictable.

◆ ◆ ◆

Dear Marilyn:
  How important in life is it to have friends?

                                                          Rhonda DeBrower
                                                          Ladora, Iowa

Dear Rhonda:
  If you don't have friends, you'll have no one who likes you for what
you really are.

◆ ◆ ◆

Dear Marilyn:
  Do you have a negative definition of the word "friend"?
                                                                Anonymous

Dear Reader:
  A friend is a person who stays by your side all through the troubles
he's caused you.

◆ ◆ ◆

Dear Marilyn:

What is the most important factor in a person's character that lets you know you can trust him?

Dorothy Marie Oakes, R.N.
Waldwick, New Jersey

Dear Dorothy:

I'd say "faithfulness."

◆ ◆ ◆

Dear Marilyn:

Which is worse—being used or being rejected?

J. J.
Santa Barbara, California

Dear Reader:

I'd rather be rejected than used because they both amount to the same thing in the end, but being used takes a lot longer.

◆ ◆ ◆

Dear Marilyn:

In terms of human relationships, we hear "opposites attract" and "like attracts like." Which is the more successful pairing?

J. T.
Carmichael, California

Dear Reader:

I think that the lower our self-esteem, the more we're attracted to our opposite, and the higher our self-esteem, the more we're attracted to another like ourselves. And couples with greater self-respect are surely going to be happier.

The above provoked a complaint from a woman with a happy interracial marriage, and we wrote to her to explain that I was referring more to "chosen" characteristics than to "given" ones. (I certainly never meant that people with brown eyes who marry people with blue eyes are insecure!)

◆ ◆ ◆

Dear Marilyn:

Do you think most people would rather be with someone who is fascinating or with someone who makes *them* feel fascinating?

Julie Gail Jarrard
Decatur, Georgia

Dear Julie:

Let's be frank. I think we can safely assume that something like ninety percent of the men in ancient Egypt would have felt that Cleopatra was a fascinating woman and would have been only too happy to express that if they had had the opportunity. But would *Cleopatra* have wanted *them*? Or would Mark Antony have looked a little better?

◆ ◆ ◆

Dear Marilyn:

Can you "will" yourself not to fall in love? This means that if the right person came into your life, he or she would have no profound impact.

C. Elizabeth
New Brunswick, New Jersey

Dear C.:

I think "falling in love" has more to do with superficial sexual attraction than it does with the profound affection, warm regard, and tenderness felt for another person based on common interest, shared intimacy, and deep physical desire. And certainly, "falling in love" cannot be applied to "family," where attachment comes about more as a result of long-term proximity. So no, I doubt that we can "will away" the insignificant sexual attraction that comes from instinct, but I do think we can "will away" mistaking it for anything meaningful.

◆ ◆ ◆

Dear Marilyn:

How does one person go about "proving" that he or she loves another person?

Confused

Dear Reader:

It's a lot easier to prove that you *don't* love someone than it is to prove that you *do*, but one of the best "proofs" I know is the desire to devote time to the person with no expectation of any sort of compensation, including gratitude, in return.

◆ ◆ ◆

Dear Marilyn:

Do people know when they are jealous, or is it generally a blind spot?

Dorothy Marie Oakes
Waldwick, New Jersey

Dear Dorothy:

Oh, I think we know it, all right. Jealousy is such a powerful emotion that I doubt we could miss it. We just don't like to admit it, either to anyone else or, more importantly, to ourselves.

◆ ◆ ◆

Dear Marilyn:

For some time, I've used the word "envy" when meaning, "I admire what you have and would like to have something like it, while feeling no resentment toward you nor desire to take anything from you." It was pointed out to me, however, that the literal meaning of the word is, "discontent and resentment aroused by another's desirable possessions or qualities, accompanied by a strong desire to have them for oneself."

Surely there is a single word in the English language that covers my intended meaning. "Admire" doesn't apply, as I might admire a five-carat diamond, but I have no desire to own one.

J. Keith
Beaufort, Missouri

Dear J.:

There's a good word, all right, but it's not too surprising that you don't use it. Although "fancy" was definitely good enough for Shakespeare, most of us just don't want to say something like, "Hey, I sure do fancy your new sixteen-wheeler, mister."

◆ ◆ ◆

Dear Marilyn:

Do you believe that we hurt the ones we love the most in the expression of that love?

Julie Bauer
Sacramento, California

Dear Julie:

Not at all. I think love is less a *reason* for deplorable behavior than it is an *excuse* for it.

◆ ◆ ◆

Dear Marilyn:

I'm engaged to a man I love more than life itself, but no matter how much he says he loves me or shows it, if he says one wrong thing or doesn't return some form of affection, I feel totally crushed. I'm insecure about my relationship. How do you deal with *your* insecurities? If you even *have* any.

M. P. Stone
North Bend, Washington

Dear M. P.:

Oh, I have insecurities, all right. Life itself is insecure, and if we don't know that, we're not in touch with reality. However, there are times when we're insecure inappropriately—that is, when the apprehension we feel doesn't match the magnitude of the event. For example, you may think it would be impossible to live without your fiancé, but have you considered the fact that every *other* woman in the world is getting along just fine without him?

◆ ◆ ◆

Dear Marilyn:

Is there a more important decision in life than the choice of a career or the choice of a spouse?

F. M.
New York, New York

Dear Reader:

Yes. The choice of which one is going to come first.

◆ ◆ ◆

Dear Marilyn:

Do you find merit in the concept of prenuptial agreements?

Peter Bollen
Lynnfield, Massachusetts

Dear Peter:

Yes. Although I don't see why people in a state of emotional bliss would be any more likely to make levelheaded judgments than people in a state of emotional discord, agreements are preferable to disagreements, especially where the courts are involved. And for those to whom financial security is more important than romance, it's the honest thing to do.

Postnuptial agreements are something else entirely. After love first blooms and before it turns rotten, they seem like the most equitable way to begin the task of breaking up a marriage, protecting a private relationship from the passions of both the insiders *and* the outsiders.

◆ ◆ ◆

Dear Marilyn:

Why are some men so smart, neat, caring, and helpful—until they become husbands?

Anonymous
Richmond, Virginia

Dear Reader:

Probably for the same reason that some women are so smart, neat, caring, and helpful until they become wives.

◆ ◆ ◆

Dear Marilyn:

My sister, with three ex-husbands, one ex-daughter, two present boyfriends, and one present daughter, has just told me that there is no way she plans to live a single person's life. "I would rather stick a knife through my heart!" she told me. Why do people feel such a compulsion to be married?

Name Withheld
Issaquah, Washington

Dear Reader:

I don't think it's a compulsion at all. Rather, society has made it very difficult for men and women to live together without it and nearly impossible for women to have babies without it. From what your sister says, it seems that she simply wants to live with a man she loves, a very natural and healthy desire.

The above reader wrote and told me he was disappointed in my answer because he feels his sister has a serious problem. That may be the case. The answer applies more to women in general than to his sister in particular.

◆ ◆ ◆

Dear Marilyn:

The basic drives of an animal are founded on its instincts for its own survival and the perpetuation of its species. Assuming the human being is a highly evolved animal, are there any ways in which we, through our ability to think, have thwarted these natural tendencies in ourselves?

C. E. Gell
Arlington, Virginia

Dear C. E.:

Don't forget aggression, in which instinct plays a very prominent role. That one is now constantly suppressed, and it may be one reason for the enormous population growth. In any event, learning can certainly repress human instinct, and, in our society, it is currently done to the extent that human behavior is primarily, rather than secondarily, dominated by learning.

It's important to remember, however, that "learning" in this context does not necessarily imply "acquiring knowledge" or even anything especially constructive. It merely implies learning behavior that is accepted by the group into which we're born.

For example, it is clear that male instincts are different from female instincts, but these differences are thwarted by social behavioral codes, which include politics and religion. As an illustration, "motherhood" is a product of nature, but "fatherhood" is a product of culture. Without a knowledge of science, a male wouldn't know which young of which female had a pipeline to the great human gene pool through him, and if it weren't for culture, he might not even care that much.

◆ ◆ ◆

I expected to receive some mail from the following reply.

Dear Marilyn:
Is man meant to be a monogamist?

Jim Brewer
Sacramento, California

Dear Jim:
Oh, probably not, but that doesn't mean you guys can't at least *try*, does it?

But instead of letters from women who thought men and women are meant to be monogamous, I received letters from men who thought they shouldn't even be expected to try!

◆ ◆ ◆

Dear Marilyn:
Is it true that if a woman does what she's supposed to do, a man won't cheat on her? (For reasons you can well imagine, I cannot sign my name.)

Anonymous
Phoenix, Arizona

Dear Reader:

No, it's not true. One of the things we must learn in life is that more often the handsome prince turns into a toad than the other way around.

◆ ◆ ◆

Dear Marilyn:

What do you think contemporary society would be like if humans had not developed sexual reproduction but instead reproduced by some kind of asexual means such as cloning?

J. Speaker
Atlanta, Georgia

Dear J.:

I think there would be far fewer of us.

◆ ◆ ◆

Dear Marilyn:

What do you think about the sperm bank in Escondido, California, that offers sperm from Nobel Prize winners to women with superior intelligence for artificial insemination? I saw you on "Nightline" talking about this, and I'd like to hear more.

Anonymous

Dear Reader:

I think these women are fooling themselves—intelligence hasn't been isolated genetically. For one thing, if the Nobel Prize winner has genetically superior sperm, why aren't his *wife's* children superior? In other words, out of the thousands of famed people in history, how many of the *children* have we heard of?

But worse, I think this attitude may fool others, and that concerns me. If just one other child in a classroom with a kid with "designer genes" is fooled into believing he or she is inferior genetically and doesn't do as well as a result, it will be more than just a harmless stunt. It will be socially irresponsible.

And speaking of social responsibility, let's look more closely at the attitudes of the proponents of this project. If their aim of breeding for intelligence is simply to improve the species, why don't they make it available to *all* women instead of just those with superior intelligence themselves?

In any case, I think the aim of breeding babies for "intelligence" shows a sick sense of values on the part of the mother. Why not for "goodness," for heaven's sake? I'd rather have a lot of good people and hope some of them are intelligent than a lot of intelligent people and hope some of them are good.

◆ ◆ ◆

Please don't ask why I occasionally answer questions like the following!

Dear Marilyn:

Generally speaking, and regardless of whether the person is a relative or friend, when does a houseguest become a freeloader? I've always been of the opinion that three days is sufficient.

James R. Pitcher
Mount Pleasant, South Carolina

Dear James:

For me, a houseguest becomes a freeloader when three conditions are present at once:

1) You want him to leave.
2) He knows it.
3) But he doesn't leave, anyway.

This can happen after a month or after an hour, depending on the person. With some people, *one's* company.

◆ ◆ ◆

Dear Marilyn:

Do you feel that you can characterize family dynamics by observing what goes on at the dinner table?

Anonymous

Dear Reader:

The person asked to say grace is seldom the person who wants to.

◆ ◆ ◆

Dear Marilyn:

What do you say to a second child of four (three girls and one boy) who says she is "short-changed" because there is a "first child," "only son," and "baby" of the family?

Helen Hammond
Atchison, Kansas

Dear Helen:

Well, *I* say, "Quit making excuses." All those "titles" she cites for the rest of the kids are used as *complaints* as often as they are for credits. You have just as much justification in telling her that means she can consider herself *lucky!*

◆ ◆ ◆

Dear Marilyn:

If a child says he didn't ask to be born and so should not be held responsible for his actions, how is a parent to answer?

J. F. M.
Syracuse, New York

Dear Reader:

Ask him for the name of anyone who *did* ask to be born!

◆ ◆ ◆

When children are young, they complain more about their parents than their parents do about them. When children are grown, however, the reverse is the case.

Dear Marilyn:

If given the opportunity, what is the most important choice that could be made in life? I think it would be to choose our parents; they determine our environment.

F. M.
New York, New York

Dear Reader:

I think your choice is good for those who are products of their environment; for the rest of us, however, it might be even better to be able to choose our *children.*

◆ ◆ ◆

Dear Marilyn:

How do loving parents stop grieving over a callous, ungrateful child (age twenty)?

Anonymous Mother
Queens, New York

Dear Reader:

This is a difficult problem, created from unrealistic expectations raised by a society that encouraged you to bet your happiness on the chance factors that combined to create any particular child. One suggestion is that you spend time developing relationships with people you choose for themselves rather than those who happened to be born in your house. Focusing your allegiance on those produced by simple sexual relationships indicates far too great a reverence for that very natural process and robs you of one of the greatest pleasures in life—the chance to associate both with people you like for themselves and with people who like *you* for *yourself*. There are plenty of people of all ages out there to enjoy, and I hope you and your husband find dozens of them.

Among others, one woman wrote to me to say that my answer had changed her life and that she and her husband's successful efforts to become involved with poor families in their area had become the subject of a news story produced by their local television station. (Although this isn't quite what I'd meant to suggest, I was still very pleased to hear from her, of course.)

But I suppose I shouldn't have been surprised to receive the following.

Dear Marilyn:

How do I determine if I am a callous, ungrateful child? My parents seem to feel as if I am, but I need a more objective measure than their opinion.

Feeling Confused
College Park, Maryland

Dear Reader:

I think you're a sweetheart to write and ask, thereby proving to *me*, at least, that you *aren't* callous and ungrateful. If you were, you wouldn't care.

◆ ◆ ◆

Dear Marilyn:

How can you intelligently stop a "nagging" mother?

Anonymous, age 13
San Diego, California

Dear Reader:

Oh, this *is* a tough one. You may as well ask how to intelligently stop a case of acne. Both are probably as attributable to bad luck as they are to anything else, some of us escaping relatively unscathed and others scarred for life. But here's a little advice: Whenever your mother talks to you, listen attentively. (This is all she really wants, anyway.) Then act according to your own very best judgment. (And this is all *you* really want.)

◆ ◆ ◆

Dear Marilyn:

I just read about a mother who murdered her own baby, and some people are saying she shouldn't be blamed because she was depressed! Does this make sense to you?

Anonymous

Dear Reader:

Not much, I'm afraid. I, also, read about a young woman who killed her child and was then vigorously defended in print by several people who called the woman a victim of post-partum depression. Looking at it as dispassionately as possible, I'd say that this may be true in a chemical sense, but it was completely unnecessary for her to choose such an inhumane behavior in response to it. A great variety of actions was open to her, ranging from the commonplace to the kind. She could have, for example, even gone so far as to give the baby to someone else to raise. I'm sure there are thousands of childless couples who would have been delighted to have it.

I expected to receive a tidal wave of opposition in response to the publication of that above answer, but the result was only a trickle. However, they were so impassioned that I want to mention them here, anyway.

"We had a similar tragedy in our family. A cousin threw her infant out the window. Be a little compassionate, won't you?"

"Post-partum depression is a severe hormonal upset that causes some women to become mentally unbalanced and delusional. Those who have killed their babies were insane at the time."

"While all women do not suffer from a truly severe post-partum depression, there are all too many that do. I know. I was one of them. It took me over a year to get pregnant, and when I found out that I was finally expecting, I was thrilled. My pregnancy was a healthy and happy one, and I couldn't wait to give birth to our first child. Everything was just perfect. My dream had come true. But what happened afterward was a nightmare. There was total and complete despair. I didn't want my son. I was terrified. I truly believed that I had made the worst mistake of my life. I had this baby—what now? I am now fourteen months post-partum and am still on medication.

"Your statement that the mother could have 'gone so far as to give the baby to someone else to raise' is totally unfounded, without merit, and spoken out of ignorance. You don't just give your baby away because you are ill."

I am well aware of the terrible phenomenon known as post-partum depression. However, the first writer's comment, *"Be a little compassionate, won't you?"* leaves me cold. Would she suggest compassion if that same woman, in the throes of that same depression, had thrown her husband out the window? Is the action less reprehensible because a new baby is more disposable?

And the second writer's comment, *"Those who have killed their babies were insane at the time,"* is just as bad. Would this writer call a woman insane who tortured her new baby or beat the living daylights out of one of her other kids? Wouldn't most of us call it *"child abuse"*?

But the third writer bothered me the most, mainly because I felt sorry for her. Her hopes were so unrealistically high that it was nearly impossible for them not to be dashed. Giving birth to a baby has nothing to do with a perfect life, and it's very sad that women have been so deeply conditioned to believe that.

We know that depression causes chemical changes as much as it results from them. To whatever extent, however small, the post-partum change in body chemistry may be aggravated by overwhelming disillusionment is the extent to which those who extol the glory of motherhood should shoulder some of the guilt. And perhaps we should begin to look into depression experienced by husbands at this time.

The last writer makes it abundantly clear that she had control of her faculties when she added, *"You don't just give your baby away because you are ill."* But if you really believe that, dear reader, then neither do you kill it.

◆ ◆ ◆

Dear Marilyn:

I have just read another child abuse story in the newspaper, and it makes me very ill. It also makes me wonder what we can do about it. Do you feel there is a proper punishment for this offense, or do you see another answer?

Nancy Van Alstine
St. Petersburg, Florida

Dear Nancy:

I do see other answers, and I'd like to focus on one of those. In addition to the many pregnancies that are actually unwanted, I suspect that a surprisingly large proportion of the "wanted" children born in this country are wanted for poor reasons, many of which have no relation to the experience of actually living with them.

Women have produced babies for reasons ranging from an unthinking acceptance of a life-style promoted as wholesome to an unconscious or conscious desire to secure long-term support, whether it's financial support from a husband to emotional support from the child itself. Instead, before deciding to have a baby, they should be asking themselves a few realistic questions like these:

Do I prefer taking care of babies and young children to other activities? (This *is* what we'll be doing, and if we don't like it, we'll be subject to acute stresses.)

Do I enjoy *all* babies and young children? (Remember, we won't have a choice. We must accept anyone who is born to us, regardless of whether we like each other.)

Does my husband *honestly* want me to have this baby? (If he was used like a sperm donor or manipulated emotionally, he'll be susceptible to dangerous disillusionment.)

In short, wanting a baby is not the issue. The point, instead, is *why*.

5.

Morals and Ethics

Dear Marilyn:

What is the difference between morals and ethics?

R. R. Quinn
La Jolla, California

Dear R. R.:

Ethics is the branch of philosophy that deals with human values in as scientific a manner as possible, independent of special interests. It tries to answer the question, "What is the highest good?" to each individual set of circumstances without regard to any personal predisposition.

Morals, on the other hand, are standards of good and bad behavior that conform to predetermined principles of what is right and wrong. Most typically, they adhere to the conventional standards of a particular social or political or religious group.

In other words, you're moral if you do what someone else thinks is right; you're ethical if you do what *you* think is right.

◆ ◆ ◆

Dear Marilyn:

What do you think are the most basic human ethics?

Glen Flax
Flushing, New York

Dear Glen:

It is possible that our most basic ethics are more like morals based on certain of our instincts. What we want most for ourselves, in other words, is what we are taught to humanely want for others. If this is the case, our most basic human ethic might be the holding dear of the survival of any human creature.

◆ ◆ ◆

When I decided to answer the following question, I must admit that I didn't really expect Parade *very much to want to publish what I had to say about it. And I was right. They didn't!*

Dear Marilyn:

Will you please distinguish between "legal" and "moral"?

Armand N. Chambers, Ph.D.
Reston, Virginia

Dear Armand:

Generally speaking, "legal" covers the hours from eight in the morning to eight at night, and "moral" covers the hours from eight at night to eight in the morning.

◆ ◆ ◆

I wrote and rewrote the following answer because I expected it to be misunderstood. Unfortunately, I was right. However, there's not enough room in any column to explain everything.

Dear Marilyn:

Having grown up in France, I cannot understand this aspect of American culture: vivid, graphic film portrayals of murder, which we consider a crime, are acceptable, while vivid, graphic scenes of lovemaking are obscene. Can you explain this to me?

Danielle Rochefort-Smith
Salt Lake City, Utah

Dear Danielle:

Americans abhor violence and consider it so much more obscene than sex in films that *the more graphic sort of violence we see on the screen is entirely faked.* Not a drop of blood is real. On the other hand, the more graphic sort of sex we see on the screen *is* real. How can you fake *graphic* sex?

In other words, I believe you're comparing "pretend" violence with "live" sex, invalidating your argument. "Live" violence, which would be the *true* counterpart to graphic sex, is *never* tolerated.

People promptly wrote to me about such atrocities as "snuff" movies, amateur films made of real murders committed for the camera, which are then sold illegally to the deeply perverted. But that's no comparison at all. Instead, it proves my point. That's the "live" violence that is not tolerated by Americans.

But I also received letters from several professors who wrote to say they would share this point with their classes.

◆ ◆ ◆

Dear Marilyn:

This question is from a philosophy major. Is morality universal or relative to the individual?

Robert B. Jennings, Jr.
Baton Rouge, Louisiana

Dear Robert:

We may have democratic morality. On the surface, it appears that morality is relative to the individual, but where there are enough individuals who think alike, for whatever good or bad reason, they conceive principles of conduct whereby they seek to influence the behavior of all. It's a little like our presidential election. We all get to vote, but the best man doesn't necessarily win. The one who gets the most votes does.

◆ ◆ ◆

Dear Marilyn:

Should our actions ultimately be guided by the answer to this question—"What would happen to humanity if everyone did what I am about to do?"

Dimitra C. Lambros
Indianapolis, Indiana

Dear Dimitra:

No, because the magnitude of an action may change not only the strength of its impact, but the direction. It's true that only *one* empty can tossed onto the ground affects the environment minimally, while the effect of thousands of cans thrown away is significantly negative. But suppose your action is to decide your career. If you became a dentist, for example, you would certainly be an asset to our society. But what if everyone became a dentist? Who would bake the bread? Who would build the houses?

♦ ♦ ♦

Dear Marilyn:

What can a person do during his or her lifetime so that he will have made his life worthwhile?

Carrie Henderson
Burgaw, North Carolina

Dear Carrie:

I think any life is worthwhile that produces more than it consumes, whether it's handbooks, harmonicas, or happiness.

♦ ♦ ♦

Dear Marilyn:

Name one good thing man has accomplished to benefit this world and not man himself.

Dawn Matthews
San Bernardino, California

Dear Dawn:

Your question had a sobering effect on me. A casual review of the most important achievements and inventions indicated a definite specialized interest on the part of man—namely, himself; a closer inspection revealed a profound disregard for the welfare of the earth. Other than attempts to control damage, I'm sorry to say that I can't find a thing.

♦ ♦ ♦

The next answer stirred quite a few men to write and express their agreement.

Dear Marilyn:

Can a person ever truly think or do anything for anyone other than himself or herself? Do we not always form thoughts or select actions that are based on the survival instinct? Isn't self-sacrifice and the giving of one's life, etc., just learned behavior?

Bob Colgan
Huntsville, Alabama

Dear Bob:

To a certain degree, yes. And I do believe that the individual can learn to value others to such an extent that when those others benefit, the individual actually still succeeds in having his or her own way.

However, this doesn't explain the behavior of the human female with her newborn. Clearly, the behavior of any male who may be with her is learned from such powerful external forces as religion and government, but isn't it just as clear that powerful *internal* forces are influencing that woman to nurse and care for her infant just when she herself is at her weakest?

◆ ◆ ◆

Dear Marilyn:

Is compassion innate?

Albert Busch
Tallahassee, Florida

Dear Albert:

If the survival of the individual is an instinct, I suspect that compassion must be learned because, in general, it runs counter to self-interest. Unless, that is, the compassion is taught to someone *else*—which may in itself be a selfish act. In other words, preaching compassion is much more natural than practicing it yourself.

◆ ◆ ◆

Dear Marilyn:

Do you believe in organ donation, and why?

Darlene C. Phibbs
Albany, New York

Dear Darlene:

It's difficult to find reasons *not* to believe in it, but in an effort to see another side, I'll try. One complaint might be that there is no fair method for the allocation of these most precious of commodities. But is there a fair method for the allocation of anything *else*? An imperfect allocation system is surely better than having nothing to allocate at all, unless the critic feels that if *he* can't have what he wants, he doesn't want anyone *else* to have it, either.

Another argument is that an unscrupulous physician might remove the organs before determining that the donor is indeed unsalvageable. But this makes as much sense as not trusting your physician to properly treat your illness because it is to his financial advantage to have you sick rather than well. And if the critic feels, as do some Asian cultures, that it's just plain wrong for someone to profit by the death of another, he should take a look around. Why, our kids do that all the time!

◆ ◆ ◆

Dear Marilyn:

Can a person—or *should* a person—bring his opposing personal values into agreement?

Karen Lucas
Oakland, California

Dear Karen:

I doubt that he can, but I think he should try. People are extremely bright, and where there is an opposition in value, making little sense intellectually, we usually find an actual value of our own and an opposing value that has been visited upon us by someone else, usually at such an early age that we don't even remember it. This can produce a life of conflict in which we find such phenomena as freedom producing guilt, calm creating anxiety, and pleasure causing pain. Life is easier when our emotions make sense intellectually.

◆ ◆ ◆

Dear Marilyn:

I've been told that because humility can be perceived as weakness, it should be hidden. Do *you* think so?

Anonymous

Dear Reader:

No. Most of us hide our humility so well that we can't find it when we need it.

6.

Religion

Dear Marilyn:
  Who were the three most influential people in world history?
                                                    Ric Whitley
                                                    Grandview, Washington

Dear Ric:
  Near the top of the list would be the Buddha, Jesus, and Mohammed.

♦ ♦ ♦

Dear Marilyn:
  In your opinion, what is the single most inaccurate or misleading piece of information circulating in the world today?
                                                    Linda Maggiolo
                                                    Santa Cruz, California

Dear Linda:
  That all religions are equally correct. That just can't be.

♦ ♦ ♦

Dear Marilyn:
  Will man ever be sure of his origins, or will that be the eternal enigma?

                                                    Robert A. Bates
                                                    Fairmont, West Virginia

Dear Robert:
  I see no conclusive reason for that to be an eternal enigma. However,

how long that knowledge actually takes to arrive may depend at least in part on whether we *like* what those origins seem to be turning out to be.

◆ ◆ ◆

Dear Marilyn:

If you were somehow given the opportunity to view any event in all of history or pre-history, which one would you choose?

John Locke
Spring Valley, California

Dear John:

I would go back and witness the creation of the universe. Just think of all the arguments I could solve.

◆ ◆ ◆

Dear Marilyn:

It is often said that we are all "in control of our own destiny," yet as religious people, we are also taught "God is the pilot; I am just the co-pilot." Are these beliefs contradictory? If so, how does one come to grips with such?

William T. Sautter
Belmont, Calfornia

Dear William:

Look, if you really believe that God is the pilot, don't be the co-pilot, for heaven's sake—be the navigator.

◆ ◆ ◆

Dear Marilyn:

This is a somewhat whimsical question asked by my then seven-year-old nephew, but it stumped us all. "If God and Superman got into a fight, who would win?" Do you dare to try to answer that one? (I'm pulling for Superman, but don't let that influence your answer!)

Stephen W. Johnson
Glendale, Arizona

Dear Stephen:

Sure I dare. Go ahead and pull for Superman—he'd need all the help he could get. Of *course* God would win! Why, he'd beat the *tights* off Superman! Making steel pretzels, skydiving without a parachute, and straight-arming runaway locomotives is *nothing* compared to whipping up an entire universe from scratch, is it? And a little kryptonite reduces him to Jell-O! Anyway, I've never trusted the kind of guy who changes clothes in a phone booth.

◆ ◆ ◆

Dear Marilyn:

I recently watched on television a tribute to Harry Houdini featuring several magicians. Why are we so fascinated by magic, but yet do not comprehend how it happens?

Carole Hopkins
Warsaw, Indiana

Dear Carole:

We are intrigued *because* we don't understand. Modern "magic" as practiced on stage and elsewhere had its beginnings in ancient religion. Would a talking idol have been anywhere as impressive if the speaker had been known to be the priestess's brother-in-law hidden in an underground chamber?

7.

Mysticism

Dear Marilyn:

Are there any people who foretell the future, such as numerologists and psychics, who have been documented as being legitimate?

Clifford C. Brown
Lynwood, California

Dear Clifford:

Nope.

♦ ♦ ♦

Dear Marilyn:

Do you feel that handwriting reveals personality and/or other characteristics?

Christine Edwards
Remlik, Virginia

Dear Christine:

Not to the extent that it would tell us anything that we don't already know about ourselves. For example, a particular sort of slanting may be characteristic of left-handedness, or excessive ornamentation may be common among the young. (I once knew a girl named Linda who dotted the "i" in her name with a tiny heart. However, she was thirteen years old at the time, and I'll bet she's grown out of the habit now, three decades later. At least, I *hope* so.)

When our handwriting departs from the way we were instructed, it may simply be due to such factors as eyesight or motor control or even whether we give a darn about it, in addition to the fact that every teacher handles the subject differently. (My own teacher used to try to grab the pencil from my hand by surprise when I was writing, and when my hand rose along with the pencil, she said I was holding it too tightly. If only she had known what it was like to sit in front of the boy who sat behind me at the time, she would have known better. We were only allowed a specified number of pencils over the semester, and he had a habit of eating his.)

I am still receiving compliments from forensic document examiners and complaints from graphologists as a result of this answer. Amazingly, one woman even wrote to say that it is possible to tell whether a man is "oversexed" by the way he crossed his "x"!

◆ ◆ ◆

Dear Marilyn:

Where does the Ouija board get its answers? Do you think spirits are really contacted?

M. M.
Pittsfield, Massachusetts

Dear Reader:

When a question is put to a spirit, the Ouija board gets its answer from the people who use their fingers to move the little platform on casters to the letters, words, and other characters printed on its surface, and from no one else. Just because the participants say that they didn't move the planchette voluntarily doesn't mean that a spirit did it for them. After all, you don't hiccup voluntarily, and that doesn't mean that some spirit somewhere has had too much to drink. It's simply hard to hold the muscles of your hands entirely still when they're not resting on something. The Ouija board may be entertaining, but the only spirits I've seen contacted there are those in a glass.

And yes, I'm still receiving mail from Ouija fans.

◆ ◆ ◆

Dear Marilyn:

Could people who get premonitions possibly have some way of "tuning in" to elements of time that most of us are unaware of?

Richard E. Brown
Bakersfield, California

Dear Richard:

If you mean the knowledge of a future event without apparent reason, I don't think so. It's more probable that most things we call premonitions are merely a result of so many people in the world thinking so many things would happen that just the laws of chance alone would dictate that their visions would occasionally come to pass.

Also, if it's true that many premonitions are felt by mothers about their children, this may be because mothers spend so much time worrying about their children that these coincidences would naturally happen more frequently to them. How often, for example, do we hear of a mother's premonition involving a *happy* event or for *another* woman's child? And more significantly, how often do their fears *not* come true?

◆ ◆ ◆

Dear Marilyn:

Is there such a thing as a sixth sense?

Anonymous

Dear Reader:

Why not? Senses are arbitrary labels. And if we're ever better able to examine any sort of extra-sensory perception, perhaps such as thinking, we will have taken a step in the direction of creating one. At that point, we would probably demystify it by giving it a name and "lowering" it to the list of senses, thus giving us, for example, the six senses HEAR, SEE, SMELL, TASTE, TOUCH, and THINK. Aspiring seventh, eighth, and ninth, etc., senses would be handled in the same way.

◆ ◆ ◆

Dear Marilyn:

Can one's spirit consciously communicate with one's self?

George Gessitz
Newton, New Jersey

Dear George:

I'd say so. One type of evidence is the physical result. For example, if we open the front door and see a lion, adrenalin will shoot through our veins. The lion, however, does not do the communicating. In fact, the actual physical presence of the lion is superfluous. Even if we only *think* we see a lion, the results will be the same. Our spirit (or mind) communicates with our self (or our physical form). The spirit can be aware of this, but is not always so, and this is certainly understandable.

In the midst of a rousing argument, it's far more satisfying to yell, "You make me sick!" than it is to yell, "I make myself sick!"

◆ ◆ ◆

Dear Marilyn:

Why can't people accept the fact that Elvis Presley has expired?

Catherine A. Smentkowski
St. Louis, Missouri

Dear Catherine:

I think nearly everyone *does* accept it. Just because there are nutty stories in tabloid newspapers doesn't mean that many people actually believe them. For example, after all the headlines I've seen about women giving birth to things like two-hundred-pound adults and space creatures and penguins, I still don't believe I could find anyone who thinks women give birth to anything other than babies.

8.

The Human Condition

Dear Marilyn:
Do you believe the saying, "Few people know how to be old?"
Julian Hammer
Carteret, New Jersey

Dear Julian:
Yes, I certainly do. It's sad to see older people who strive to look and act like younger people when the best thing about being young is simply that the body has more time left. And they haven't affected *that*, have they? Aside from physical aging, I'd rather be older than younger. If we've managed our circumstances well, we have more knowledge, more understanding, more financial security, more accomplishments, and more friends. And with the heightened perspective, living grows more poignant each year. On the other hand, if we've managed our circumstances poorly, we'll be left with the superficiality of youth, but old bodies.

◆ ◆ ◆

Dear Marilyn:
What is the best chronological age in a person's lifetime?
Paulette J. Di Meola
Parlin, New Jersey

Dear Paulette:
If you mean the age at which personal happiness should reach its

peak, I believe this would be the oldest possible age before the onset of physical debility, but only in people who have successfully avoided believing Madison Avenue's claim that physical beauty is more important than mental beauty. When comprehension becomes more important than reproduction, as it should have done long ago, growing older will become delightful. After all, we already have more than enough people in the world, but less than enough wisdom.

◆ ◆ ◆

Dear Marilyn:
   Why does society put such a high emphasis on physical beauty?
                                                    Stephanie Siler
                                                    West Mifflin, Pennsylvania

Dear Stephanie:
   Maybe because it's the easiest thing to first notice about a person. That says a lot about its value, doesn't it?

◆ ◆ ◆

Dear Marilyn:
   Why are there no more renaissance men? Are people just lazy?
                                                    Abraham Ziffel
                                                    Fort Wayne, Indiana

Dear Abraham:
   There are no more renaissance men because we've progressed so far into the complex. In other words, when comparatively little was known, one could much more easily be an expert in numerous disciplines. Pretending to be a renaissance man or woman today, however, insults the specialists of this world—now the majority instead of the minority.

◆ ◆ ◆

Dear Marilyn:
   My definition of success is fulfilling one's capabilities. What do *you* think?

                                                    Jay B. Gailey
                                                    Paramount, California

Dear Jay:
   That sounds like a good *goal*, but there are far too many circumstances beyond our control for me to see it as a definition of an individual's success. Rather, I think success may be the ability to be happy with whatever we're stuck with.

◆ ◆ ◆

Dear Marilyn:

Competition, they say, is good, but is there such a thing as too much of it, say, in the young?

E. M. Wolf
Mazomanie, Wisconsin

Dear E. M.:

Oh, I certainly do think so, and I'd say the danger point is reached when the emphasis turns from a desire for our own success to a desire for another's failure.

◆ ◆ ◆

Dear Marilyn:

Do you have a negative perception of mankind?

David G. Brown
Enumclaw, Washington

Dear David:

No. I have a positive perception of humankind, but not universally so, and I believe that's shared by nearly everyone. Otherwise, we wouldn't have *apart*ments, would we? We would have *together*ments!

◆ ◆ ◆

Dear Marilyn:

In a barrel of a hundred apples, if one apple is bad, it is supposed to spoil the whole barrel. Why can't the ninety-nine good apples make the bad one fresh, instead? Is it true that the natural order of the universe is toward destruction?

Frank Scarola
Queens, New York

Dear Frank:

Not according to your example. The same natural order that makes apples rot also makes brand new apples!

◆ ◆ ◆

Dear Marilyn:

What would be the most significant change in the way we live our lives if all human beings were to become absolutely honest?

Rebecca L. Avalone
New York, New York

Dear Rebecca:

Well, the divorce rate would probably go through the roof.

◆ ◆ ◆

Dear Marilyn:

Why do people not fully acknowledge their less physically adept brothers and sisters? Why does an apparent attitude of condescension exist? Is it only because we disabled persons remind the more able-bodied individuals of the frailty of the human condition?

Prince Tyrone Williams
Orange, New Jersey

Dear Prince Tyrone:

I think it may be due to the "squeamishness" brought about by being sheltered from the less pleasant aspects of life and death. The child looks toward the pain of his first injection, but his mother tells him to look away. Eventually we sicken at the sight of a skinned knee, many of us going so far as to wince even when someone else yanks off a Band-Aid. The occasional individual is cruel, yes, but many of the rest of us are just ill at ease.

◆ ◆ ◆

Dear Marilyn:

Why does society, which thrives on variation, hate eccentricity so much? Why should it be wrong to be an eccentric? Or why should it not?

John A. Pickard, Jr.
Matthews, North Carolina

Dear John:

I think the major reason society doesn't tolerate eccentrics well is that they represent the range from a simple lack of success in the socialization process to a complete loss of power over the individual. Any person who is "out of control" is threatening, whether physically or psychologically. If someone is eccentric in merely a whimsical or odd way, we can consider him or her harmless, and we laugh to mask our discomfort. But if that person is eccentric in a way that shows disregard or even contempt for current customs or restraints, we may be frightened, and understandably so. The human being is the most dangerous animal on the earth.

I think it is no more right or wrong to be eccentric than it is to be conforming, but it appears that defiance for the sake of it is probably even less productive than compliance for the sake of it. In other words, if you don't rebel *with* a cause, you shouldn't rebel at all.

◆ ◆ ◆

Dear Marilyn:

What's the difference between a subculture and a bunch of weirdos?

David C. Morrow
Corpus Christi, Texas

Dear David:

The weirdos are the ones you *don't* like.

◆ ◆ ◆

Dear Marilyn:

How would you characterize the difference between an ordinary nice neighborhood and a pretentious one?

Anonymous

Dear Reader:

When it's hot in an unassuming neighborhood, you can fry an egg on the sidewalk. In a pretentious one, they make you fry an omelette.

◆ ◆ ◆

Dear Marilyn:

Are you missing the finer things in life when you can barely make enough money for the necessities?

Mary Grzymala
St. Petersburg, Florida

Dear Mary:

No. Almost all of the finer things in life are free or nearly so. You don't have to pay for the sky at night or snow in the morning or a kiss on the nose when you're sick. Forgetting that may put you at the mercy of those who seek to profit by convincing you to want whatever it is they have to sell.

◆ ◆ ◆

Dear Marilyn:

What do people the world over share most in common?

Colleen Kelley
Spokane, Washington

Dear Colleen:

In addition to instinct, perhaps the most widespread trait is the love of freedom (and maybe ice cream).

◆ ◆ ◆

Dear Marilyn:
Which is more important: love or freedom?

                                        Randall Jewell
                                        Silver Spring, Maryland

Dear Randall:
Freedom. Otherwise, kids would never leave home.

Quite a few mothers wrote in response and said that children would not leave home if given enough love. Well, I suppose that's right. Anyone who doesn't leave home because of motherly love can certainly be called a child, all right.

◆ ◆ ◆

Dear Marilyn:
Is there any aspect of human behavior or action that produces only advantages or disadvantages?

                                        Fred Iyasere
                                        Sacramento, California

Dear Fred:
If you're a negative person, I suppose you can find something bad in everything, and if you're a positive person, I suppose you can find something *good* in everything, but I have great difficulty finding anything bad in healing the sick and anything good in wearing high heels.

I wear high heels myself only when the occasion seems to require it. Like a wedding. My own, that is.

◆ ◆ ◆

Dear Marilyn:
Do you think it's possible that women in our lifetime will be looked upon as true equals? I'm so sick of men stereotyping women—noticing and commenting first on face and figure.

                                        Anonymous
                                        Raleigh, North Carolina

Dear Reader:
I would be flabbergasted if this occurred. But as you've requested anonymity, I feel free to ask this without concern for embarrassing you.

Do you wear makeup? Do you wear clothing that draws attention to your figure? If so, you're part of the problem, and you should keep that in mind when you complain.

◆ ◆ ◆

Dear Marilyn:

Is there really equality of the sexes? Or is it just a myth pushed by the female of the species?

> Edward T. Garafano
> Naugatuck, Connecticut

Dear Edward:

Why are you asking *me*, Edward? Why not some *guy*?

No, I *don't* think the sexes are equal. I think they're different, but in ways that just don't adequately account for the gulf that separates men and women in our society.

◆ ◆ ◆

Dear Marilyn:

If it's "ladies first," why is it still called a *man's* world?

> Kelly Marrapodi
> Tucson, Arizona

Dear Kelly:

Because being on the *receiving* end of a social gesture means nothing compared to being on the *giving* end.

◆ ◆ ◆

Dear Marilyn:

What would happen if all the men disappeared from the face of the earth?

> Jan Jonsson
> Duluth, Minnesota

Dear Jan:

All of the windows in the world would eventually become stuck shut.

9.

Human Biology

Dear Marilyn:

If all the people on earth were to die, how many people would it take to repopulate the earth again (without the danger of incest)? I had always thought it would just take two, but then the children would have to marry each other, and so on.

Anonymous
Brush Prairie, Washington

Dear Reader:

Then let's start with four unrelated people, two couples. If each woman has only one baby, the population will diminish. If each woman has only two babies, the population will stay the same. To repopulate, then, let's begin by presuming that each woman will have a minimum of three babies, one of them having two females and a male, the other having two males and a female. This is how the first pairing would look:

F(1)M		F(2)M
F	(3)	M
F	(4)	M
M	(5)	F

Of couples number 3, 4, and 5, the women have the following babies:

F(3)M	F(4)M	F(5)M
F	F	F
F	M	F
M	M	M

But the children can't marry because they're all first cousins. (And with nine of them, one would be very unhappy, anyway.) So let's try three unrelated couples, the women having the following babies:

F(1)M		F(2)M		F(3)M
F	(4)	M		F(6)
F	(5)	M		F
M(6)		F	(7)	M

They pair off again, (with one going off to the convent), the women having the following babies:

F(4)M	F(5)M	F(6)M	F(7)M
F	M	F	M
F	M	F	M
M	F	M	F

But the children can't marry because they're still all first cousins. So let's try four unrelated couples, the women having the following babies:

F(1)M		F(2)M		F(3)M		F(4)M
F	(5)	M	*	F	(8)	M
F	(6)	M	*	F	(9)	M
M	(7)	F	*	M	(10)	F

And here is where everyone will have to cooperate. If the children resulting from #1 and #2 will promise not to marry the children resulting from #3 and #4, the results will be the following:

F(5)M	F(6)M	F(7)M		F(8)M	F(9)M	F(10)M
F	M	F	*	M	F	M
F	M	F	*	M	F	M
M	F	M	*	F	M	F

None of the children resulting from #5, #6, and #7 can marry because they're first cousins. Likewise, none of the children resulting from #8, #9, and #10 can marry because they're also first cousins. However, they can cross over like this:

F(5)M		F(8)M	F(6)M		F(9)M	F(7)M		F(10)M
F	(11)	M	M	(14)	F	F	(17)	M
F	(12)	M	M	(15)	F	F	(18)	M
M	(13)	F	F	(16)	M	M	(19)	F

The children resulting from #11, #12, #13, #14, #15, #16, #17, #18, and #19 could then intermarry because they would be only "second cousins," a term used for people who have a grandparent who is a sister or brother of the other's.

But with regard to the incest taboo, you might be interested to know that it is no longer widely considered to guard against negative biological consequences. Instead, most social scientists today believe that its primary purpose is to guard against jealousy!

So, we'll need eight people to repopulate, which means that if it begins to rain very hard, you should build the ark about four times as large. (That is, unless you have different social standards for bunnies.)

◆ ◆ ◆

Dear Marilyn:
I've heard no two individual human beings are alike. How many humans have ever existed?

Jerry Choiniere
Fort Worth, Texas

Dear Jerry:
The figure is surprisingly low, considering that more than five billion are alive right now: about eighty billion, all told. But even more shockingly, the increase in world population just since 1950—only forty years—equals the total increase over the millions of years from when the human species first appeared.

◆ ◆ ◆

Dear Marilyn:
Do you believe that human life begins at conception?

Jeri Holzgen
Grand Rapids, Michigan

Dear Jeri:
Human life is certainly present *before* conception—in the form of the living egg and sperm. However, yes, I believe that the life of an *individual* human begins at the event itself and that efforts to label it something else until a future date is a well-meaning attempt to attain a desired social goal despite an emotionally charged reality perceived, rightly or wrongly, to be lying squarely in the path. Those who are in favor of abortion would far better serve their cause by presenting arguments that take reality into consideration instead of avoiding it, which only inflames those who *aren't* in favor of it.

◆ ◆ ◆

Dear Marilyn:
How limited or unlimited do you think brain function actually is?

Laura Stanley, Neuroscientist
Little Rock, Arkansas

Dear Laura:

I suspect it is far more limited that we would like to believe. A fish is unaware that it can't understand spoken language like a dog, a dog is unaware that it can't understand mathematics like a human, and a human is unaware that it can't understand . . . who knows what?

◆ ◆ ◆

Dear Marilyn:

Which do you feel adapts faster to environmental change, the mind or the body?

Danielle Rose
San Jose, California

Dear Danielle:

It appears that the mind adapts very quickly, but the body lags behind, from a minor to a major degree, ranging from seconds to millennia. Even when we *miss* an accident, our hearts still pound minutes after the fact.

◆ ◆ ◆

Dear Marilyn:

In sports, where you race against the clock, will there ever be a record that cannot be broken? Will a human ever be able to run a mile in a second?

E. J. Plovanich
Pittsburgh, Pennsylvania

Dear E. J.:

Whether clocked or not, I believe records will be set that can't be broken, and I don't believe a human will ever be able to run a mile that fast, both for the same reason. Biological substances, like any other materials, are subject to the laws of physics. This means that there are definite limits to their strength and their ability to withstand stress and strain. Human bone, for example, is actually a naturally occurring polymer composite. At some point, the spirit may be willing, but the flesh *will* be weak.

◆ ◆ ◆

Dear Marilyn:

Many years ago, theaters carried live acts on their bills, one of which was often a contortionist. The claim would be that he or she was "double-jointed." Is there such a thing?

Walter Efimetz
Livonia, Michigan

Dear Walter:

No. These people simply manage to stretch their ligaments farther than the rest of us and probably were born with more slack. However, I don't see why this should make today's professional circus contortionist any less intriguing to see. We're fascinated by the sight of the feat itself, not by the inner workings that make it possible. (Personally, I don't get any more excited by joints than by ligaments, do you?)

◆ ◆ ◆

Dear Marilyn:

The human body is a marvelous machine, but it sometimes arrives with handicaps and is subject to disease and accident. What changes would you make if you were to design a new "man"?

N. C. Grieninger
Somerville, Alabama

Dear N. C.:

I don't think the human body is all that good a machine; it seems extremely fragile to me. If I were able to make a change, though, I'd start with a body that doesn't age. I think aging is the worst disease known to mankind because everyone gets it, and it's a universal killer. And it doesn't even kill you mercifully all at once when you're a hundred years old; instead, it takes seventy or eighty years of increasing debility to do it.

◆ ◆ ◆

Dear Marilyn:

What is the single greatest flaw that the human race possesses?

Christine Vernon
Irvington, New Jersey

Dear Christine:

I think it may be the susceptibility to aging. All things considered, this is the cause of most death, just about the worst thing that can happen to any of us. And when I hear someone say that death is good for the species because it makes way for new people, I always wonder why such a person thinks that new people are going to be any better than we are. And if they're talking about evolutionary changes that will occur over the eons, I'd have to say that I'd rather not wait quite that long. The only way to speed up the process is to encourage reproduction as soon as possible, and then get rid of ourselves afterward. And so what? All Pacific salmon die immediately after spawning, and they haven't come out so darned great!

Well, I'm glad I finally had a chance to say that. People who can applaud the concept of death must be able to justify anything, stretching rationalization past its breaking point.

◆ ◆ ◆

Dear Marilyn:

How come more people die in hospitals than at home?

Julian Hammer
Carteret, New Jersey

Dear Julian:

I don't know what statistics you're using to formulate your question, but hospitals are full of sick people! When your doctor is really worried about your health, does she tell you to go *home*? When your ambulance driver extracts you from your crumpled automobile, does he take you *home*?

A few emergency medical service technicians wrote to express their dismay at being called mere "ambulance drivers," but I've decided not to apologize for this one. Everyone knows they're more than chauffeurs the way everyone knows that airline pilots do more than just steer the plane. Have a little confidence, all you emergency medical service technicians out there! (And come up with a shorter title!)

◆ ◆ ◆

Dear Marilyn:

I've heard a medical expert on television state that there is no such thing as a cure for a viral disease, though there may be a vaccine and treatments. Is this true?

Mary Anne Landers
Russellville, Arkansas

Dear Mary:

For the most part, yes. There are very few drugs that can be used to directly fight an invading virus, mainly because viruses have such an intimate relationship with the normal cells that drugs that interfere with the development of the virus also interfere with the function of ordinary cells. This is not to say that there are no measures that can be taken; there certainly are—among them, vaccines, immune globulins, chemoprophylaxis, and chemotherapy. However, so far, no antibiotic has been found to be effective, as a virus is not a bacteria.

◆ ◆ ◆

Dear Marilyn:

Should you feed a fever and starve a cold, or should you feed a cold and starve a fever?

Anonymous
Pittsburgh, Pennsylvania

Dear Reader:

Neither. This is just one of those old husbands' tales.

◆ ◆ ◆

Dear Marilyn:

Do you believe in human spontaneous combustion? If so, what do you think is the cause?

Jim Broderick
San Jose, California

Dear Jim:

I don't know of any verified cases where a *human being* has burst into flames without heat from an outside source, but such fires are certainly a very real and dangerous phenomenon in the home and on the farm.

Some folks think that rags containing substances such as oil, paint, or polish should be stored away from their living quarters merely to avoid accidentally igniting them with a candle or a cigarette. This is not so; the situation is far more unpredictable than that. They may ignite *entirely on their own.* Coal is also subject to this problem, as is hay in the barn.

---

*Some folks wrote to me enclosing newspaper clippings reporting alleged occurrences of spontaneous human combustion, but none of them were substantial enough to make me believe it. After all, I remember walking by one newspaper with a headline that read something like, "*ALIEN BASEBALL FOUND ON TOP OF MOUNT EVEREST.*"*

◆ ◆ ◆

Dear Marilyn:

How does the human body produce its temperature?

S. Dombrowski
Tijeras, New Mexico

Dear S.:

Nearly all of the actual physiological generation of heat is achieved by the combustion of food, releasing heat almost the same as if it were burned. The process has something in common with a fire except that the body uses chemicals instead of striking a match.

When my editor at Parade, *Sara Brzowsky, read this one, she laughed and said that my wording made it sound as if we're all ready to explode! (Well, maybe I'd better read up on human spontaneous combustion a little more!)*

◆ ◆ ◆

Dear Marilyn:

Let's say that the manufacturer of a food product advertises that it contains 100% of the recommended daily requirements for the day. If this is so, why would we have to eat any other food to survive?

Mrs. J. McCormack
Phoenix, Arizona

Dear Reader:

A single serving of that food may indeed contain all you need of *some* U.S. recommended daily allowances, but it won't contain all you need of *all* of them. In addition to oxygen and water, mammals need a very complex mixture of chemicals, including carbohydrates, fats, vitamins, minerals, and amino acids (more commonly known as protein). Cereal, for example, may be fortified with the equivalent of a vitamin pill, but it's so low in protein that you'd have to eat a couple of dozen bowls of it to satisfy that particular need. And by then, it would be far more appropriate to call it "feed" instead of "food"!

◆ ◆ ◆

Dear Marilyn:

How is it that the foods that taste the best are actually the worst for us? I wouldn't think that Mother Nature would be out to fool us in this way.

Stewart Glanzman
West Orange, New Jersey

Dear Stewart:

Don't blame Mother Nature. Farmers don't raise hamburgers, French fries, and soda.

Would you believe a fellow (whom I will mercifully leave unnamed) wrote to me and said, "Just who does raise potatoes (French fries) and beef (hamburgers) if farmers don't? Do city girls still think these things come from the supermarket?" And he inscribed, *"You blew it again"* on the outside of the envelope. *Well, he missed the point. Turning low-calorie potatoes into fatty French fries is what the* cook *does, and that's why I said, in essence, "It's our own fault."*

◆ ◆ ◆

Dear Marilyn:
  Does odor have weight?

                                                    Tony Calabrese
                                                    Glenfield, Pennsylvania

Dear Tony:
  I know this answer is going to draw a loud, "Oh, y-u-c-k!" when everybody thinks about it, but I'm afraid it *does*, however little, and for the following reason. Odor is the name of the phenomenon produced by airborne particles (and the name of the particles themselves) actually coming into contact with areas inside the nasal passages. Even though their number is relatively minute, smelling an odor is like inhaling an infinitesimal amount of whatever is generating it. (Clearly, this is *not* a piece of information you want to remember when you're stuck in a station wagon with a wet dog.)

10.

Animals and Plants

Dear Marilyn:
Do you like nature?

Aretha Washington
New York, New York

Dear Aretha:
I love it. But people are a part of nature—to me, the most important, most fascinating part. I would rather spend time with a thousand people than with a thousand trees. A national park is a nice place to visit, but I wouldn't want to live there.

◆ ◆ ◆

Dear Marilyn:
What is the purpose of evolution?

Anonymous

Dear Reader:
I don't believe that evolution has a purpose because it is not a being with personal intentions. Of course, if evolution were placed in motion by a distinct being, that being certainly could have had intentions, but that isn't the question. If, instead, evolution exists on its own, as a natural process and without a purpose, it would still, however, lead to a consequence. In the past, it may well have resulted in the survival of the fittest, but this is no longer the case. Human kindness is working to change this to the survival of any human creature.

◆ ◆ ◆

Dear Marilyn:

I recently spent a small fortune to purchase a two-volume, 1100-page, 5400-footnote critique of Darwin's major work. If evolution is a "fact" or even a reasonable theory, why is there so much scientific opposition to it?

John Weldon
Chattanooga, Tennessee

Dear John:

Charles Darwin was not merely a proponent of evolution. He postulated a specific *cause* of evolution, namely, natural selection. Most of the scientific opposition is not to the theory of evolution in general, but to Darwinism in particular, regarding such things as the rate of change or the manner of it.

◆ ◆ ◆

Dear Marilyn:

What initiates a cell to evolve? Adaptation doesn't seem to be a good enough reason.

Sarah Hutchens
Galax, Virginia

Dear Sarah:

According to scientists, accidents called "mutations" and sexual recombination of genes are the raw material for this process.

◆ ◆ ◆

Dear Marilyn:

As dolphins are the smartest known creatures after humans, why didn't man evolve from them instead of apes?

Elaine M. Drotzmann
Yakima, Washington

Dear Elaine:

I don't believe dolphins are that intelligent. Although those that have been studied in captivity do indeed rank higher than the dog, the cat, and the horse, they're not on the level of primates. Next to human beings, apes are probably the most intelligent creatures, with chimpanzees commonly considered to be the brightest of them.

◆ ◆ ◆

Dear Marilyn:

Do fish ever drown?

Sheila Lyons
North Mankato, Minnesota

Dear Sheila:

In a way. Fish must extract oxygen from the water in order to live the way we must extract oxygen from the air. And if by "drown" you mean the commonly accepted definition of dying from suffocation in water (or another liquid) because access to oxygen is prevented, fish can very easily drown in water that is poor in oxygen content. That's why we must take care to aerate our aquariums.

◆ ◆ ◆

Dear Marilyn:

Why do birds fly?

Randy Harris
Greensboro, North Carolina

Dear Randy:

Most of the time, they fly because it doesn't occur to them *not* to, having inherited an instinct that makes them use their wings to stay out of the clutches of their predators. Presumably, birds that instead tried to run away from a cat fared less well overall.

Some of the time, however, at least judging from what I've seen in a summer sky in the morning, I think they're just showing off.

◆ ◆ ◆

Dear Marilyn:

I've been trying to find the answer to this question for over a year. Can you help? Why don't birds fall out of trees at night while they sleep?

Lee M.
Honolulu, Hawaii

Dear Lee:

My first inclination was to assume that birds don't fall out of trees at night for the same reason that we don't fall out of bed. They're asleep, but they're not *dead*. However, after a little investigation, it turns out that the foot of a bird is particularly adapted for perching in such a way that when the ankle is bent, the toes are, too. In other words, the weight of a crouched bird keeps his toes clenched around the perch. Now, I have a question for *you*. Why have you been trying to find this answer for over a year?

◆ ◆ ◆

Dear Marilyn:

The only time you see a dead bird is if it has met with an accident.

What about when they die of "old age"? What happens to them?

R. K. Marvin
Joplin, Missouri

Dear R. K.:

And even with an accident, you won't see it for long. That's because birds generally are fragile little creatures with no teeth and are easily eaten by others, most notably cats, rats, dogs, pigs, goats, and opossums, at least in the civilized areas. If they can't fly, they're quickly eaten, and a bird that becomes prevented from taking wing by either the progress of illness or the advance of old age is gulped down before it can lie down. (Not without exception, of course. Even if you live next door to a zoo, your cat will never drag home an elderly ostrich.)

◆ ◆ ◆

Dear Marilyn:

Why don't we ever see baby pigeons?

J. W.
Freeport, New York

Dear Reader:

Because we so seldom hang around rocky cliffs and the man-made equivalent of bridges and the like—pigeons are "ledge nesters." And, difficult as this may be to believe, they were considered *sacred* in ancient times, but for a reason that won't surprise us at all: they were associated with fertility!

◆ ◆ ◆

Dear Marilyn:

Does the beautiful butterfly as he flutters in the spring remember his former life of drudgery as a lowly caterpillar, or, during that wondrous time of transformation in the cocoon, is his mind transformed as is his physical body? Please answer, as our friendship is being strained by this dilemma.

Paul Duke and Daryl Schwartz
Chapel Hill, North Carolina

Dear Paul and Daryl:

I'm afraid I don't know for sure, but I doubt that he'd remember even if his mind *weren't* transformed. Memory may be defined as the persistence of learning, and I don't think a butterfly is capable of learning much of anything. And even if he *did* remember, I wouldn't feel too sorry for him, if I were you. With people, life isn't so predictable. Some of us start out as caterpillars and become butterflies, but others of us start out as butterflies and become caterpillars.

◆ ◆ ◆

Dear Marilyn:
   What makes a lightning bug light up at night?

Janice Jorn
Virden, Illinois

Dear Janice:
   Males and females each have a distinctive flash, and it's generally accepted that this is how they attract each other. It's a little like smiling.

Part Two

Politics and the Press

11.

Leaders

Dear Marilyn:
What quality do you think a good leader should have?

Sharon Kocher
San Francisco, California

Dear Sharon:
A good leader needs to stand behind his or her followers as often as he or she needs to stand in front of them.

◆ ◆ ◆

Dear Marilyn:
Regarding leadership for our country, what qualities, education, and religious training do you consider important?

Timi Zeiders
Vernal, Utah

Dear Timi:
For personal qualities, I think we need likeable problem-solvers. Charisma alone can bring votes, but it doesn't bring progress, and ability alone doesn't bring progress if it can't bring votes. For professional qualities, I'd like to see both intellectual *and* down-to-earth credentials. The first could be demonstrated by a college degree in the humanities or by the production of thoughtful work, and the second by practical experience in managing an organization such as a business or a charitable institution. As for formal religious training, the less, the better. After

all, who's religion would it be? However, while these requirements considerably narrow the field of candidates, anyone who doesn't feel he or she quite fits the bill shouldn't feel too bad. Mankind needs more followers than leaders, anyway.

◆ ◆ ◆

Dear Marilyn:

If you were on a committee to question members of both houses of Congress to determine if they were qualified to serve, what would you concentrate on first?

> Anonymous
> Florence, South Carolina

Dear Reader:

I would concentrate first on integrity, and by that, I mean the individual's trustworthiness in adhering to his or her principles. To be prudent, however, I would concentrate next on learning what those principles *are*.

◆ ◆ ◆

Dear Marilyn:

Should governmental officials be given tests for competency before taking their jobs?

> Anonymous

Dear Reader:

If we believe that if competency tests should not be required of voters, we should not require them of office-holders, for the same reason—the danger of using the tests in order to prevent certain people from gaining power.

◆ ◆ ◆

Dear Marilyn:

If there were more females in public office, would the United States have a better economic situation, and would the entire world be more peaceful?

> Gayle L. Anderson
> Lino Lakes, Minnesota

Dear Gayle:

In the short term, I don't think so. At present, women are far less experienced than men in handling economic affairs. Also, the majority of our public officials have little effect on hostilities outside our borders. In the long term, however, while I see no evidence that women can handle economic matters *better* than men, they do appear to have a more peaceable nature.

It always surprises me when a woman will write and say something like, "How could you say that about women? You're a woman yourself!" as though it's desirable to be biased toward whatever group of which we may happen to be members!

◆ ◆ ◆

Dear Marilyn:

What title will we use to refer to the husband of the first woman president of the United States? "First Gentleman" hardly seems appropriate.

Vivian Goff
Akron, Ohio

Dear Vivian:

"First Gentleman" may sound silly, but it's obviously the correct counterpart to "First Lady," and it's a very sad realization that the position and corresponding title that have always been considered desirable for a woman would be considered degrading to a man.

◆ ◆ ◆

Dear Marilyn:

Do you believe in the saying, "Behind every successful man, there is a woman"?

Anonymous

Dear Reader:

No. But I'm beginning to wonder if "Behind every successful man, there is a politician."

◆ ◆ ◆

Dear Marilyn:

Are we a country without heroes?

Julian Hammer
Carteret, New Jersey

Dear Julian:

I don't think so. We just don't recognize them for what they are after they've been torn apart by both the press and even their so-called relatives and friends in some cases. A country that supports a sensational media deserves the heroes it's left with.

◆ ◆ ◆

Dear Marilyn:

Who is more effective at getting things done, a good listener or a good talker?

Peter Eager
San Diego, California

Dear Peter:

Looking back throughout history, I find only Great Communicators. Caesar was one; Churchill was another. Great Listeners may get things done, but they don't get famous for it. Maybe it's because a good talker can affect thousands of people, but a good listener can affect only one.

◆ ◆ ◆

Dear Marilyn:

Is there a way to determine which person will become a good leader and which one will not?

Manuel H. Moraleda
Battle Creek, Michigan

Dear Manuel:

There may be ways to determine whether people have the potential to become leaders because the trait is often evidenced early in life, but it's much more difficult to determine whether they'll become *good* ones. Unfortunately, we have the tendency to view leadership ability as a universally positive trait instead of a potentially dangerous one.

◆ ◆ ◆

Dear Marilyn:

How in the world do you account for the rise to power of a man like the former Ayatollah Ruhollah Khomeini of the Shiite Muslim clergy?

Adam Warle
Chicago, Illinois

Dear Adam:

Even a five-watt bulb looks bright at night.

◆ ◆ ◆

Dear Marilyn:

When they write history in 2092, who currently alive will be remembered as outstanding contributors?

Art Ruben
Seattle, Washington

Dear Art:

Unfortunately, outstanding contributors to history are not the same as outstanding contributors to mankind. Instead, they are merely the ones who have had the most publicity. With that criterion in mind, Muammar al-Qaddafi and Princess Diana will be right up there with President Bush and former Prime Minister Thatcher.

◆ ◆ ◆

Dear Marilyn:

If one is unhappy about something done or not done by the government, what is the best way to show opposition? Writing one's representatives in Congress does little or no good. Their clerks simply send a form letter of acknowledgement and file your letter in the wastebasket. How can I make my point carry weight?

Frances Adcock
Lake Charles, Louisiana

Dear Frances:

Go to the press. Right or wrong, the press gets the attention of lawmakers because it has influence far beyond its actual numbers. First, find the name of the government official most responsible for the action and then write a letter to the editor of your local newspaper mentioning his or her name. After you see how that looks in print, write another letter, this time to the editor of the biggest city newspaper nearby. And after you see how *that* looks in print, write two or three *more* letters, but this time to the editors of the most influential newspapers in the country, such as *The New York Times* and the *Washington Post*, enclosing clippings of any letters that were published.

Be vigilant at your local newsstand for those major publications, and then write a final letter directly to the government official himself or herself, enclosing every clipping you've got.

◆ ◆ ◆

Dear Marilyn:

If I had a plan that would solve the problems of the world, what are the chances of the "powers that be" taking it seriously?

Kathy Brown
Parish, New York

Dear Kathy:

Honestly? Zero. Unless you yourself are one of those "powers." Anyone who truly believes he or she has such a plan should run for political office.

◆ ◆ ◆

Dear Marilyn:

Why should governors and presidents have the power to pardon a person who has been given every legal opportunity to prove his innocence and has been found guilty?

Carl L. Schaefer
Hammond, New York

Dear Carl:

It is my understanding that pardons have less to do with the guilt or innocence of the person involved than they do with serving a worthy purpose that does not fall within the scope of the law. Unfortunately, the worthiness of the purpose is not always clear to the rest of us.

This question didn't get published before the reader became too impatient to wait any longer, and he wrote again, so I took the opportunity to expand a little on what I said.

Dear Marilyn:

I have a question that has been bothering me for ages. Why do chief executives like governors and the President have the power to free felons who were given every opportunity to prove their innocence and were found guilty?

Carl L. Schaefer
Hammond, New York

Dear Carl:

The pardon, it seems to me, should provide that one narrow avenue of escape from the law for those who have no other recourse, but deserve it. An example might be a person who has done something in the public interest that is also illegal. However, pardons are more often granted for other reasons, including clemency or a belief in the accused's innocence. Clemency makes a modest amount of sense to me, but only if it's exercised equally among all those who apply; otherwise, it would be painfully capricious at best and a euphemism for favors to friends at worst. Believing in the accused's innocence, however, makes the least sense of all. A chief executive doesn't know anything that all the rest of the people involved don't.

12.

Government

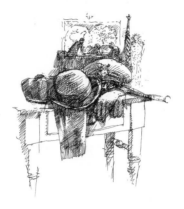

Dear Marilyn:
What is the essence of our America?

Kenneth R. Huebner
San Antonio, Texas

Dear Kenneth:
The essence of our America is finding and maintaining that perfect, delicate balance between freedom "to" and freedom "from."

◆ ◆ ◆

Dear Marilyn:
I have read on several occasions that our 200-year-old government is on the decline. What, realistically, can we as individuals do to improve our nation's future?

C. Johnston
Joplin, Missouri

Dear C.:
I think that one of the best things we can do for our nation's future is to stop voting out of self-interest. It is a far more honorable act to vote in the *country's* interest, instead.

As an example, I was recently discussing with a pacifist the pros and cons of armed conflict, and she said to me, "But what if it were *your* child who had to go into combat? Wouldn't you be against it?" I replied that using this kind of personal appraisal as the basis for evaluation

would be one of the most selfish possible ways of making a judgment
that would affect us all. War itself is not the issue here; nor are any of
the other serious matters that press the more concerned among us.
What is at stake is the process of making responsible political decisions,
and neither senator nor citizen does that by being self-serving.

◆ ◆ ◆

Dear Marilyn:

Imagine you have discovered documented evidence that your country's government has engaged in a colossal fraud. The result is honest
people driven to depression and suicide, others sent to jail, destroyed
businesses, and the cheating of the public of trillions of dollars over the
last seventy-five years. Assume also that the court system and the news
media are involved in the deception and cover-up. How would you go
about informing your fellow citizens?

David B. Baker
Crofton, Maryland

Dear David:

I would go to communications media that are not involved with the
news, a top-quality book publisher probably offering the best opportunity. However, I wouldn't bet that they're going to publish the book
unless you have a truly unique perspective on the 16th Amendment to
the U.S. Constitution, which was ratified around that time and to
which I suspect you're referring. After all, *everyone* gripes about income
tax.

◆ ◆ ◆

Dear Marilyn:

Could you define the term "government" in terms of its purpose and
its function without making any judgments as to which philosophy of
government is best, but providing a framework of goals and methods by
which judgment of such philosophies can be made?

Raymond G. Wilkinson
Montvale, New Jersey

Dear Raymond:

Philosophically speaking, I believe "government" could be defined as
the effective leadership of a society that acts as the parent to a national
family, performing many of the same functions. This leadership may
range from excellent to poor throughout the world, but all have one

thing in common—they act with authority to control behavior. We are born as arbitrarily to a government as we are born to a parent, neither of us choosing the other. Allegiance develops through familiarity, not through objective evaluation. Ultimately, the goal of the government is to take care of the citizenry; the goal of the citizenry is not to need care.

◆ ◆ ◆

Dear Marilyn:

Which kind of political representative is more befitting a democracy: a delegate-type representative who votes as the constituents demand, or a trustee-type who votes out of his or her own free will?

John D. Portelli
Albany, New York

Dear John:

Here's another possibility to be considered—one that I think may have the best of both: an "administrator"-type representative who votes as he or she believes the constituents *would* demand *if* they had access to all the information that the representative has.

◆ ◆ ◆

Dear Marilyn:

Imagine that a genetic engineer creates a breed of chimpanzee that has twice the normal brain mass. The chimps learn to communicate, seem intelligent, and express concern over their own mortality. Would you support the granting of full constitutional rights to these chimps?

John Steimke
North Augusta, South Carolina

Dear John:

Oh, you've come up with a dandy, all right. I'd say "no," however, because it would set a dangerous precedent to use intelligence as the criterion for granting constitutional rights. In other words, just because chimps are dull compared to humans isn't the reason they don't have constitutional rights now. And intelligence clearly isn't the reason that even the slowest-witted human being *does* have those rights.

◆ ◆ ◆

Dear Marilyn:

If pollsters are as accurate as they claim—plus or minus 4%—why can't we allow them to conduct national elections? It would be easier and cheaper.

Harry Kleinman
Bradenton, Florida

Dear Harry:

In a way, the Nielsen rating has already obtained that kind of power over television programming, their particular measurement performed with boxes that are attached to selected television sets to record which channels are being watched.

But even if the political pollsters are as accurate as the figures you mention, that isn't accurate enough for our elections. For example, if they gave Candidate Smith 52% instead of his actual 50% and gave Candidate Jones 48% instead of her actual 50%, it would appear to be a solid victory for Smith, but in reality was an even match. Or worse, if Smith actually had 51% but was given 49%, and Jones actually had 49% but was given 51%, the victory would go to the wrong person and the results would be just the opposite of the voting.

◆ ◆ ◆

Dear Marilyn:

Using only objective reasons—no subjective ones—can you name a single flaw with majority rule?

Anonymous

Dear Reader:

Sure. The majority may be wrong.

◆ ◆ ◆

Dear Marilyn:

I am not a communist or a pessimist. However, isn't it inevitable at some point that some form of socialism will rule most of the planet?

David Marks
Largo, Florida

Dear David:

Ideologically speaking, it may already. Although communism as a system of government has failed, socialist doctrines are among the most popular and widespread political views in the world today. And they have deeply penetrated other ideologies as well, capitalism included. Even conservatives in this country, for example, now accept many features of the welfare state.

◆ ◆ ◆

Dear Marilyn:

What do you think about the future of capitalism in this country?

Anonymous

Dear Reader:

We Americans seem to have developed a great love/hate relationship with capitalism. In these vacillating times, we love things for ourselves, but hate them for business, as if capitalism were un-American, instead of just the opposite. We love tax breaks for ourselves, but hate them for business; we love legislation for ourselves, but hate it for business; we love loopholes for ourselves, but hate them for business. In other words, we like to invite businessmen to dinner, but we don't really want them to eat.

◆ ◆ ◆

Dear Marilyn:

Is it possible for capitalism to exist without an underclass? Is an underclass essential to capitalism?

Manuel Jauregui
Elk Grove, California

Dear Manuel:

Let's first agree on terms. I see "underclass" more as part of a *social* system and think of it consisting of people such as drug dealers, prostitutes, and thieves. On the other hand, I see "lower class" more as part of an *economic* system and think of it consisting of people who have substantially less money than average for a variety of reasons.

But you asked about an *underclass* related to an *economic* system. Yes, I think capitalism can get along quite nicely without an outlaw class. I can't imagine any economic system that requires one, but neither can I imagine any economic system completely without one, unless it exists with an extremely repressive social system.

◆ ◆ ◆

Dear Marilyn:

Who is more compassionate—the liberal or the conservative?

M. Mueller
Fayetteville, Arkansas

Dear M:

The conservative seems more *deeply* compassionate, but the liberal seems more *broadly* compassionate. In other words, the conservative is probably more compassionate with those generally considered to be more deserving, and the liberal is probably more compassionate with those generally considered to be less deserving. Either way, I believe that compassion can be misplaced.

◆ ◆ ◆

Dear Marilyn:

Why is it that so often it seems that the outstanding quality of a person, institution, or concept is both its greatest strength *and* its greatest weakness? I mean things like a person's sense of compassion or society's liberalism or democracy's freedom.

Bonnie L. Fortini
Limington, Maine

Dear Bonnie:

Because you can so often have too much of a good thing. And that usually happens when the good thing stops being used as a means to an end and instead becomes an end in itself. This is the point where we lose control over ourselves, making it easy for others to use our own strong points against us.

◆ ◆ ◆

Dear Marilyn:

Do you think we are moving toward the future depicted in the novel called *1984?*

Anonymous

Dear Reader:

George Orwell's *1984* details a society in which every person is observed in totality and every thought is controlled. While the threat of a "Big Brother is watching you" mentality looms large in the American consciousness—a warning against absolute control by either left or right—I think we may be moving more toward the sort of society depicted in Aldous Huxley's novel called *Brave New World* in which individual identity is eliminated and people are treated as herds of animals. To avoid emotion, people simply take a drug, and especially noticeable is the way happiness is achieved—through sensory gratification. Sounds familiar, doesn't it?

◆ ◆ ◆

Dear Marilyn:

Do you think that people who hijack airliners for political reasons are mentally ill?

Anonymous

Dear Reader:

Well, if they aren't exactly mentally ill, they are certainly stupid. How else can you explain the reasoning behind people who will release the sick passengers for humanitarian reasons and then proceed to kill the healthy ones?

◆ ◆ ◆

Dear Marilyn:

Was the kidnappings of civilians by the Middle East terrorists an intelligent bargaining chip used against the rigid Establishment in order to gain the release of imprisoned comrades?

Leonard Faymore
Oxford, Wisconsin

Dear Leonard:

I don't believe the kidnapping of civilians is intelligent because it fails to take the long-term ramifications into account. The practice is universally despised, and courses of action that produce public hatred could not easily be considered intelligent, if, indeed, they are political. Short-term, it could be superficially successful—like extortion—but as extortion is highly unlikely to ever win the support of the people, neither will kidnapping.

◆ ◆ ◆

Dear Marilyn:

I don't know that much about what's going on in Northern Ireland these days, but I'm beginning to wonder about the psychology of zealotry in general. Do you have anything to say about it?

Anonymous

Dear Reader:

One difference between a political zealot and a religious zealot is that the former can afford more machine guns, but the latter will use them more quickly.

◆ ◆ ◆

Dear Marilyn:

What's the opposite of an extremist?

Helen Baer
La Mesa, California

Dear Helen:

A passivist. (Not to be confused with "pacifist" or "passive resister."

A pacifist doesn't want to make war; a passive resister doesn't want to make way; a passivist doesn't even want to make lunch.)

Both pacifists and passive resisters wrote to complain about my reply to this question, mainly because each thought I didn't give them enough credit, but no passivists wrote! See what I mean?

◆ ◆ ◆

Dear Marilyn:
I'm not satisfied anywhere on the political spectrum. Does this mean I'm mixed up?

Anonymous

Dear Reader:
I don't think so. The concept has great limitations. From left to right, its range covers only a single issue well—political power—but we tend to try to define all our opinions in terms of that criterion, as if it were the only one. Of course, we could add dimensions like a vertical line representing freedom, with one end "freedom *to*" and the other end "freedom *from*," and then we could call ourselves "upper leftists" or "lower rightists." Or we might wonder why politics should have a shape at all, and at least be thankful no one has given us a historical square or an economic oval.

◆ ◆ ◆

Dear Marilyn:
Are the terms "democratic" and "republican" synonymous? It appears that "democratic" applies to the theory of "one man, one vote," whereas "republican" refers to "the good of the public."

Charles J. Hallett
Babylon, New York

Dear Charles:
Both Democrats and Republicans alike believe in modern "democracy," a concept of government in which the important policy decisions are directed by a majority of the adult citizens. Likewise, they both believe in the modern "republic," a form of government in which the head of state is not a monarch, and the ruling power resides in the citizens entitled to vote, exercised by elected officials who are accountable to them and who govern according to law. A democracy may not be a republic, and a republic may not be a democracy. However, our

country is both: a democratic republic (or a republican democracy.)

"Democrats" as people often characterize themselves by their desire for social and economic equality. "Republicans" as people often characterize themselves by their desire for restricting the role of government in the affairs of the citizens.

And this is where the confusion arises: the word "democratic," when used to refer to the concept of "democracy," doesn't have anything more to do with the Democrats than it does with the Republicans. They *both* believe in democracy. Only when the word "Democratic" is capitalized and used in reference to party politics does it refer to one group and not the other.

Here are eight words we should know better than we do:

democracy	a concept of power in government
democratic	referring to the above
republic	a structural form of government
republican	referring to the above
Democrat	a member of one political party
Democratic	referring to the above
Republican	a member of another political party
Republican	referring to the above

◆ ◆ ◆

Dear Marilyn:

How can everyone make a profit? Doesn't someone lose when another gains?

Alton Lohner
Virginia Beach, Virginia

Dear Alton:

If you're talking strictly about dollars, theoretically someone must indeed lose for another to gain, assuming the supply of both money and people remains the same. If you're talking about "value," however, everything is different. Dollars symbolize value because they can buy some of it, but most of value can't be purchased. We can buy clothes for our bodies, but not health. We can hire employees to obey us, but not love. We can buy vacations in our old age, but not peace of mind. Everyone can make a profit by gaining happiness without causing unhappiness to others.

◆ ◆ ◆

Dear Marilyn:

When do stepping stones become stumbling blocks?

Mrs. Marjorie Richmond
Utica, Kentucky

Dear Marjorie:

A stumbling block is a stepping stone that has been through a congressional committee.

◆ ◆ ◆

Dear Marilyn:

I recently read that before Ferdinand Marcos died, his wife pleaded with President Aquino to allow them back in the country so he could die in his homeland. But she refused. Don't you think this was heartless, or, at the very least, weak of her? How could she be afraid of a dying old man?

Anonymous

Dear Reader:

Maybe she wasn't afraid of a dying old man; maybe she was afraid of a vigorous young wife. After all, Corazon Aquino didn't climb the Philippine ladder to power on her own merits; she was brought there by her husband, Benigno Aquino, the political opposition leader who was assassinated upon his return after three years of voluntary exile here in the United States. If she allowed the return of Ferdinand Marcos, she might soon have been face-to-face with another very powerful widow: Imelda Marcos.

◆ ◆ ◆

Dear Marilyn:

Is there any truth to the rumor that a peace treaty was never signed with Germany after World War II?

Anonymous
Vincennes, Indiana

Dear Reader:

No rumor, really—it's just another historical fact that, although the Allies cooperated in many ways, a serious estrangement grew between the U.S.S.R. and the other major Allies. This manifested itself in the failure to achieve a peace treaty with Germany or to establish a central government for the zones into which Germany had been divided. Instead, the Western powers combined their territory to form West Germany, and the Soviets retained East Germany. This whole situation played an important part in the Cold War.

◆ ◆ ◆

Dear Marilyn:

There is overwhelming evidence that this planet is being visited by civilizations from outer space. When do you think the American government will finally admit it?

Michael H. Landwehr
Kingman, Arizona

Dear Michael:

Well, if they'd just spend a summer evening at a sidewalk café in Greenwich Village looking at the people who walk by, as I've often done, I believe they could rapidly become convinced.

◆ ◆ ◆

Dear Marilyn:

What would happen to our world if it were suddenly stricken with a virus called "truth and honesty"? Could the major establishments survive? Could the average citizen survive?

Chalis W. Myers
Moncks Corner, South Carolina

Dear Chalis:

Truth and honesty are very different concepts. People can be perfectly honest without knowing the truth. And they can be perfectly knowledgeable about the truth without telling a word of it. Religious power structures tend to fall into the former category; unfortunately, political power structures tend to fall into the latter category. And private citizens who both know the truth and are honest about it are seldom heard. But if we put these two powerful principles together, I think the majority of the power structures would be in critical condition, with most eventually dying, but the average person would simply be "under the weather" for a while and would ultimately recover completely, to feel better than ever before.

◆ ◆ ◆

Dear Marilyn:

Do you believe that the ultimate end of any advanced civilization is its own destruction?

Barry J. Swink
Canton, Georgia

Dear Barry:

To me, this doesn't follow logically, but as it has happened so often, we should ask ourselves why, assuming that by "destruction," we mean that a great civilization fell and was replaced by an inferior one. In general, there would be four main ways for a civilization to fall: violently from the outside, peacefully from the outside, violently from within, and peacefully from within. As we're excluding outside reasons, however, we have to concentrate on the latter two. Looking back at history, it appears that a government may fall violently when it refuses too much to its people, and it may fall peacefully when it gives too much to its people. If that is the case, being advanced has less to do with internal destruction than failing to maintain that delicate balance.

13.

War and Peace

Dear Marilyn:

As nuclear disarmament of nations holding stockpiles would still leave those nations with the knowledge and capability of generating new weapons, what significance does disarmament have for world peace other than removing the impulsive capability?

Randall Denham
Bayou La Batre, Alabama

Dear Randall:

You make a good point, but I see the scenario a little more optimistically. Reducing and then eliminating stockpiles would be only a first step, to be followed by reducing and then eliminating capacities. Key knowledge would always be kept, of course, but gearing up the machinery of implementation would require such effort that it could hardly be done without thoughtful cooperation.

◆ ◆ ◆

Dear Marilyn:

All my life, I've believed that if men refused to fight, there would be no wars. All my life, I've been told it's not that simple. Why not?

Karleen Sheppard
St. Paul, Minnesota

Dear Karleen:

If every man and woman refused to fight, there would, indeed, be no more wars. But consider the price to be paid for this sort of peace. We would be easy prey for any madman. A leader could rise quite peacefully to power, acquire the necessary following, then inform all the members of a particular religion that they would be incarcerated in concentration camps until they died. To these people, and to many more, the presence of war in their lives might be preferable to the absence of dignity.

◆ ◆ ◆

Dear Marilyn:
When you come right down to it, all wars are alike, aren't they?
Anonymous

Dear Reader:
I don't think so. For example, religious wars have the potential to last much longer than political wars because they are less subject to the vagaries of public popularity. The war in Vietnam was perceived as political, but the wars in the Middle East were perceived as religious. Young men will die far more easily for gods than they will for congressional representatives.

◆ ◆ ◆

Dear Marilyn:
How can the universal desire for peace become effective?
Steve Sherry
Berkeley, California

Dear Steve:
The desire for peace may be universal, but nearly as universal is the desire for peace on one's own terms, and therein lies the problem: we fight for our own version of peace. For example, if people are quietly held in concentration camps and later exterminated, is this an acceptable peace? So rather than aiming at peace itself, I think it may be wiser to target nonpartisan communication among the world's peoples, the first step toward understanding differences.

◆ ◆ ◆

Dear Marilyn:
Is world peace possible? If so, what initial steps must be taken by governments and individuals to achieve this goal?
Rose Edwards
Severn, Maryland

Dear Rose:
I'd say the best chances for world peace lie with world interrelation-

ships. To take the first steps to achieve this, different governments could promote cooperative efforts with other governments, such as joint research programs. Diverse individuals could encourage collaborative projects with other individuals, such as shared literary and artistic endeavors. This can range from something as small as two youngsters across the ocean becoming "pen pals" to something as large as two publishers printing translations of each other's literary works regardless of whether it will make them a profit.

◆ ◆ ◆

Dear Marilyn:

If I had but one wish that would be granted for mankind, I would wish there to be no more wars. What would yours be?

Johnny Walker
Fort Wayne, Indiana

Dear Johnny:

Sometimes I just wish that we would all get what we deserve.

14.

The Press

Dear Marilyn:

The "news" is very depressing! In your opinion, is there more bad in this world than good, or are we just led to believe so?

Marge Bowsher
Phoenix, Arizona

Dear Marge:

Oh, I'm completely confident that there is *far* more good than bad, but one of the problems is that the good stuff is seldom as "immediate" as the bad stuff, and so it lends itself less to media attention. When a celebrity is healthy all of his life, no one notices, but when he has a heart attack, *everyone* does. (If the smog ever disappears from Los Angeles in the same amount of time that the oil was spilled off the coast of Alaska, it *will* be in the news.)

◆ ◆ ◆

Dear Marilyn:

Nearly all of the well-known journalists in this country are politically liberal and slant the news to the left. How can such a small part of the population have the same attitudes? Is it the fault of our journalism schools, or is it a genetic problem?

Scott Clay
Granbury, Texas

Dear Scott:

A genetic problem?! I hope you'll bear with me while I overgeneralize (distort, to be frank) to reply without writing a book. Liberals thrive in journalism because the sort of thing they write is so popular. More people want to read negative rather than positive things about those in power, for various reasons. And if you're negative about those in power, you're considered liberal, even if those in power are already leftist. This is one of the reasons that the changes that occurred in the U.S.S.R. were called "liberalization," a term that might otherwise seem oddly out of place. In other words, it is the readership that makes journalism a liberal profession.

◆ ◆ ◆

Dear Marilyn:

News reporters have a propensity for sticking cameras and microphones in the faces of friends and family members of victims of such tragedies as the crash of Pan Am 103 as soon as the event is known. What do they hope to achieve by this outrageous assault on the shocked and grieving? What good is done?

Roberta Maged
Roselle, New Jersey

Dear Roberta:

You asked two separate questions. First, they hope to achieve personal benefit from the situation, such as getting another byline or selling more newspapers. Second, no good is done, unless you consider the foregoing good.

But you should have asked a third question, "Is harm done?" I believe it is. In addition to the disgraceful violation of the privacy of those directly involved, there is "a greater harm"—the harm done by training the public taste to personal tragedy.

◆ ◆ ◆

Dear Marilyn:

You always hear that newspapers spell people's names wrong. Is it because they just don't care?

Anonymous

Dear Reader:

For the most part, it's because a misspelled name so often doesn't look wrong to anyone but its owner. Errors that creep into names through ambiguous handwriting and typographical accidents are more likely to remain than those that creep into ordinary words. After all, if you were proofreading an article, you wouldn't notice if "Mr. Marks" should have read "Mr. Parks," but you *would* notice if, instead of saying "Thomas Parks picks his successor," it read "Thomas Parks *kicks* his successor." (Even if it turned out to be true.)

15.

Issues

Dear Marilyn:

After having been poor, sexually and physically abused all through childhood; entering single motherhood as a teenager; having three babies approximately nine years apart; supporting them for twenty years by welfare (the sexual abuse being the factor in not sending them to day care in order to work); having been raped, homeless, and friendless during my adult years; *never* having outside help—financial or otherwise; never knowing that I was loved or cared for (ever!); never knowing what it was like to be able to pay your bills or dress nicely; how realistic is it to consider that a person like myself could possibly break the chain of poverty and trouble that seems to follow me throughout my very existence? Answers . . . please!!

Lotus
Enumclaw, Washington

Dear Lotus:

I have questions of my own first: 1) Why did you have the second two babies? 2) What does the sexual abuse have to do with not sending them to day care in order to work? And why didn't you work when they entered elementary school? 3) Why don't you think welfare is outside help?

When you can answer these honestly, you'll be able to gain control of your life again. Thank goodness it's not too late. You're still young (38, you added), and your grammar, spelling, and handwriting indicate that you'd be an acceptable employee. *Please* try to get any kind of beginning clerical position and write back to let me know how you're doing. A job will send your self-esteem soaring.

◆ ◆ ◆

Dear Marilyn:

Suppose that poverty were impossible to eradicate completely by any means under any sort of economic setup. In the long run, what effect would this have on society in general?

Joe Eastman
Colorado Springs, Colorado

Dear Joe:

The only way I can conceive of the poor being an immutable constant is by defining them as those people who, *through no fault of their own*, are unable to satisfy basic human needs. As living standards rise, and the gulf between them and the rest of us widens, I believe they will become more and more sharply defined as a special group of people— like children or the aged—who need special protection. And the wider the gulf, the sharper the definition, and the more that society will be able to afford to provide that protection.

◆ ◆ ◆

Dear Marilyn:

Why must we pay to live?

Kathleen Bainbridge
Birdsboro, Pennsylvania

Dear Kathleen:

Considering food, shelter, and clothing to be basic needs, everything that we need is already owned by someone else, and we must pay these people to let us have it, unless they are willing to give it to us free, of course, but the choice is not ours.

For shelter, we must have land, and for land, we must have money. Clothing must be purchased if it is not made by hand, but even making clothing requires materials. While those materials don't grow on trees, they *may* grow on animals, but animals require land, and land requires money. And food must also be purchased if it is not grown, but even though food *does* grow on trees, trees require land, and land requires— guess what—money.

◆ ◆ ◆

Dear Marilyn:

I've read that it is possible to distribute more evenly the very uneven distribution of wealth in this richest of nations. This is a *deep* concern of mine. What do *you* think?

Mrs. Mary Colello
Altoona, Pennsylvania

Dear Mary:

There's no doubt in my mind that this is possible. However, are you sure this is what you want? If so, why should the wealth remain inside this one country? If it is right to redistribute wealth evenly throughout the country, wouldn't it be far more right to redistribute it evenly throughout the world?

In that case, all the citizens of the United States—and all other wealthy countries—would be required to give up everything above a bare subsistence level, and that would then be redistributed among the poor people in the Third World countries in order to bring them *up* to that same subsistence level.

◆ ◆ ◆

Dear Marilyn:

Millions of dollars are spent on the Olympics, and of course, these games are very exciting. I have problems, however, with all this hoopla being made over sporting events. If someone runs faster than someone else, or if someone dives better than someone else, what substantive good has this done, other than boost that individual's vanity? It seems to me that all the money, time, and effort could have been better spent helping the homeless or starving ones in our world. There would be real joy in giving someone hope who has none. Can you help me understand the importance of competitive sports?

Lenny Moore
Huntsville, Alabama

Dear Lenny:

I doubt there's much actual importance, but if we eliminated all activities that did not produce substantive good, it would be a bleak world, indeed. Entertainment, sports included, would be among the first to go, all right, but art and literature would not be far behind. After all, Shakespeare's plays provide no food to the hungry of this world, do they? And as far as the average person is concerned, what real good does it do to dance? Or to eat popcorn? Or to wear green on St. Patrick's Day?

◆ ◆ ◆

Dear Marilyn:

The study of archaeology is very interesting, but can the expenditure of funds and expertise be justified? Could you cite a few examples of how any of the findings have benefitted mankind? Possibly the money and manpower could be put to better use solving some of the problems of current times.

Douglas L. Griffin
North Windham, Maine

Dear Douglas:

With all the ridiculous expenditure of funds on other nonsense, how can you target so fascinating and illuminating a discipline as archeology? Are art museums a waste of time and money? Would you prefer that paleontologists leave dinosaurs hidden in the dirt? Would the world be a better place *without* King Tut's treasures or the entire city of Pompeii?

◆ ◆ ◆

Dear Marilyn:

How much would each person pay to provide enough money for the government if they all paid the same amount?

Anne Tansey
Candler, North Carolina

Dear Anne:

In 1988, the government collected about 400 billion in individual income taxes. With a population of about 250 million, this means that if every man, woman, and child paid $1,600 each and no more, the government would receive the same amount of money. And back as recently as 1950, with government revenues of 17 billion and a population of 150 million, that figure would have been only $113 per person.

◆ ◆ ◆

Dear Marilyn:

If I place a sum of money in a drawer indefinitely, would our government make money, lose money, or wouldn't it make any difference?

T. V. Riddle
Clifton Forge, Virginia

Dear T. V.:

It would make a difference, both to you *and* to the government. As far as *you're* concerned, if you put your money in a drawer, it won't earn interest, of course, and with an interest rate of seven percent, for example, money will double in ten years. But one of the most important functions of interest, besides encouraging savings, is allocating savings funds to those sectors of the economy where savings can be used most profitably, a significant factor in achieving economic growth.

◆ ◆ ◆

Dear Marilyn:

Would changing the tax structure from taxing income to taxing spending have a beneficial effect on this country?

Margaret Lang
Leucadia, California

Dear Margaret:

I'm not a scholar of tax theory, but this may make for a better answer in certain ways. Students of taxation generally like tax; you don't become a veterinarian because you dislike animals. Those of us who are "outsiders" may well be necessary.

In particular, the income tax is not a fact of life. Not only is it relatively new in history, the top rate was only 6% in its early days in the United States, increasing to a minimum of 23% and a maximum of 94% by the end of World War II.

It seems reasonable to argue that income taxes are less favorable to economic growth than expenditure taxes because income taxes reduce money that is saved and thus available either for direct investment or for lending to direct investors such as financial institutions. However, we must keep in mind that taxes serve not only the purpose of economic growth, but those of governmental fiscal requirements and income redistribution, both of which can interfere with it.

In other words, the answer to your question must ultimately lie in what you consider just, and in the modern welfare state, other goals more and more often give way to that of the reapportionment of personal resources among the population. If that's not your idea of justice, you're going to condemn the very taxes that others applaud.

◆ ◆ ◆

Dear Marilyn:

Can you say something about the subject of money?

Claudia Eve
Newport Beach, California

Dear Claudia:

The number of a person's relatives usually becomes directly proportionate to the size of his estate.

◆ ◆ ◆

Dear Marilyn:

Can you explain why gold was and is considered the most precious metal? Why not silver, for example?

Ethel Christian
Alanson, Michigan

Dear Ethel:

Gold was one of the first few metals used by humans in its elemental form, the others being silver and copper, because it could be found uncombined and needed no sophisticated refining techniques. All three are attractive to man. However, unlike silver and copper, gold does not tarnish. Combining that trait with the fact that gold is also the most workable of metals, it seems only reasonable that it would soon become accepted in exchange for goods and services, eventually assuming its present stature by sheer force of its long-standing reputation.

◆ ◆ ◆

Dear Marilyn:

What is your definition of profit?

Bruce C. Benke
Belle Mead, New Jersey

Dear Bruce:

Profit is what we have left after we make a donation to a worthwhile cause.

◆ ◆ ◆

Dear Marilyn:

I think we're a bunch of hypocrites! If not, why do people always say, "Money isn't everything," when, in reality, money is all that seems to concern today's society?

N. Stevens
Youngstown, Ohio

Dear N.:

I think the people who don't have money say it because they hope it's true, and the people who *do* have money say it because they *know* it's true.

◆ ◆ ◆

Dear Marilyn:

If money, politics, federal, state, and local law were no object, how would you help the street people?

> Don Volker
> Ormond Beach, Florida

Dear Don:

There appear to be two main reasons for the existence of homeless people. For one, there is the policy of discharging many of the mentally ill from hospitals under the assumption that with the powerful new medications now available, these people could be released from the institutional environment where they could become part of the community. For another, there is the major reduction in the availability of low-income housing due to significant cutbacks in federal funding for subsidized housing and local factors such as the renovation of urban property by middle- and upper-income people, transforming low-income neighborhoods into areas of attractive, but expensive homes.

With the above in mind, and with your lack of restrictions, I would first fund community mental health services and shelters for the people who are ill. I would then fund job training for those who are not. Third, I would provide dormitory housing for those who become employed, to be supported by their earnings.

There are numerous people who are capable of productively filling the less sophisticated jobs always available in complex societies. They shouldn't be forced to live with birth relatives like children or on the streets and in the parks like wild animals because of current economic conditions or restrictive zoning laws meant to prevent people from "living in sin." But neither do I find having your own private apartment to be a basic human right.

◆ ◆ ◆

Dear Marilyn:

Why is it that the homeless on the streets are increasing, as are the dollars we pour into the problem, when each day's paper contains columns of "help wanted" ads? Granted, some of these jobs may not be in desirable fields, but common sense seems to dictate *any* job rather than the risks inherent in street life.

Isabelle White
Prescott, Arizona

Dear Isabelle:

If sociologists are correct in evaluating homeless people as either mentally ill or unable to afford housing, it appears to follow that the former group would be incapable of holding the jobs you mention, of course, but that the latter group would be unable to earn enough money at them to support themselves independently, anyway. A more pointed question would be to ask why those in this latter group aren't both holding those jobs and living with others.

◆ ◆ ◆

Dear Marilyn:

What could or would happen if everyone in America had a job?

Tiny Jaudon
Midlothian, Virginia

Dear Tiny:

If you mean those who are willing and able to work, economists traditionally say that full employment generates pressures for higher wages, higher prices, and a decline in productivity as the motivation to work hard decreases with the need to do so in order to remain employed.

◆ ◆ ◆

Dear Marilyn:

More and more labor is done by machinery, but the forty-hour work week has stayed the same for decades. Where does the extra work go?

Lawrence Fleming
Pasadena, California

Dear Lawrence:

It goes into progress.

◆ ◆ ◆

Dear Marilyn:

Greatness in musical composition, conducting, and with notable exceptions, performance, has been primarily a male phenomenon through the years. Aside from the obvious discriminatory policies of

which our society has always been guilty, are there other factors that
contribute to this whole lopsided affair?

Ronald T. Michalak
Pine Rush, New York

Dear Ronald:

There's the behavior of women themselves to consider. Greatness is
more likely to arise in proportion to the number of those making the
requisite effort in the field. Maybe it's on the way!

♦ ♦ ♦

Dear Marilyn:

Why do you think the majority of women are still discriminated
against in the workplace? Will we ever make what men do, despite
taking time off in the childrearing years?

Kim Foster
Baltimore, Maryland

Dear Kim:

Let's be realistic. If one woman works for ten years straight, and
another woman works for two years, takes off six to rear a child until
he or she enters elementary school, then goes back to work for two
years, which woman is going to have a greatly superior position in the
workplace? The first one, of course, and we don't hold it against her—
it only makes sense. So why should we hold it against a man?

♦ ♦ ♦

Dear Marilyn:

How would you resolve the apparent conflict between women's rights
and the lack of gender-free singular third-person pronouns?

Richard de Mille
Santa Barbara, California

Dear Richard:

I'd coin new words, introducing them into the language one at a
time, and beginning with the use of "s/he" for each instance where the
dual-gender phrase "he or she" would be appropriate. (Other pronouns
could follow later.) This means that usage would be strictly limited to
such contexts as, for example, "Executive power of the United States
of America shall be vested in a president. S/he shall hold this office for
a term of four years." It would not, of course, replace the *individual-
gender* words "he" and "she," such as in "Margaret Thatcher was the
British prime minister from 1979 to 1990. She was born in 1925."

In looking for possibilities, I considered dozens of new combinations, but "s/he" was an easy winner on several counts. It's easy to say, (seh-HEE), it's easy to write, and it conveys the message clearly. Of course, it took many years for "Ms." to be fully accepted, but we have to start *sometime*.

◆ ◆ ◆

Dear Marilyn:

Where is the line that distinguishes between a person who is preju-diced and a person who has made an honest evaluation?

Eugene Bernhard and David Hauser
Wesleyville, Pennsylvania

Dear Eugene and David:

The judgment of a prejudiced person is inferior due to being either premature or unwarranted. That is, he or she has made a decision either *before* getting the facts or *despite* getting the facts. What is usually overlooked, however, is that there is prejudice "for" just as there is prejudice "against." For example, women who cannot speak ill of women are as prejudiced as women who cannot speak well of blacks. All types of prejudiced people, then, may be distinguished from all types of people who've made honest evaluations simply by seeing if they apply the same standards to "their own."

◆ ◆ ◆

Dear Marilyn:

What can blacks do individually and collectively to assimilate into the American and world mainstream rapidly? Please avoid most of the stock answers.

John Spence
Altadena, California

Dear John:

The quickest way for anyone to assimilate into a group is to become as much like the group as possible. This would include manner of dress, behavior, and even thought processes, such as value systems. We should keep in mind, however, that the quickest way to a goal is not always the best way. For example, the mainstream might be badly flawed and not all that desirable to join as it is. In addition, there are many people who actively dislike being part of *any* mainstream, preferring instead to trickle off in their own unique way.

◆ ◆ ◆

Dear Marilyn:

Do you have a constructive remedy for disillusionment in today's seemingly self-destructive society?

Scott Eugene Stickney
Portland, Oregon

Dear Scott:

In your spare time, read a little history about the classic civilizations of the world, and things won't look so bad these days.

◆ ◆ ◆

Dear Marilyn:

I have very serious concerns for the future of this nation and wonder if there is any hope for America regarding its destructive drug problems. If you could decide the next major step to take to stop the importation of drugs or stop individuals from dealing drugs or putting a stop to this whole corrupt situation, what step would you take?

Extremely Concerned
San Diego, California

Dear Reader:

If you're asking *me*, you're probably looking for a different approach, something other than all the methods that are already being tried and aren't working, and I'm going to give that to you. This is a novel strategy to consider, one that may seem startling at first, but could become more interesting on further examination: the government could contaminate the drug supply.

◆ ◆ ◆

Dear Marilyn:

At the rate the world's population is growing, will we run out of food or room first? Or will a nuclear bomb or a disease such as AIDS solve these problems for us?

J. W.
Glen Easton, West Virginia

Dear Reader:

Food, for sure. Famine problems are already widespread, killing multitudes of people, but space problems are much less severe and aren't killing people even where they are occurring. And if predictions are correct, and the world population does indeed stabilize by the end of the 21st century at about 10 billion, there will still be enough physical space for them. A plentiful supply of food, however, seems far less likely. But I don't see how nuclear mayhem or catastrophic disease can be called solutions; they seem like *problems* to me!

◆ ◆ ◆

Dear Marilyn:

Given problems such as pollution, crowding, fuel and food shortages, etc., are you optimistic or pessimistic concerning the quality of life in, say, a thousand years from now?

Kenneth E. Burch
Arlington, Texas

Dear Kenneth:

Oh, optimistic, definitely. There have been difficulties pressing people since ancient times—even the Romans living in 200 B.C. bemoaned the polluting of the Tiber and complained about the crowding and the noise of all those oxcarts, wagons, and chariots clattering around the city—but things have always gotten better *so far*, haven't they?

◆ ◆ ◆

Dear Marilyn:

Why can't important problems, such as environmental pollution, be managed so that they don't need major overhaul every few years? In other words, why do we seem to prefer short-term planning in most of our affairs?

Byron Hess
Northridge, California

Dear Byron:

Maybe because the physician must closely follow the progress of his case. Too much medication will often damage the patient more than the illness will.

16.

Laws and the Courts

Dear Marilyn:
If humans were devoid of feelings, would we have any need for laws?

Jim Green
Hayward, California

Dear Jim:
I think so. Keeping in mind that emotions prevent crime as well as cause it, we'd also need to consider the world of instinct—those inherited behavior patterns that function to promote survival, most noticeable in combative and sexual activity. These patterns may be tempered by the learning process, and the higher the animal form, the more pliable the behavior. Among humans, most of all, learned behavior prevails over inherited behavior, and laws stand tall among the processes by which society can exercise its influence.

◆ ◆ ◆

Dear Marilyn:
What do you tell an eighteen-year-old who faces death by execution (or spending the rest of his life in prison without the possibility of parole) about the value of his future?

I represent such a boy in a death penalty case, and I'm enclosing material to substantiate that for you.

Name Withheld
Attorney and Counselor-at-Law
City and State Withheld

Dear Reader:

You tell an eighteen-year-old the same thing you tell a thirty-eight-year-old or a fifty-eight-year-old: The value of a life lies less in how long it is than in how good it is, and freedom has never been a prerequisite of personal worth.

Any determination of value, however, must be made within context to be worthwhile, linking our future inextricably with our past. We cannot cordon off a piece of it to suit our convenience. Should Hitler be judged by his final days? Or should he be judged by *all* of them?

Just as the lives a physician saves remain indelibly with him or her, so are the lives an individual murders never forgotten. Ultimately, our future is like a mirror. Whenever we face it, it always reflects what we left behind.

◆ ◆ ◆

Dear Marilyn:

Can a person in his "right" mind commit a *premeditated* murder?
                                    A. J. D'Atri
                                    Daytona Beach Shores, Florida

Dear A. J.:

Sure. Soldiers kill people as a matter of course, and we don't question their sanity. The only difference between "murder" and "killing" is that "murder" is against the law, but breaking the law certainly isn't considered a definition of mental illness.

◆ ◆ ◆

Dear Marilyn:

What kind of world would it be if there were no laws? There are those in the world who think that all laws are an infringement on one's rights.

                                    J. Ambrosio
                                    Ozone Park, New York

Dear J.:

Maybe they are, but I, for one, am very happy to see an infringement on a Jeffrey Dahmer's so-called "rights."

◆ ◆ ◆

Dear Marilyn:

As society is made up of individuals free in thought and choice, can institutions such as law enforcement agencies ever provide us with a crime-free life, or would it be just a crime-controlled life?

John W. Krzywicki, Jr.
Wilkes-Barre, Pennsylvania

Dear John:

I want to make it clear that I disagree with your assessment of society, but even if it were true, criminals are those who are unsuccessfully controlled *regardless* of the level of individual freedom involved. In other words, just because people are free doesn't mean they're free to be criminals. That means the difference in the level of crime might simply be due to the difference in the level of enforcement. It is seldom the case that a permissive society has a strict judicial system or that a strict society has a permissive judicial system. But it could be done. Depending on what we want and how much we're willing to pay for it, I suspect we can *choose* our crime rate.

◆ ◆ ◆

Dear Marilyn:

Why do you think this country is so soft on crime? By that, I mean why is the penal code so lenient? And are the judges giving as much punishment as the law allows?

Bill Sorrelle
Frederick, Maryland

Dear Bill:

Looking at this objectively, it would appear that one of the reasons the penal code is more lenient in this country than in many other parts of the world is because Americans believe, accurately or not, that there is less personal responsibility on the part of the criminal than those others believe. These days, society itself is often considered the offender here, and judges just reflect the current attitudes when sentencing.

◆ ◆ ◆

Dear Marilyn:

Do you think it possible that what appears to be good or evil to us might not be what those on another planet see, where justice and injustice may be reversed?

S. E.
Lewcadia, California

Dear Reader:

Yes, but we don't have to go as far as another planet to find an example. Among our closest neighbors, we find both those who see society as the victim of the criminal and those who see the criminal as the victim of society.

◆ ◆ ◆

Dear Marilyn:

If justice is blind, how can we expect fairness?

Lois Gronauer
San Marino, California

Dear Lois:

According to American sentiment, justice is considered to be blind *in order* to be fair. In other words, it is supposed to make judgments based only on the facts and not on the people involved. However, people are also bundles of facts themselves, and leaving them out of the analytical process forces us to make decisions with less information than we have available.

◆ ◆ ◆

Dear Marilyn:

Do you agree that the right of every citizen to a jury of his peers is a fallacy and that the jury system ought to be composed of professional retired people? For example, when a doctor is tried for malpractice, there is never a doctor on the jury panel.

Norman L. Koch
Kensington, Maryland

Dear Norman:

It's my understanding that the jury must simply be representative of the community, not of our peers. In any event, I don't see why our peers should be defined by our profession. After all, we have political peers and religious peers and ethnic peers, too.

◆ ◆ ◆

Dear Marilyn:

Here in the United States, due to the separation of church and state, I say it is not legal for the court system to require a person to take an oath based on faith in God. I believe this is a clear violation of our rights. What do you say?

Raiden Trujillo
Pueblo, Colorado

Dear Raiden:

I know this is going to annoy you, but I personally don't see the oath as based on God; I see it as based on tradition. The whole point of it, after all, is simply to force a person to tell the truth with the hope that this might be better accomplished if he or she fears some sort of divine retribution.

The following is a very common oath: "I do solemnly swear that the testimony I am about to give will be the truth, the whole truth, and nothing but the truth. So help me God." If you remove the last sentence, the church might be more separated from the state, but the state might very well be more separated from the truth. Do you mind paying that price?

Oh, did I ever hear it when that appeared. The letters were divided among people who felt that I didn't realize that the court system does not require an oath based on God and those who simply detested my answer. One reader wrote, "I have no qualms separating the church from the state—religion's record of persecution, crusades, holy wars, and corruption hardly make it an admirable bastion of truth."

But I had stated that the religious oath was a common one, not the only one. That is, I didn't feel the reader was asking whether people are required to take a religious oath, but whether such an oath should be illegal. I should have made that more clear. And for not doing so, I was blasted from everyone from an angry Madalyn Murray O'Hair, the atheist activist, to a thoughtful American Civil Liberties Union, and many readers wrote to express their extreme distaste for any kind of reference to religion whatsoever.

So, to clarify any misunderstanding, here's what I do mean: I don't believe it serves the cause of truth to make it illegal to require a religious oath of a religious person. (That's not the same as requiring a religious pledge of allegiance from everyone, for heaven's sake.)

◆ ◆ ◆

Dear Marilyn:

Criminally speaking, what difference, if any, is there between "innocent" and "not guilty"?

Jud Shrader
Aviston, Illinois

Dear Jud:

Outside a court of law, I would say that "innocence" is freedom from guilt through lack of fault, and "not guilty" is freedom from guilt through lack of proof.

◆ ◆ ◆

Dear Marilyn:
   Where does all the money go that is collected in courts for fines?
K. Buhl
Scottsdale, Arizona

Dear K.:
   The fine in a criminal case, other than the amount of damages, is always paid to "the state," regardless of who is actually the damaged party. But the identity of "the state" varies. In some of the larger cities, the traffic and parking fines bring in enough funds to run the whole traffic court system, which seems innocent enough. In some of the small towns, though, fines may be such a significant source of revenue that they pay the salaries of local officials, which seems far less innocent.

17.

Work

Dear Marilyn:

Doctor, lawyer, laborer, U.S. president, educator—of these five, whose work is the most important?

T. W. Koskinen
L'Anse, Michigan

Dear T. W.:

If we think of these as groups, I'd say the most important work is done by presidents, followed by laborers, without whom nothing gets done at all. But as individuals, I'd say the most important work is done by a president, followed by an educator, each of whom is personally responsible for shaping hundreds of minds.

◆ ◆ ◆

Dear Marilyn:

Do you think anyone can achieve any job goal if he or she has enough incentive? Or are we limited by our intelligence? For example, if I want to be a doctor, but have only average intelligence, can I achieve it through sheer determination?

Karen Fleming
Akron, Ohio

Dear Karen:

While I'm completely confident that normal intellectual capacity is

far greater than is necessary for nearly all jobs, I'm also confident that
nearly all of us reach our limits of motivation, hard work, and perseverance far before we reach our limits of intelligence. In other words, our
attitudes hold us back more than our aptitudes.

◆ ◆ ◆

Dear Marilyn:

Could you please tell me what is the most dangerous job in the world
today? I might want to fill out an application if the pay is okay.

Craig A. Thornton
Chicago, Illinois

Dear Craig:

According to my information, firefighting ranks all the way down
at the bottom of the desirability list with regard to stress level, job
environment, and physical demands. However, with a little effort, I'm
sure you could easily find plenty of individual jobs that could surpass it,
such as official taster for Fidel Castro.

---

*And would you believe that firefighters wrote me to complain?! Why did I
rank them at the bottom? they asked, insulted. Did I have something against
firefighters?! Well, what should I have written? That firefighting is relaxing,
safe, and effortless? I'll bet they'd have written to complain about that, for
sure!*

◆ ◆ ◆

Dear Marilyn:

I am always looking for a job. The main reason is because employers
either do not tell me the duties or deceive me when I am interviewed.
Can you tell me how to spot this and how I can avoid it in my future
undertakings?

Ellen M. Koenig
Clark, New Jersey

Dear Ellen:

My advice is to continue attending interviews as usual, but whenever
you're actually offered a position, *tell that employer just what you told me.*
They're unlikely to retract the offer once they've decided upon you,
and they'll be put on notice that you really need to have an inside look
at the job before you accept it, which they'll now be more likely to
provide. There are few things more irritating to an employer than
spending months or years training an employee only to have him or her
quit.

◆ ◆ ◆

Dear Marilyn:

During the last year, I've gone on a lot of interviews, but I haven't been able to get a decent job. What can I do to increase my chances? Doesn't the law of averages work here?

Corlis Mitchell
Portsmouth, Virginia

Dear Corlis:

I'm afraid not. Employers hire by choice, not by chance, and if you're not what they want, it's all over. But here's a suggestion that can't hurt. It appears that your written application is good enough to get you interviews, but your interviews may not be good enough to get you a job. The next few times you get turned down after an interview *with a noticeably helpful or friendly person*, give him or her a call afterward and ask if you can come in again, but just briefly. If you're lucky enough to get a "yes," explain when you get there that you understand you're not the right person for that particular job, but that you'd greatly appreciate any one tip he or she might give you to improve your chances of getting the *next* one. (And then listen!)

◆ ◆ ◆

Dear Marilyn:

What is the best answer to give when an interviewer asks you, "Why do you want this job?"

Anthony Grimes
Norfolk, Virginia

Dear Anthony:

For a beginning job, you might tell the interviewer that you actually enjoy doing that sort of work, making it likely that you'll be a very good employee in many ways, from showing up on time to working with enthusiasm. But only say this if it's true. If it isn't, do both of you a favor and look instead for a job you *do* like.

◆ ◆ ◆

Dear Marilyn:

Can people really be thoroughly evaluated through interviews? I personally think that trial and error is still the best system for evaluating anything. What do *you* think?

Marvin Pepper
Greenville, South Carolina

Dear Marvin:

Trial and error may be all right for chocolates, puppies, and blind dates, but extensive interviewing is in order for baby-sitters, doctors, and basement-waterproofing specialists.

I'm still wondering why I didn't hear from the basement-waterproofing specialists about that one.

◆ ◆ ◆

Dear Marilyn:

What characteristics would you look for to evaluate a person's intellectual ability?

Doris Bailey
Evansville, Indiana

Dear Doris:

If people know "what" happens, they have average ability; if they know "how" it happens, they have superior ability; if they know "why" it happens, they have exceptional ability.

◆ ◆ ◆

Dear Marilyn:

Is it true that you learn more from your mistakes than from your successes?

John Wilkie
San Diego, California

Dear John:

I don't think so. If this were the case, the people who make the most mistakes would be our most learned, and the people who have the most successes would be our least learned. In other words, our Supreme Court Justices would know nothing compared to the people in prison! It might be more accurate to say that the kind of person who is capable of learning from his or her mistakes doesn't make all that many.

◆ ◆ ◆

Dear Marilyn:

Why is it so hard to live in today's world? Is it because we are never taught that a great deal of individual initiative is needed?

M. J. Reynolds
San Antonio, Texas

Dear M. J.:

Sometimes I wonder if it's because we *are* taught. The faster the horses run, the harder it is to win the race.

◆ ◆ ◆

Dear Marilyn:

Should I feel dissatisfied if I haven't chosen a specialty area to work in by the age of forty? What is your advice?

Allen M. Roberts
Tinker Air Force Base, Oklahoma

Dear Allen:

Don't be too hard on yourself. Where would an orchestra be without its conductor? And what would a football team do without a coach? There are "generalists" in this world as well as "specialists," and we need them both.

But if you simply can't tolerate staying put for very long, how about looking into a job that *requires* travel (instead of one that doesn't, the way most people do)? That way, instead of moving around from job to job, your *job* will move around with *you*!

◆ ◆ ◆

Dear Marilyn:

Where is the best place to live, and why?

Regina Love
Springfield, Oregon

Dear Regina:

The best place to live is wherever you will be challenged to develop your finest element or skill to a level significantly broader or deeper than it is now. Personal or professional growth is not only exciting, it makes you both independent *and* desirable, two qualities that grow more valuable with each passing year.

Happily, there should be numerous cities that will satisfy this requirement for most of us, and here are two personal suggestions for choosing among them. First, concentrate on the best aspects of the place, not the worst. When you're feeling good about yourself, annoyances fade into the background and can even turn into an amusement. And second, don't take fear of the unfamiliar into consideration. Just because you were born into a city doesn't mean cities like it suit you. That was your *mother's* choice!

◆ ◆ ◆

Dear Marilyn:

I know this question is different from most that you answer, but I'm a thirty-year-old actor and have a problem with agoraphobia. How does one get over this? I just auditioned at Yale Drama School and felt too far away from home and insecure.

Name Withheld
West Hartford, Connecticut

Dear Reader:

Psychiatrists have various methods of helping people cope with the fear of leaving home, but I personally know of none better than to repeatedly place yourself in the situation. In other words, don't wait for the next audition to go away, even if it's just taking a train to a nearby city to spend the weekend as often as you can. Whether personally or professionally, this will be money well spent. There's a *very* thrilling world out there. (But don't feel too bad. *Anyone* would feel insecure auditioning at the Yale Drama School!)

18.

School

Dear Marilyn:

If a student plans on a career which doesn't require much education, is it important to do well academically?

Shannon Mullis, student
Lincoln Elementary School
Bedford, Indiana

Dear Shannon:

Whether a career choice requires sixteen, twelve, or only eight years of education is not the significant factor. Any number of years spent should be spent well in order to gain the most benefit from them. Even if all you really need to do is learn how to read, write, and use basic mathematics, it's best if you know how to do it well.

◆ ◆ ◆

Dear Marilyn:

What kind of educational system would best meet the needs of current and future society?

Niela Miller
Nagog Woods, Massachusetts

Dear Niela:

I think the best kind of educational system is one that clears a path and lights the way for every individual to reach his or her potential, but neither chooses nor channels. Inner needs should be satisfied first, because if the individual members of a society aren't happy, adding increasingly sophisticated technology becomes pointless. The success of a society shouldn't be judged on whether the average citizen drives a car with a dashboard that resembles a cockpit; rather, it might be judged on, among other things, whether he or she sleeps peacefully at night. With this in mind, I'd recommend an educational system that relies heavily on encouraging individual motivation in the early years rather than pushing or pulling youngsters along a precocious path by teaching them as much as they'll tolerate. I'd rather see more happy people than yet another communications satellite sent into orbit.

◆ ◆ ◆

Dear Marilyn:

What do you see as the most important function of the elementary school?

> Pat McAlister, Principal
> Lincoln Elementary School
> Bedford, Indiana

Dear Pat:

One of the most useful would be to instill motivation.

◆ ◆ ◆

Dear Marilyn:

As a former high school teacher, now an instructor of the disadvantaged wishing to upgrade themselves, I *hate* deciding on grades. "The curve" has much to recommend itself. Should we lean toward expecting more and grade harder, or encourage more and build confidence? (I try to do both.)

> J. Hall, Jr.
> Pasadena, Texas

Dear J.:

I think it would be helpful if the grading procedure changed its entire emphasis to one of encouragement. This would mean that teachers would be free to grade students on a completely individual basis according to whether that student needed a bit of ordinary confidence or a realistic recognition of effort or perhaps a little prodding to go on to even greater achievement, forgetting curves, straight percentages, and everything else. Then they could leave the final assessment to the standardized tests such as the College Boards.

Goodness knows there's already far too much assessment in life and precious little encouragement.

◆ ◆ ◆

Dear Marilyn:

Do universities such as Harvard and Stanford and Yale have admission standards that are too high?

Anonymous
Cedar Rapids, Iowa

Dear Reader:

I don't think so. If they lowered them, they would still have only the same number of positions to fill and would naturally select the best of the available candidates, wouldn't they?

◆ ◆ ◆

Dear Marilyn:

What is the value of the social and behavioral sciences in America's colleges and universities?

G. Edward Montgomery,
Associate Professor of Anthropology
Washington University
St. Louis, Missouri

Dear Edward:

If it weren't for the broad perspective of the social and behavioral sciences, I see no discipline offering understanding of the whole of social interaction, the elementary component of human civilization. Such phenomena as social inequality and stratification, ethnic and racial relations, and crime and deviance studied in isolation can be of little value outside the framework that can create, maintain, or mitigate against them.

The only shortcoming I can find is that critics question the applicability of scientific method here, but I don't find this a worthy criticism. Application of the scientific method is not wholly appropriate to numerous other worthwhile disciplines, and I see no reason to regard it as a prerequisite. How in the world are we to employ the scientific method to the study of history, for example?

◆ ◆ ◆

Dear Marilyn:

How can we teach children and adults to be more responsible?

David P. Marshall
Santa Ana, California

Dear David:

There are many ways to be responsible, but one of them lends itself to rational training especially well, and that is the understanding that a person is answerable for his or her own behavior. To encourage that, we need only to interfere less, in order to make sure that we don't separate behavior from its consequences. When a child breaks a toy, whether by accident or on purpose, if we promptly replace it for him, he doesn't learn that mishandling a possession may result in damage or loss. Instead, he learns that it doesn't matter much because someone else will fix it for him. Fortunately, childhood is a fine time to learn these lessons because there are so many "small" consequences that will loom large to the child.

◆ ◆ ◆

Dear Marilyn:

What are two of the worst things that we commonly teach our children?

Francis J. Gribbin
Wilmington, Delaware

Dear Francis:

That a knowledge of science is nice, but not necessary, and that a knowledge of sex is necessary, but not nice.

What? No mail on that one?

◆ ◆ ◆

Dear Marilyn:

If our children were taught creativity, would we be a happier and more fulfilled people?

Janet Pizzo
Cornwall-on-Hudson, New York

Dear Janet:

If by "creativity," you mean the ability to produce something new, traditionally within the purview of the arts, I'd say "yes," adding that I would go a major step further and encourage creativity in all other areas as well, including the sciences. I think it's very possible that the creative person in art will generate a painting, and the creative person in science will generate an invention.

◆ ◆ ◆

Dear Marilyn:

Is life a constant conditioning experience?

Terrence J. Crowley
Bellwood, Illinois

Dear Terrence:

I'm afraid I believe so, but it doesn't have to be nearly as invasive a phenomenon as it is. If we all had as much instruction in *how* to think as we already do in *what* to think, the situation would be much different.

◆ ◆ ◆

Dear Marilyn:

What's the difference between an error and a mistake?

Art Bullock
Medford, Massachusetts

Dear Art:

An error becomes a mistake when we refuse to admit it.

◆ ◆ ◆

Dear Marilyn:

Is it true that you learn something new every day?

Paul Bagnall
Arlington, Virginia

Dear Paul:

Only if you're speaking of inconsequential things. But learning of even minor significance takes effort, not the mere passage of time.

◆ ◆ ◆

Dear Marilyn:

A human from another world offers you a teaching position on his home planet. Your safety is guaranteed. The only catch is that you would have to leave immediately and secretly, severing all communication with Earth and leaving everything behind. Would you do it, and if so, why? If not, why not?

Timothy A. Davis
Seattle, Washington

Dear Timothy:

I wouldn't do it. And substituting the word "country" for "world" might put things into better perspective by taking away some of the mystique. The catch is deceptively significant. Not only would I not want to leave my loved ones behind nor would I want to cause them suffering in exchange for what amounts to novelty, however intriguing, I wouldn't even be able to communicate anything I learned to anyone *else* back here. So where's the gain? Anything I might be able to contribute to *them* would be offset by not contributing it *here*.

◆ ◆ ◆

Dear Marilyn:

What do you think of the statement, "Those who can, do; those who can't, teach"?

Anonymous
Topeka, Kansas

Dear Reader:

It's nonsense. If you can't explain a subject, you don't know it, and if you *can* explain it, you do. The ability to explain and impart should be highly prized in society, and that's the reason I have such respect for the teaching profession. In other words, I believe teaching *is* doing, and of the highest order.

◆ ◆ ◆

Dear Marilyn:

I just don't know who to believe any more. My friends tell me one thing, and my teachers tell me another, but I know that my teachers can be wrong. What I am supposed to think?

Lucy Greenbaum
Albuquerque, New Mexico

Dear Lucy:

Education comes from listening to your teachers; experience comes from listening to your friends.

◆ ◆ ◆

Dear Marilyn:

If I'm forced to choose, whom do I follow—my parents or my teachers?

Belinda Landes
Washington, D.C.

Dear Belinda:

If you choose your parents, you'll probably suffer the least loss. After all, your parents are your teachers, but your teachers aren't your parents.

◆ ◆ ◆

Dear Marilyn:

Is it improper for a child to correct an adult when the child knows the adult is wrong? Under what circumstances would it be appropriate?

Riley Casey
Iron Station, North Carolina

Dear Riley:

I think a child should correct an adult in much the same manner as an adult should correct an adult, that is:

1) If the adult is the student, or
2) If the adult is the employee, or
3) If the adult just enjoys being corrected, or
4) If the health or safety of the adult is at risk.

◆ ◆ ◆

Dear Marilyn:

Do you think gifted children should be treated differently from other children in the home?

Tessa Cherney
Prince George, Virginia

Dear Tessa:

No, and they shouldn't *act* differently, either. Home should be both their refuge from the world and the world's refuge from *them*.

◆ ◆ ◆

Dear Marilyn:

I have two intellectually gifted children, and I'd like to know what you think is the most important thing I can give them. Would it be things to study, for example, or the best teachers or the best schools?

Anonymous
Kelso, Washington

Dear Reader:

I think the best thing you can give gifted children is the motivation to be self-reliant instead of expecting other people to give them things. And perhaps the best thing you can give *normal* children is the motivation to be self-reliant instead of *wanting* other people to give them things.

◆ ◆ ◆

Dear Marilyn:

Do you feel that gifted classes or enrichment classes are only for high-I.Q. individuals?

Marcia B. Ward
Urbana, Ohio

Dear Marcia:

Definitely not. A high I.Q. should be only one of the factors considered. The schools are full of budding young Edisons who may not happen
to test well, which I strongly suspect happens far more often than we
think. Achievement might be another factor, motivation still another,
perseverance yet another. After all, human qualities such as devotion
to a cause and love of mankind aren't on the tests, but I still think
Mother Theresa is one of the most gifted individuals in the world.

◆ ◆ ◆

Dear Marilyn:

I was disturbed last week, while watching a television program, to
see a very bright boy being forced by his father to excel in school without
the benefit of friends or fun. What do you think about pushing gifted
children?

Victor Sentry
Sommerville, Massachusetts

Dear Victor:

Well, I've seen one or two that I'd like to push, all right. Officially,
however, I don't see why we should push bright people any more than
we should push anyone else. In other words, if we're going to push
"gifted" people to perform *difficult* jobs on a broad scope, maybe we
should also push "nice" people to accomplish *good* works of great impact.

◆ ◆ ◆

Dear Marilyn:

Do you think a child should be forced to attend college as soon as he
graduates from high school? My son is only seventeen and isn't at all
decided on what he wants to be, but my husband is very angry and is
demanding that he start achieving.

Anonymous
Portland, Maine

Dear Reader:

I think it's perfectly fine for a teenager not to have decided what he
or she wants to be. Judgments about a life-long profession made too
early in life often lead to disillusionment later. However, this has little
to do with beginning college. In fact, going to college is probably the
best starting point for this exploration.

On one hand, I don't agree that a seventeen-year-old is a child, but
on the other hand, I don't think anyone should be forced to go to

college. It's all too likely to be a waste of time on his or her part, a waste of money on the part of whoever is paying for it, and a source of great tension for all concerned. My suggestion is that the young man consider a part-time start, including a favorite subject.

◆ ◆ ◆

Dear Marilyn:

Are we flunking many valuable students who are talented but are simply not "book smart"?

Elenore Bedell
Escalon, California

Dear Elenore:

I'd say so. The person who can read many books is less valuable than the person who can write only one.

◆ ◆ ◆

Dear Marilyn:

Do you think it is proper to participate in professional sports if you are considered "gifted"?

Nick Rhoton
Scott County, Virginia

Dear Nick:

Sure. In this country, we're not interested in classifying people for public use. You may be able to dig ditches faster than anyone in town, but you're welcome to be an opera singer instead. And even if you're extremely tall, it's just fine to be a small-particle physicist instead of a basketball player.

◆ ◆ ◆

Dear Marilyn:

If you were an Indian citizen and had an excellent chance to get a superior education in the United States, what would you do? Would you leave your own country for your own selfish interest or would you make use of the opportunity to become a bigger person overall by turning it down?

Amit Bhandari
Exchange Student from India
Hicksville, Ohio

Dear Amit:

Go for the education. When you better yourself, you better your country. After all, what's to stop you from becoming educated here and then taking that fine education back to your home country afterward? What a greater asset you'd be than without it!

◆ ◆ ◆

Dear Marilyn:

For a high school student, what is the most effective way of studying?

Julayne Austin
Oakland, California

Dear Julayne:

With the time you have available, read the subject matter twice instead of once. Generally speaking, and especially with difficult material, you'll understand more by reading the text straight through without stopping and then reading it again, both in the same amount of time that you normally would take to read it only once (but more slowly and stopping frequently to try to puzzle things out).

◆ ◆ ◆

Dear Marilyn:

What course of action or study do you think would be most useful to the average individual in developing clarity and precision of thinking? If you say "the study of mathematics," I'm going to be terribly depressed.

David McAlister
Hapeville, Georgia

Dear David:

Uh, oh. Better get out your handkerchief. The study is mathematics is just about the best for this, all right, but cheer up. There are plenty of other methods, too. Studying physics or chemistry is also excellent, but if you'd rather avoid anything that reminds you of school, how about chess? (You're probably reaching for a *second* handkerchief by now, aren't you?)

◆ ◆ ◆

Dear Marilyn:

How is it possible to understand something, but be consistently wrong when applying that understanding? Last year, I tutored people in chemistry, and they got A's while I got approximately three correct answers. And it's starting to happen this year in physics, too.

Brenda Somes
North Palm Beach, Florida

Dear Brenda:

Here's one possible explanation. Your problem may be that you're spending too much time tutoring. If, for example, you successfully help three people learn basic principles by spending an hour a week with each of them, you've spent three hours with those principles, but they've spent only one, freeing them for further study while you're remaining with familiar material.

◆ ◆ ◆

Dear Marilyn:

Is there any way to straighten out one's orientation on the map once it has been turned wrong? Mine has been turned wrong since grade school, when we faced east and our maps faced north. I'm always readjusting my senses.

Patty Kranz
Richland, Washington

Dear Patty:

Wow, have you got a chronic case! But let's give it a try using a method that may work for less long-standing cases. First, take your desk at home and face it due north. Second, get a big, rectangular, topographical map of the United States, but one with as little detail, including words, and clutter as possible. (Certainly nothing cute like pink states and green states and blue states.) Finally, affix it to the top of your desk, right over the work surface, where you can see it beneath you each time you work. After a few months, replace it with a map of your state and its neighbors, and eventually replace that with a map of your city and its suburbs.

◆ ◆ ◆

Dear Marilyn:

What is one of the most effective things I can do to help increase my memory and intellectual level?

Charmaine K. Kuhn
Yakima, Washington

Dear Charmaine:

Read more. It's far easier to remember and understand in context, and reading gives you that background. Consider how difficult it is to remember and how impossible it is to understand six simple Chinese characters when you're not at all familiar with Chinese. The same phenomenon holds true when you read the newspaper. You will not understand or readily remember what happened in Jerusalem this morning unless you know something about Israel.

19.

Talking and Listening

Dear Marilyn:
   If you had to pick four books, and these four books were the only books you would be allowed to keep, which ones would you choose?
                                                      Roland O. Beauchesne
                                                      Manchester, New Hampshire

Dear Roland:
   I'd choose the following:
   1)   *Webster's Dictionary,*
   2)   *Roget's Thesaurus,*
   3)   *Bartlett's Familiar Quotations,* and
   4)   the *New York City Yellow Pages.*

◆ ◆ ◆

Dear Marilyn:
   What do you consider the most practical invention of all time?
                                                      Bobby Miller
                                                      Sherman Oaks, California

Dear Bobby:
   Writing. It added a timeless dimension to oral communication, enhancing its capabilities the way mathematics enhanced counting on our fingers and toes, and made possible our modern world.

◆ ◆ ◆

Dear Marilyn:

Which is greater, the spoken word or the written word? I realize the written word gives the history of civilization, but the spoken word takes care of the present.

Arthur W. Dake
Portland, Oregon

Dear Arthur:

The written word, by far. It's of better quality, having benefitted from planning, organization, and revision, it has greater stability, making our memories look ephemeral by comparison, and it can reach more people over the course of time, including those not even born yet.

◆ ◆ ◆

Dear Marilyn:

Why is it that the proportion of really good books that make a lot of money is so small compared to the trashy, flashy best-sellers?

Anonymous

Dear Reader:

Probably because the supply of wisdom is always greater than the demand. However, making a lot of money has little to do with value, and we should keep in mind that the best-seller lists define the number of copies sold, not their intrinsic worth. In other words, they measure "value in"—to the book producers—instead of "value out"—to the book buyers. As for me, I'd rather give a lot of value to a few people than give little of value to a great many.

◆ ◆ ◆

Dear Marilyn:

Is it correct to say that dictionaries are nothing but continuous loops because all the words are defined by other words and vice versa?

T. Crisan
Masury, Ohio

Dear T.:

I'd say instead that there are primary words we've assigned to represent basic concepts. These words are then used to define less-basic concepts, to which we've assigned more words. All of these are then used to define even less basic concepts, to which we've assigned still more words, the process continuing this way to the level at which brand-new words are formed for concepts unknown before that point, but able to be defined with existing words. In other words, the dictionary seems to me to be more of a loom than a loop, showing us a dazzling array of patterns to be found in the fabric of life.

◆ ◆ ◆

Dear Marilyn:

Is there such a thing as a misspelled word? I maintain there is *not*—it can't be a word if it is misspelled! Only words are shown in any dictionary; therefore, the absence of any "word" that is misspelled is proof that it isn't actually a word. Am I correct? A case of beer is riding on this!

David C. Graham
San Diego, California

Dear David:

Sorry, but maybe you can talk your friend into giving a little party with the case of beer and inviting you. Of *course* there is such a thing as a misspelled word, and now I have the job of convincing not just you, but all the others who wrote with this same question. For one thing, dictionaries do contain more than words; they also contain symbols ("O" for oxygen) and abbreviations ("mph" for miles per hour), for example. *They* aren't words, are they?

But more importantly, as far as the absence of words is concerned, weren't there words *before* there were dictionaries? And weren't there words even before there was written language? Saying a word isn't a word if it's misspelled is a lot like saying a word isn't a word if it's mispronounced.

◆ ◆ ◆

Dear Marilyn:

There are three _____ in the English language. They are to, too, and two. How do you spell the word for the blank?

Wm. Bruce Damron
Sarasota, Florida

Dear Bruce:

"Too." This is because the sentence communicates a sound in the blank space, not a word, and the phonetic spelling for that sound is "too."

◆ ◆ ◆

Dear Marilyn:

"Their is four errers in this sentence."

Since the above sentence makes a specific claim—and hence must be either true or false—I would like for you to tell me if it's true and explain your choice.

Dann Walker
Waco, Texas

Dear Dann:

I believe the claim is false because I see only three errors. Corrected, the sentence would read, "*There are four errors in this sentence.*" We can't call the word "four" an error any more than we can call the word "sentence" an error without changing the claim itself. If we could, we may as well say the sentence should read, "*There are four ducks in this bathtub,*" and call the claim true. That is, of course, if your bathtub does indeed contain four ducks!

◆ ◆ ◆

Dear Marilyn:

How did people think before the invention of language?

John Czarnek
Houston, Texas

Dear John:

They were probably dependent on the most primitive forms of intuition and insight, neither of which would enable them to travel very far intellectually no matter how naturally intelligent they were. Thinking without words is like doing mathematics without numbers.

◆ ◆ ◆

Dear Marilyn:

Does thought form language, or does language form thought?

Jennie L. Brown
Woodinville, Washington

Dear Jennie:

In contemporary society, it appears that the *controlling* individuals use thought to form language and the *controlled* individuals use language to form thought. Unfortunately, whether an individual controls has little relation to whether he or she is, in fact, correct.

◆ ◆ ◆

Dear Marilyn:

Does intelligence breed language, or does language breed intelligence?

Douglas J. Ellis
Spokane, Washington

Dear Douglas:

It seems to me that the ability to speak and thus to form a language—exhibited by normal human beings, but by no other animals—produces the ability to learn and solve problems more than the other way around. Intelligent behavior does exist in other species, but only to a very small degree by comparison. Most animal "learning" appears to be simply the development of habits as a direct or indirect result of ordinary reinforced behavior. Interestingly, the same is true of human babies before they begin to use language. Like mathematics, language is an intellectual tool that we can use to grasp what we can't reach without that help.

◆ ◆ ◆

Dear Marilyn:

I read that if wild animals had the ability to speak, they would likely be the masters of humans. What do you think?

Raiden Trujillo
Pueblo, Colorado

Dear Raiden:

Look, if lions could speak tomorrow, what could they possibly say? "Hungry"? "Ouch"? They don't even have the intellect to say, "Wanna go bye-bye" let alone something like, "Hey, if we play our cards right, the next thing you know, we'll be running the *Fortune* 500 companies!" Despite any physical superiority, wild animals are just too darned *dumb* to push us around.

That answer angered a few people who wrote to state that other animals are much smarter than humans and kinder, in addition. While I feel that we should treat other animals with appropriate compassion, I believe those statements are incorrect.

◆ ◆ ◆

Dear Marilyn:

Assuming, as some people do, that languages are but a fragment of true communication, then what form would pure, full communication take?

Mike Lusk
Havelock, North Carolina

Dear Mike:

The best I can envision would be mind-reading, bearing in mind that you specified true communication and not truth itself. What's in our minds has far less relation to the truth than we would like to believe.

◆ ◆ ◆

Dear Marilyn:

Mathematicians say that since nouns and verbs used in ordinary human reasoning are subject to different interpretations, why not replace them with symbols as unambiguous as numerals and with operations as unambiguous as addition and multiplication. What do you think?

Robert W. Dufresne
St. Paul, Minnesota

Dear Robert:

I don't see how writing the word "beauty," for example, as something like "58"—or tapping it out in Morse code, for that matter—helps to eliminate different interpretations. Even if we had different numbers for the different meanings of beauty, as the dictionary does, "beauty #1" would be distinguished from "beauty #2," but my interpretation of "beauty #1" would still not be distinguished from my neighbor's interpretation of "beauty #1."

◆ ◆ ◆

Dear Marilyn:

Which do you consider more important—language or mathematics?

Noralee Lund-Garner
Long Beach, California

Dear Noralee:

Language, by far. Without it, we can neither benefit from all the knowledge accumulated in the world since the beginning of recorded history nor can we pass on that which we gain ourselves either to our contemporaries or to future generations.

◆ ◆ ◆

Dear Marilyn:

I have a profound hearing impairment, and people tell me that I must be very smart to know how to lipread, but I say it was something I had to do. What do you think?

Arlene Miller
Pittsburgh, Pennsylvania

Dear Arlene:

I strongly suspect that if people are telling you you're smart—no matter what the reason—you probably are.

◆ ◆ ◆

Dear Marilyn:

Why is listening—the most essential communication skill—continually described in terms such as "the most used and the least taught," "forgotten" and "neglected," and "the secret skill"?

> Charles H. Swanson, Professor
> Department of Speech & Communication
> Fairmont State College
> Fairmont, West Virginia

Dear Charles:

I suppose it's assumed that the capacity for listening is natural, and it probably is, but that doesn't mean that listening *well* is natural. *Speaking* well certainly isn't!

The intellectually vital techniques of speaking and listening have been neglected ever since the invention of the printing press put a schoolbook on the desk of every student in addition to the desk of every teacher, and this educational omission has been very unfortunate. As reading means little without adequate comprehension, so is listening useless without understanding.

And if listening is called "the secret skill" in communication, it may very well mean that of the four basic ones—writing and reading, speaking and listening—the last is so often overlooked that anyone who gains proficiency in it will be at a distinct advantage in life. For example, unlike writing and reading, speaking and listening are the social communications, necessary if we're to succeed in cooperation with others.

If it makes sense to offer courses in Public Speaking, it makes sense to offer courses in Comprehensive Listening, too. After all, how can anyone be an effective speaker without an effective listener?

◆ ◆ ◆

Dear Marilyn:

Why is there so much foul language in the movies these days? So many good ones are ruined by this.

> D. B.
> Salt Lake City, Utah

Dear Reader:

For the same reason that extra salt and sugar are added to food—to sell it, regardless of whether it's healthy.

Part Three

Nature at Work
and at Play

20.

Physical Sciences

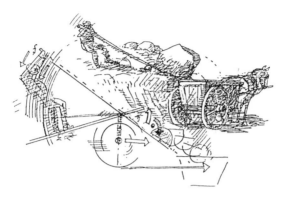

Dear Marilyn:

If "the truth will set us free," why has every great advance in science met with such opposition?

Ronald Scott Pettis
Lancaster, Pennsylvania

Dear Ronald:

Some people make a living or an identity by criticizing the work of others, generally a fairly effortless thing to do. After all, which is easier: building a house or burning one down?

The light bulb, for example, is far from perfect. It may light a little room, but it won't light your whole house, will it? And it'll break when you drop it, shattering into sharp pieces. But so what? The critic remains silent in darkness, but curses the light bulb as soon as somebody invents it. In science, those who can, do; those who can't, criticize.

◆ ◆ ◆

Dear Marilyn:

I want to know why we study science.

Amy Hermes
Carlsbad, California

Dear Amy:

Even if we're not going to become scientists, the problem of scientific illiteracy bears heavily on our understanding of everyday life and on our ability to cast a respectable vote. For example, it is socially irresponsible for citizens who don't even know what a laser is to be making decisions on the Strategic Defense Initiative ("Star Wars"). In a nationwide survey reported in *The New York Times*, researchers for the National Science Foundation discovered that 21 percent of Americans polled don't even know that the earth revolves around the sun rather than the other way around.

◆ ◆ ◆

Dear Marilyn:

Does America have an abundance or a shortage of capability in scientific fields, such as math, chemistry, and physics?

Sam Smith
Pittsburgh, Pennsylvania

Dear Sam:

We have an abundance of capability, but a shortage of trained personnel. A significant part of this problem is due to the fact that, although a huge talent pool exists among women, blacks, and Hispanics, it is practically invisible, at least in the sciences. As the years go by, this situation becomes more and more relevant: in 1985, one in every five eighteen-year-olds was black or Hispanic; by the year 2010, one in every three will be. And by the year 2000, it is predicted that half of the work force will be women.

Contrast those burgeoning percentages with the fact that out of the 341 people who earned Ph.D.'s in math in 1988, only one was black, and three were Hispanic. We can no longer afford to ignore this situation. If we don't look to females and minorities here in the United States, we're going to be looking at Japanese superiority.

◆ ◆ ◆

Dear Marilyn:

Given recent disasters and the proposition that today's equipment is so complex that no one person or group can have a handle on the entire system, is it possible that we have reached the limit of our technological ability?

James Burnip
Santa Barbara, California

Dear James:

I don't think so. It seems to me that we have already been successfully managing systems beyond our grasp since the beginning of our time.

The human body is an example. No one physician knows as much as all the specialists, and even the specialists themselves are groping in the dark much of the time. It should be far easier to handle what man himself has created, but with the immense complexity involved, management skills will be as important as scientific ones. That is, the chief executive officer of a major electronics firm will not know how to actually create any individual component himself, but he "knows how to manage" those who "know how to manage" those who "know who to manage" those who do.

Man-made disasters are deplorable, of course, but extremely rare compared to man-made successes. When that proportion changes significantly, *then* we will have reached our "limits."

◆ ◆ ◆

Dear Marilyn:
Do you know of any real weaknesses in the scientific method?

Anonymous

Dear Reader:
The way a chain is only as strong as its weakest link, the scientific method is only as strong as the individual using it. When the procedure is to formulate a hypothesis and then try to prove it, there's a significant tendency to have far more of them "proven" than there should be, even given the greatest effort at objectivity. Our excessive fondness for preconceptions, however, seems only to apply to our own and not to our associates', so maybe one way to increase rigor in science would be to trade our theories with our neighbors!

◆ ◆ ◆

Dear Marilyn:
What one discovery or event would prove all or most of modern scientific theory wrong?

Jennifer W. Webster
Slidell, Louisiana

Dear Jennifer:
Here's one of each. If the speed of light were discovered not to be a constant, modern scientific theory would be devastated. And if a divine creation actually did occur, modern *scientists* would be devastated.

◆ ◆ ◆

Dear Marilyn:
What do you think about discoveries that seem to contradict history

as we know it, such as the skull of a long-extinct animal that apparently died of a gunshot wound long before man existed?

David Reyes
Elsa, Texas

Dear David:

If the finding appears to contradict history, it suggests that either we are "wrong" about the finding or we are "wrong" about history, neither of which would be very surprising in most cases. And the less surprising of those two is the most likely. For example, if that animal were found with what appeared to be a crude bullet lodged in its skull, it would be more likely that a non-human force shot a pebble there—the way a tornado drives a nail into a tree—than that our dating system is almost comically flawed.

◆ ◆ ◆

Dear Marilyn:

Scientifically speaking, I believe an exception disproves any rule. Do you agree or disagree with this?

B. Miller
Chicago, Illinois

Dear B.:

For the most part, I agree. In science, at least, a rule with an exception is a lot like a rooster that lays eggs.

◆ ◆ ◆

Dear Marilyn:

Can the whole be more than the sum of its parts?

Stephen K. Williams
Norfolk, Virginia

Dear Stephen:

In a way. Addition of parts does not necessarily describe a whole. For example, when the nuclei of the isotopes of certain light elements collide, resulting in the redistribution of their protons and neutrons, a nuclear fusion reaction is produced.

◆ ◆ ◆

Dear Marilyn:

Will we eventually find a way to neutralize nuclear waste so that it is harmless and useful?

Jean Stonecipher
Chesterton, Indiana

Dear Jean:

My guess is "yes" on making it harmless, but I'm far less optimistic about making it useful. We haven't even found a way to make *old shoes* useful.

◆ ◆ ◆

Dear Marilyn:

Why isn't solar power more prevalent?

Kathy Babb
Rolla, Missouri

Dear Kathy:

Mainly because it's still so expensive. Although the conversion of solar energy to thermal energy in order to heat a house, for instance, has its share of problems, they pale in comparison to the difficulty of economically converting solar energy to electrical or mechanical energy, the area where most of humankind's energy needs exist. As an example, the cost of electricity from a solar cell is more than a hundred times its cost from traditional sources.

◆ ◆ ◆

Dear Marilyn:

Everyone is talking about the "greenhouse effect" and how it may melt the polar ice caps. This will supposedly cause the oceans to rise, inundating beachfront property. But since ice occupies *more* volume than water, won't the oceans *drop* if the ice melts? A tumbler full of ice doesn't overflow when it melts.

John Starrs
Pasadena, California

Dear John:

About ninety percent of the world's glacial ice is in the Antarctic ice sheet, but only about ten percent of that ice is floating on the sea; the remainder of it rests on the land. So even though water is somewhat denser than ice, most of that ice isn't already in the water, but would run off into the ocean if it melted, raising the seas about 200 feet, according to current calculations.

The havoc this would wreak transcends the imagination. When thinking about beachfront property, consider Manhattan, for example, an international port at sea level. A "meltdown" of this magnitude would bring the Atlantic up to the sixteenth story of the Empire State

Building and two-thirds of the way up to the torch of the Statue of Liberty!

◆ ◆ ◆

Dear Marilyn:

Why is it that wheels in a movie often appear to be rotating backwards?

Leon H. Moyer
Quakertown, Pennsylvania

Dear Leon:

This is called a "strobe" effect. As a motion picture is really a sequence of still pictures shown at the rate of twenty-four per second, the rotation of the wheel must synchronize with the shutter speed of the movie camera in order to look stable. This means that when the wheels travel more slowly, they will appear to be moving backward; when they pick up speed, they will appear to be stationary; and when they travel even faster, they will appear to be moving forward. At none of these times, however, will they seem to match the true speed of the vehicle.

And yes, this is the thing that makes dancers in some discos look so weird. (*One* of the things, that is.)

◆ ◆ ◆

Dear Marilyn:

When I am six cars back, waiting at a stop signal, I've often wondered why all six cars cannot move all at once when the light turns green. Do you know?

Shirley Thomas
Ontario, Canada

Dear Shirley:

Only the first driver looks at the green light as his signal to go ahead. The second driver looks at the first car, the third driver looks at the second car, and so forth, slowing down the whole process greatly. This is initially due to the understanding that if the second through the sixth driver steps on the gas and just one driver in front of him doesn't, he'll have an accident.

And then, even when each driver *can* begin to move forward, the rate of acceleration of the car in front of him must first be witnessed, then followed, but with a delay, in order to avoid equally unpleasant results. It may be all right for cars to be only a few feet apart when they're at a stoplight, but just think how you'd feel if you were traveling in that tight a knot at forty miles an hour.

◆ ◆ ◆

Dear Marilyn:

My mother was the victim of an auto accident, and since I had to go through the scene of the accident each day to visit her, can you tell me which is the safest lane to drive in?

Gina Hernandez
McLean, Virginia

Dear Gina:

The National Safety Council recommends using the right lane for most two-lane (in the same direction) driving. In the case of three or more lanes, it suggests that motorists choose one that lets them move smoothly within the flow of traffic (and the speed limit, of course). This will often be the lane that is the second from the right. However, there is no "safest" lane.

◆ ◆ ◆

Dear Marilyn:

I live on the island of Hawaii and have driven around the island on the coastal road several times. I have noticed that the waves always seem to be coming directly at the beach. How is it possible that the waves can be coming at this point in the ocean from all directions at the same time?

Jerry Moulton
Hilo, Hawaii

Dear Jerry:

Waves travel more slowly as they enter shallower water, and as a wavefront approaches a coastline at an oblique angle, the portion nearer to the shore slows down before the portion farther away. This swings the wave around until it faces more nearly toward the shoreline, thus making life far more convenient for sea turtles and surfers all over the world.

◆ ◆ ◆

Dear Marilyn:

Suppose you are standing in an ocean off the continental United

States at exactly noon. Using only your view of the ocean, can you name the ocean in which you are standing?

Gary R. Leister
Mifflin, Pennsylvania

Dear Gary:

Assuming both a sunny day and a north/south shoreline, yes. Turn the same direction as the waves are moving, and if your shadow points toward your right, you're in the Atlantic Ocean; if it points leftward, you're in the Pacific Ocean.

That's because if you're so close to shore that you can actually stand, facing the direction the waves are moving will face you to the shore. Then, as shadows point toward the north at noon in the northern hemisphere, if your shadow falls toward your right, you must be facing the east coastline, placing you in the Atlantic; if it falls leftward, you must be facing the west coastline, placing you in the Pacific.

◆ ◆ ◆

I made a mistake on the next one, which was pointed out by only one alert reader. Do you see it?

Dear Marilyn:

I can see bubbles of air coming up and out of boiling water, but I can't see the air going down *into* the water to create them. Where do they come from?

Sonia Lea
Bonita, California

Dear Sonia:

Those bubbles are the water itself escaping from the liquid state to the gaseous state. (You see the end results of this whenever you leave the teapot on top of the stove for too long and *all* the water escapes.)

You put a tea kettle on the stove, not a tea pot. A teapot is what goes on the table!

◆ ◆ ◆

Dear Marilyn:

In a flame, which color is hotter—blue, red, yellow, or orange—and which is cooler?

Clint Vittum, age 13
Carlsbad, California

Dear Clint:

Generally speaking, a flame is a layer of hot gas around a core of cool gas, but as there are many distinctions between various sorts of flames, it would probably be more useful to refer instead to "color temperature." In this concept, red is the "coolest," yellow is hotter, white is hotter still, and blue is even hotter than that. Here's a sentence I've made up for you to help you recall the sequence: (R)emember (Y)our (W)ay (B)ack.

◆ ◆ ◆

Dear Marilyn:

Why do objects of the same temperature feel cooler or warmer than one another? That is, a bath rug feels "warm," but a tile floor feels "cold," even though both are in the same 70° room.

Anonymous
Pennsylvania

Dear Reader:

Because heat flows naturally in the direction of decreasing temperature, and some objects conduct it better than others. Try this at home: Step onto the tile with one bare foot and onto the rug with the other. Because your feet are nearly 30° warmer than what they're standing on, and the tile is a more efficient conductor, it will transfer heat away from the foot on the tile faster, making that foot feel cooler than the one on the rug.

◆ ◆ ◆

Dear Marilyn:

Why is glass clear?

Genevieve Haviland
East Grand Rapids, Michigan

Dear Genevieve:

It isn't. Ordinary window glass only *seems* clear because it transmits light rays well enough so that objects on the other side of it may be distinctly seen. It's "clearer" than water, but not as "clear" as air.

◆ ◆ ◆

Dear Marilyn:

Why does a mirror reverse our image from right to left, but not up to down?

Anonymous

Dear Reader:

A mirror doesn't reverse images at all; it reflects light directly backward at us. The error results from our assuming the image faces us. Instead, the image faces forward, just as we do. This is because the mirror "sees" what the camera does. If it were transparent, like a slide, we would know, almost instinctively, that we would need to walk around on the other side of it to see ourselves the way others see us.

◆ ◆ ◆

Dear Marilyn:

I need glasses to see things at a distance. When I look in the mirror, I can see my face clearly. When I look at the things reflected in the room behind me, they appear fuzzy, yet the distance is an illusion, and all objects reflected are an equal distance from my eyes. Can you tell me why this is so?

Mary Murphy
Upland, California

Dear Mary:

The realization of this is amazing, but the distance is not an illusion. You're looking at rays of light actually coming from the distant objects, merely diverted by the reflecting surface of the mirror. In other words, you may not be facing in their direction physically, but you're looking at them just as much as if you were!

If your vision problem prevents your eyes from handling the angle of the light rays coming from the buildings across the street, it will prevent them from handling those same rays after they've bounced off a mirror because the angle of reflection will be the same. So, if you can see well at, say, six feet, and you stand only three feet away from the mirror, you'll have no problem seeing your face because the light will travel three feet to the mirror, then three feet back to your eyes, a total of six feet. But if you don't see well at sixty feet, you'll have difficulty seeing the house across the street because the light must travel a couple of hundred feet to the mirror, then three feet back to your eyes, a total of far more distance than your eyes can handle. And if there's a spot on the surface of the mirror, it will look only three feet away because the light isn't being reflected at all.

This is why a mirror, especially one facing a window, makes a room seem larger, but a photograph doesn't. With a mirror, you're actually looking at the landscape, not the mirror!

◆ ◆ ◆

Dear Marilyn:
What color are things in the dark?

Sadie Porter
Millbrook, Alabama

Dear Sadie:
Current theory contends they are colorless. Color depends on light for its very existence, changing according to the source. (An apple that is bright red in sunlight will find its color greatly diminished in fluorescent light. Under a mercury-arc lamp, that same apple will look white.) By "dark," I assume you mean the absence of all kinds of light, not just sunlight. And as color is a property of light, then with no light at all, color ceases to exist.

◆ ◆ ◆

Dear Marilyn:
This may seem like a silly question, but I mean it seriously. Why is it that so many things seem to stop working right when you need them?

Eric Jens
Salt Lake City, Utah

Dear Eric:
We're often unaware that something isn't working until we try to use it. The air conditioner, for example, doesn't let us know in March that it won't work when we turn it on in July. And then there's the stress of start-up to be considered. A reasonable time for the hair dryer to stop working is when a sudden jolt of electricity shocks it into action. In addition, there's the strain of continued operation. Pants don't split in the closet.

In other words, I think it's *normal* to find out things don't work when we try to use them. And now that we have automobiles that tell us when they're going to run out of gas, maybe someone can go to work on one that will say, "Don't bother heading for your mother's house next Sunday morning. I'm going to stop dead after twenty minutes, stranding you on the highway with a dozen jelly doughnuts."

◆ ◆ ◆

Dear Marilyn:

If it was 0° F on Christmas day and twice as cold on New Year's Day, what would be the temperature?

John Bolman
Honolulu, Hawaii

Dear John:

If the temperature could get that low, it would be under −27,000,000° F. However, it can't according to current theory, which puts the lower limit at a comparatively balmy −459.67° F. As you know, zero degrees doesn't mean an absence of temperature; rather, it's a point on a scale ranging from "hottest" (with no present limit) to "coldest." Cooling all the way from "hottest"—the center of the sun is estimated to be about 27,000,000° F—down to the temperature you've chosen is already a great jump; twice that would definitely put a strain on the AAA. Humans live within a very narrow temperature range, a mere wafer-thin slice of the whole. When the temperature rises from 1° F one day to 2° F the next, it isn't twice as warm. It's only a degree warmer, a very slight change.

◆ ◆ ◆

Dear Marilyn:

I've heard that if you're in a falling elevator, you should jump up and down repeatedly so that when the elevator touches the ground, there's a good chance you'll only be a few inches in the air and will land harmlessly. Is that true?

Anonymous

Dear Reader:

No. Even if we're only six inches from the floor right before we land, we'll still be injured. After all, a person who falls out of a fiftieth-floor window also will be only six inches from the concrete right before he lands. The strength of our muscles is the problem. Gravity is at work inside the elevator just as it is outside it, and objects pick up speed as they fall. We'd need the lift of airplane engines to jump up while falling, and if we had that, we wouldn't need elevators.

◆ ◆ ◆

Dear Marilyn:

You once answered a question regarding the speed of a bullet coming down after being shot straight up into the air. You said it wasn't very dangerous (or something like that), but I've seen articles in magazines reporting deaths from falling bullets! Can you comment?

Sharon Yamasaki
Santa Clara, California

Dear Sharon:

This question is clearly important enough to require clarification. If shot straight up into the air, a bullet will come down *far* slower than it went up, but that's still fast enough to be hazardous. And if shot at an angle, as nearly every bullet is, it's much more dangerous. DON'T DO IT!

◆ ◆ ◆

Dear Marilyn:

If you had a completely enclosed truck with birds inside, would the truck weigh the same if the birds were in flight?

Patrick Moretta
Chino, California

Dear Patrick:

If the truck is perfectly sealed—not allowing the escape of even one molecule of air—the flying birds' weight would be supported by the air trapped inside the truck the way it would be supported by a crate that provided a place to sit. In that case, the weight would remain the same.

At least, that's the accepted answer to this "trick" question. But as usual, there's more. While a flock of birds fluttering around has this effect overall, it doesn't work quite that way with each single bird. Downward acceleration reduces the weight of the system, and upward acceleration increases it. (And if a bird is in free fall, his weight isn't felt at all.)

◆ ◆ ◆

Dear Marilyn:

If I'm flying in a Concorde from London to New York at the speed of sound, and I see a fly buzzing around in the cabin, does that mean the fly is flying at the speed of sound?

Frank Ziegler
Baltimore, Maryland

Dear Frank:

In a way. The entire environment captured inside the plane is flying at the speed of sound relative to the earth, but the fly is only humming along at his usual rate compared to the enclosed surroundings.

◆ ◆ ◆

Dear Marilyn:

If I'm on an airplane flying at a normal speed, could I get closer to the back of the plane simply by jumping up real high and letting the plane fly under me? If not, why not? (I tried doing this, but got too many stares.)

Audrey Schaper
Florissant, Missouri

Dear Audrey:

No, because the body of the airplane shields you from the air resistance that would slow you down otherwise. (And I certainly hope you won't try to check this by opening a door!)

◆ ◆ ◆

Dear Marilyn:

What happens to the sound waves coming from a jet traveling at *twice* the speed of sound? Where would the sonic boom occur?

Gary Bridgestock
Klamath Falls, Oregon

Dear Gary:

Contrary to popular belief, a sonic boom does not occur at one particular place just when the jet passes through the sound barrier. Rather, when an aircraft flies faster than the speed of sound, it generates waves that are dragged along with it, not unlike a speedboat. Wherever this wave collides with the ground, we'll hear a sonic boom if the aircraft is close enough, but only a sonic whisper if it's farther away.

◆ ◆ ◆

Dear Marilyn:

Why can't wind be seen?

James Prince
Clifton, New Jersey

Dear James:

Because our eyes aren't good enough. Wind is just air in motion, and air is a mixture of gases whose particles are so small and so rare in concentration that they can't be seen with the unaided eye.

◆ ◆ ◆

Dear Marilyn:

When Roald Amundsen planted the flag of Norway at the South Pole on December 14, 1911, was his body weight substantially greater than that which it would have registered when he crossed the Equator?

My argument is that when he stood at the Equator, the centrifugal force exerted by the rotational speed of the earth's surface would have reduced his weight from that taken at the Pole, where centrifugal force is zero. If this is true, what would be the difference between the two readings?

Kenneth S. Christensen
Slidell, Louisiana

Dear Kenneth:

This will surprise a lot of people, I know, but yes, he weighed more at the South Pole than he did at the Equator. To a scientist, the difference is significant, about 1 part in 300. However, if Mr. Amundsen weighed 150 pounds at the Equator, that means he would only weigh 150½ pounds at the Pole, probably not even enough to induce him to give up dessert.

◆ ◆ ◆

Dear Marilyn:

Why is the speed of the earth's rotation constant?

John Purvis
Mobile, Alabama

Dear John:

It isn't—it's slowing down gradually. I just hope that when it finally comes to a stop, it's on a Saturday.

◆ ◆ ◆

Dear Marilyn:

Why is the world round?

Bridget McConnell
Scott County, Virginia

Dear Bridget:

According to Newton, gravity, acting inward in the direction of the center of the earth, tends to make the planet spherical. On the other hand, centrifugal force, acting outward from the earth's axis of rotation, tends to make the planet oval. As a result of these forces combined, the planet has taken the form of a very slightly flattened sphere, which some people see as a football, but is actually more like a fat hamburger bun. In other words, like many of its inhabitants, the earth itself bulges in the middle.

◆ ◆ ◆

Dear Marilyn:
Hot and cold, positive and negative, good and bad. Can you name one thing that exists without an opposite?
R. L. Jackson
Hendersonville, North Carolina

Dear R. L.:
It seems to me that *most* tangible things exist without opposites. What is the opposite of a clock, for example? Or a compact disc player? Would it be a bunch of people humming in the living room? And there seem to be plenty of intangible things, too. What is the opposite of mathematics, for example? Or music? (And don't tell me it's what's typically played on radio stations.)

◆ ◆ ◆

Dear Marilyn:
How would you define what is functional and what is not functional?
Robert D. Kauffman
Asheville, North Carolina

Dear Robert:
If something is functional, it performs pretty well even if it doesn't look too good. If something is *not* functional, it looks pretty good even if it doesn't perform too well. Generally speaking, everything else gets thrown away.

◆ ◆ ◆

Dear Marilyn:
What is the difference between a spacemaker and a spacesaver?
Jane Vangelor
Syracuse, New York

Dear Jane:
A spacemaker makes use of *unused* space, like that in the top of a closet. A spacesaver makes more efficient use of space *already* in use, like that in the bottom of a closet. A spacewaster is often what's hanging in the middle.

◆ ◆ ◆

Dear Marilyn:

What scientific theory can prove that "no two snowflakes are alike"? I contend that all the snowflakes have never been examined and compared.

Claire Rayner Lowe
Muscatine, Iowa

Dear Claire:

Photomicrography has shown that there is far more minute variety than we had ever dreamed possible, and it is now understood that as a growing snowflake drifts downward, what occurs to its rapidly branching crystals during every instant depends with incredibly acute sensitivity upon the combination of conditions it encounters such as humidity, temperature, turbulence, and impurities in the air. Each flake, then, is a nearly unbelievable record of its own personal experience, and the possible combinations boggle the imagination, making "infinite" a descriptive, if not provable, adjective.

◆ ◆ ◆

Dear Marilyn:

Is it really true that there are no two snowflakes exactly alike?

S. Torrens
Emporia, Kansas

Dear S.:

Probably, but no people and no parakeets and no pickles are exactly alike either. We don't walk around looking at trees, for example, and saying to ourselves, "Gee, out of the thousands and thousands of trees I've seen in my life, I've never seen two totally identical trees!" So why is it such a big deal for snowflakes?

21.

The Sun, Moon, and Stars

Dear Marilyn:
Where does the *sun* get its fuel?

Edward H. Wolfe
Laguna Hills, California

Dear Edward:
From within. The sun has such tremendous temperature and density that thermonuclear reactions converting hydrogen into helium take place, sending energy streaming outward.

◆ ◆ ◆

Dear Marilyn:
Considering that the sun emits in all directions, what portion of the sun's total output does the earth receive?

Bill Elmendorf
Lebanon, Illinois

Dear Bill:
The earth receives less than half of one billionth of the sun's power!

◆ ◆ ◆

Dear Marilyn:
Why does the sun sometimes turn a fiery red when it sets?

Alta Palaski
Torrington, Connecticut

Dear Alta:

The dramatic colors seen at sunset are caused by particles in the atmosphere—mainly water and dust. When the sun nears the horizon, the shorter wavelengths of light are absorbed by the particles in the greater distance they must travel, creating the splendid glows we all enjoy. In other words, some of the most glorious sights on earth are caused by pollution!

◆ ◆ ◆

Dear Marilyn:

I know our sun is about 1,000,000 times larger than our earth and that the earth is in orbit about 93,000,000 miles away from the sun, and I can visualize the earth as small as a BB or a pea, but not a grain of sand, the way it's usually described. Using a BB or a pea to represent the earth, can you put this size and distance on a scale that I can visualize?

Chester B. Dean
Akron, Ohio

Dear Chester:

Oh, boy, is *this* going to be an approximation. For a stellar salad, if the sun were a pumpkin about a foot in diameter, Mercury would be a tomato seed about 50 feet away, Venus would be a pea about 75 feet away, Earth would be a pea about 100 feet away, Mars would be a little raisin about 175 feet away, Jupiter would be an apple about 550 feet away, Saturn would be a peach about 1025 feet away, Uranus would be a plum about 2050 feet away, Neptune would be a plum about 3225 feet away, and Pluto would be smaller than a strawberry seed nearly a mile away.

◆ ◆ ◆

Dear Marilyn:

If it were possible to concoct a liquid that would destroy anything with which it came into contact, would it also be possible to find a container in which to store it?

J. Foulds
New York, New York

Dear J.:

Maybe, but we won't find it in the garage or the attic. One sort could be a "living bottle," a container that reproduces on the outside as fast as it's destroyed on the inside. Another could be a "force basket," a container that controls without touch. Gravity and centripetal force, for example, do a fine job of holding the sun and planets in place.

◆ ◆ ◆

Dear Marilyn:
    Ptolemy believed that the Earth was the center of our solar system. Copernicus showed that Ptolemy was wrong and said that the planets moved in circular orbits around the sun. Kepler showed that Copernicus was wrong and said that the planets moved in elliptical orbits around the sun.
    Einstein believed that the speed of light was absolute, that nothing with mass could ever go faster than light, and that with increasing speed, objects would increase in mass and experience time more slowly. Do you believe that someone will someday show Einstein to be wrong? And if so, will his errors be as major as those of Ptolemy or as minor as those of Copernicus?

Dennis Sherman
Arvada, Colorado

Dear Dennis:
    And Kepler thought that the stars were all contained within a thin shell somewhere outside the solar system. My best guess is that, yes, someone will someday show Einstein to be wrong. And as errors tend to grow smaller with time, which is how we make progress, after all, they will probably be less earthshaking than the discovery for which Copernicus was condemned by religious authorities, continuing nearly three hundred years after his death.

◆ ◆ ◆

Dear Marilyn:
    How many stars are in the sky?

Andrew Cross
Jonesboro, Tennessee

Dear Andrew:
    All of them.

◆ ◆ ◆

Dear Marilyn:
    Where do stars go when they fall?

Mary Lou Boyle
Cleveland, Ohio

Dear Mary Lou:

"Falling stars" are not stars at all. Instead, they are solid objects passing through the earth's atmosphere. Occasionally, they even survive the trip and land on the surface of the planet. In other words, it's actually possible (although unlikely) to "catch a falling star and put it in your pocket."

◆ ◆ ◆

Dear Marilyn:

How far away is the horizon, assuming my eyes are a few feet above the ground and ignoring any hills or valleys, etc.?

Patrick C. Madden
Whippany, New Jersey

Dear Patrick:

The horizon, by which we mean the place where the sky appears to meet the ground or the sea, is not as far away as we might expect—only about 2.8 miles if our eyes are about five feet above the surface. The higher our eyes, however, the more distant is the horizon, but again, not as much as we might think. If we're up as high as 10,000 feet, for example, the horizon is still only 126 miles away.

On other heavenly bodies, the principle is the same, but the distances will differ with the size. If we're standing on the moon with our eyes about five feet above the surface, the horizon will be only 1.4 miles away, about half of that on the earth.

◆ ◆ ◆

Dear Marilyn:

Why is the sky blue?

Catrina Fendley
Ventura, California

Dear Catrina:

The blue color of the sky is actually the "color" of the atmosphere that surrounds the earth, thinly composed of things such as air molecules, water droplets, and tiny particles. When sunlight passes through it, this very small volume of matter makes it easy for the light—and the spectrum of resultant colors—to be scattered in all directions. The shorter the wavelength of the light, however, the more effectively it is scattered. Blue light, the shortest, is scattered about nine times as much as red light, the longest. Therefore, on a normal, clear day, the sky will appear to be generally blue to us.

◆ ◆ ◆

Dear Marilyn:
  Where does space end?

                              Ben Aiken, age 7
                              Baton Rouge, Louisiana

Dear Ben:
  Space ends in lots of places—it ends wherever something else begins. However, when thinking about the notion of an infinite space, it might be useful to consider space to be the "nothing" that is between the "somethings." I think it's easier to conceive of an infinite "nothing" called space than an infinite "something else" called space. When someone asks us how much we paid for a gift we received, we reply, "Nothing" and have no trouble with the extent of it. Is there an end to that nothing? No. And it doesn't seem to bother us.

◆ ◆ ◆

Dear Marilyn:
  Is there anything that is absolutely still?

                              Mark Harper
                              Lincoln, Nebraska

Dear Mark:
  Cats in windowsills notwithstanding, the modern scientific theory of an expanding universe says no.

◆ ◆ ◆

Dear Marilyn:
  It has been stated that every force in the universe has an opposite: good/evil, matter/anti-matter, strong/weak, etc. Is it then possible that anti-gravity could exist?

                              Allan Bentley
                              Riverdale, Georgia

Dear Allan:
  I don't believe your three examples *are* forces, at least in the most commonly accepted sense of the word. However, even if we accept the hypothesis that every "physical" force—such as gravity—has an opposite, it doesn't follow that the opposite is at all likely to actually exist outside of theory. It would even seem that opposites would be *less* likely to exist if for no other reason than because they "oppose" rather than "fit" conditions. Just because we find a raging fire doesn't mean that we're ever likely to find ashes transforming themselves back into trees again, even though we can readily envision such a thing. If anti-

gravity is out there, it'll probably be for a different reason than simply because gravity itself exists.

◆ ◆ ◆

Dear Marilyn:

Why isn't there gravity in space?

Paul Sauer
Sayreville, New Jersey

Dear Paul:

According to theory, there *is* gravitational attraction in space, although not at the same value as the gravity we're accustomed to here on the earth. On the moon, the gravitational force is only one-sixth that of the earth, on Jupiter, it's over two and a half times as much, and starlight nearing the sun appeared to be "bent" by gravitation during the solar eclipse of 1922. But even in "deep" space, the recession of galaxies is said to be slowed down because they attract one another. None of this, however, is without controversy about both cause and effect. Maybe gravity is just nature's way of keeping us humble.

◆ ◆ ◆

Dear Marilyn:

Newton's law describing the force of gravity states that every body attracts every other body with a force that is proportional to the mass of the body. Why is a one-pound iron bar more attracted to a one-pound magnet that to a one-pound block of wood? Doesn't this disprove Newton's law of gravity?

Jack E. Reinhard
Dover, Delaware

Dear Jack:

No, your example refers to magnetism, and electromagnetic fields are *far* stronger than gravitational fields. Also, your example refers to weight, but weight is not the same as mass.

◆ ◆ ◆

Dear Marilyn:

I have a magnet that is still good after a number of years. Why don't magnets ever wear out like so many other things do?

Joe Kent
Fort Worth, Texas

Dear Joe:

Well, they do, actually, or at least they tend to, but how long that takes, if it happens at all, depends on such things as the material of which they're made, the shape of the magnet itself, and how they're handled. Even "permanent" magnets tend to demagnetize themselves with time, and if you treat a magnet roughly, heat it, or expose it to another magnetic field, you may very well hasten the process considerably.

◆ ◆ ◆

Dear Marilyn:
   Which is the more powerful force—gravity or magnetism?
                                             I. J. Armstrong
                                             Staten Island, New York

Dear I. J.:
   Gravity is feeble compared to magnetism. At equal distances, if we give gravitation interaction a value of 4, we'd have to give electromagnetic interaction a value of, incredibly, 10,000,000,000,000,000,000,000,000,000,000,000,000. (Just think— you can overcome the force of the entire earth's gravity with the little magnet that you stick onto your refrigerator!)

◆ ◆ ◆

Dear Marilyn:
   The highest tides are during the full moon. I know the moon's gravity affects the oceans, but why more so during the full moon?
                                             David Hill
                                             Prescott, Arizona

Dear David:
   Because it has the help of the sun then. The sun affects the oceans too, and most of the time, the sun and the moon pull in different directions, but at new and full moons, they're lined up in such a way that they pull together.

◆ ◆ ◆

Dear Marilyn:
   Since Albert Einstein has said that nothing is so complex that it cannot be answered simply, can you explain this question in a relatively simple way? Why are there two high tides and two low tides every day?
                                             Aaron H. Holtzman
                                             East Windsor, New Jersey

Dear Aaron:

No, I can't. The subject of tides is excessively complex. I don't come anywhere near doing it justice when I say that the tides are caused by the gravitational action of the moon and sun upon the revolving earth and that the moon pulls up water on the side nearest it while the water on the other side is spun outward, causing two great tidal waves to arise at the same time on opposite sides of the planet. The statement that nothing is so complex that it cannot be answered simply may sound catchy, but I think it's just plain wrong.

◆ ◆ ◆

Dear Marilyn:

If you woke up tomorrow morning and everything in the world, including yourself, were twice as large, would you notice the difference?

Gary S. Kimball
Albany, New York

Dear Gary:

You bet. Unless the earth expanded too, we'd have a crowding problem that would make sardines look comfy. And if the planets and sun were included, suntanning would no longer be voluntary.

Actually, there's a much longer answer to this question, but I decided not to pursue it because of its wildly speculative nature. That is, for example, if atoms were twice the size they are, would the laws of physics change proportionately? If not, the difference in our world would be beyond imagination.

◆ ◆ ◆

Dear Marilyn:

If we claim that there is other life in the universe, then why haven't we discovered them or vice versa?

Brian Cruz
Havelock, North Carolina

Dear Brian:

Just because we think the chances are good that other life forms exist doesn't mean the chances are equally good that one will discover the other. In fact, the chances of the latter happening are far less. The detection of others is contingent upon them already being there, but their existence isn't contingent upon any sort of observation, past, present, or future.

◆ ◆ ◆

Dear Marilyn:

Why is it, as scientists widely contend, a theoretical impossibility for man to ever travel at the speed of light?

Carol Puschaver
Gathersburg, Maryland

Dear Carol:

This is less a stand-alone statement of fact than it is a dependent one. In other words, the special theory of relativity makes it impossible for an object to travel at a rate of speed exceeding that of light without it (the theory, that is!) falling apart mathematically.

◆ ◆ ◆

Dear Marilyn:

Is there a fourth dimension?

James H. Smith
New Port Ricky, Florida

Dear James:

I'd say yes, but we don't yet know what it is. This is because we don't "find" dimensions; we "identify" them. Put another way, planets are discovered; dimensions are named. As soon as everyone can agree on what the fourth dimension should be, we'll have one. However, this will probably be dependent to a great extent on whether or how well it can be measured with current instruments. After all, an unmeasurable dimension may be a contradiction in terms. At this point, time seems to be the front-running favorite.

22.

Time

Dear Marilyn:
Please define time without speaking of the measure of it by man.
Terry McGee
Makanda, Illinois

Dear Terry:
Time is the distance between the beginning of a state and the end of it.

♦ ♦ ♦

Dear Marilyn:
Could you tell me when time began and when it will end?
Harry Faulkner
Albany, New York

Dear Harry:
I believe that time, like mathematics, is a logical construct, a concept devised to intellectually organize a valid phenomenon. Asking when time began is something like asking when mathematics began.

♦ ♦ ♦

Dear Marilyn:
Is there a present time? Since the past is a time gone by, and the future a time to come, where is the present? In a split second, the future is upon us. Conversely, in a split second, it is past us.
Roy Scott
Sharon, Massachusetts

Dear Roy:

Cosmologically speaking, I'd say the present is a point that spans no time, but doesn't mean it doesn't exist. After all, like the boundary between properties, how else could we define what is "past" and what is "future"?

◆ ◆ ◆

Dear Marilyn:

Does time always move forward?

Anonymous

Dear Reader:

I believe time doesn't move at all. Instead, we can view it as a sort of ruler laid out over the whole of events, both known and unknown, past and future, as an aid to our comprehension of their relationship to each other. As we don't yet know when the first event occurred, it has been useful to select a date such as the designated birth year of Christ and place the ends of two rulers at that point, one measuring the sequence of events before it and the other measuring the sequence of events afterward. If we discover "more past," we lengthen that ruler; as "more future" happens, we lengthen the other one.

◆ ◆ ◆

Dear Marilyn:

Can we ever travel back in time?

Anonymous

Dear Reader:

In a way, we already do. Even now, we don't really witness events as they occur. We witness them *afterward*, when the light and sound waves reach us. But I suppose if we could ever travel faster than the speed of light, we could, at least in science fiction, race away from the earth, then stop and watch the past happening. Hearing it would present other problems, complicated by the fact that sound waves are not known to travel though space. But even if they did, light and sound travel at such differing speeds that we would see the past, but not hear it until much later. So, in theory, we might find ourselves in the position of watching Julius Caesar speaking to his Senate with the voice of an early cave-woman scolding her children.

◆ ◆ ◆

Dear Marilyn:

Time is considered the best test for most things; can you give us some examples of things where it is not?

Brent Paul Williams
Pullman, Washington

Dear Brent:

Yes: flowers, fashion, and fish.

◆ ◆ ◆

Dear Marilyn:

Why do people seem to experience car accidents in slow motion when it's happening?

Sandy Snapp
Denver, Colorado

Dear Sandy:

I don't know for sure, but it may be related to the phenomenon whereby an hour in the dentist's chair seems so much longer than an hour at the amusement park. Perhaps it's simply that situations that evoke fear stir our survival instinct, causing us to "tune in" so closely that we attend to sixty details in a minute rather than a less frightening sixty details in an hour or a completely comfortable six details in an hour, corresponding roughly to the accident, the dentist's office, and a combination of laughing friends and cotton candy.

◆ ◆ ◆

Dear Marilyn:

We have metric measurements for just about everything except time. Why is there no mention of metric time?

E. M. Henderson
Nassawadox, Virginia

Dear E. M.:

Shhh!! They might hear you!!

◆ ◆ ◆

Dear Marilyn:

What age are we in? (Examples would be "ice age," "space age," etc.)

Greg Bitter
Davis, California

Dear Greg:

I think we could call this the "information age" because, for the first time in history, the average person has access to nearly all of the collected information of humankind. Unfortunately, a great deal of it is inaccurate and misleading, but, what the heck, you can't have everything, can you?

23.

Days and Dates

Dear Marilyn:

Do you suppose a society that does not celebrate individual birthdays could ever come into being?

Chris Morrow
Carlsbad, California

Dear Chris:

It already has. Celebrating the anniversary of the day of birth is an old custom, but not as widespread as we might think. And in the classical civilizations of Egypt, Greece, and Rome, the birthdays of gods and kings were duly noted, but it was far less important to pay attention to the birthdays of ordinary people, with those of women and children considered downright trivial.

◆ ◆ ◆

Dear Marilyn:

I'm reasonably certain that when Christ was crucified, his disciples didn't say, "Here it is, A.D. 33." I've asked many people and checked several encyclopedias, but no one has been able to give me the answer to this question: who initiated numbering the years of the calendar from when Christ was believed to have been born?

Thomas P. Scanlon
Valley Stream, New York

Dear Thomas:

In ancient times, calendars were generally renumbered with each new ruler, so it was not without precedent that around what is now known as A.D. 525, a monk named Dionysius Exiguus proposed that years be counted from the birth of Christ. This was adopted throughout the Christian world over the following 500 years. Modern chronologists, however, position the occasion closer to 4 B.C., several years earlier.

◆ ◆ ◆

Dear Marilyn:

If the current year is 1992, what was the year 1,992 years ago?

Sporty Peters
Baltimore, Maryland

Dear Sporty:

There was no year called "0," so the answer would be the year 1 B.C. because that's the designation for the year that fills the time period. Here's a way to visualize this:

[3 B.C.] [2 B.C.] [1 B.C.] [A.D. 1] [A.D. 2] [A.D. 3]

If we were in the midst of A.D. 3 and went back one year, we would be in the midst of A.D. 2. If we went back two years, we would be in the midst of A.D. 1. If we went back three years, we would be in the midst of 1 B.C. And so it follows that, if we are in the midst of A.D. 1992 and go back 1,992 years, we would also be in the midst of 1 B.C.

◆ ◆ ◆

Dear Marilyn:

This one couldn't be solved by anybody around here, even after a trip to the library. How would you write the Roman numeral "1999"?

Susan M. Alinder
Liverpool, New York

Dear Susan:

The usage of Roman numerals has changed throughout the ages, but in modern form, I'd vote for MDCCCCLXXXXVIIII, which means "1000 + 500 + 100 + 100 + 100 + 100 + 50 + 10 + 10 + 10 + 10 + 5 + 1 + 1 + 1 + 1." An alternate form, called "subtractive," would be MCMXCIX, which would mean "1000 + 900 + 90 + 9," but I didn't choose it because it seems less clear to me, even though it has the advantage of being shorter.

◆ ◆ ◆

Dear Marilyn:

In an earlier column, you gave a "preferred" outlandish group of Roman numerals for 1999. Although correct, I'm surprised that you didn't offer the more conventional MCMLXXXXIX.

R. B. Worland
Franklin, North Carolina

I was always taught that it is totally incorrect, when writing Roman numerals, to write more than three like numerals consecutively. MCMXCIX would be correct. Do you have what it takes to print a correction?

Susan Oshinsky
Sugar Land, Texas

I wondered why you wouldn't write it MCMIC since anytime a smaller number precedes a larger one, it would be subtractive. It would also be a lot easier to figure out when reading the year a movie was made at the end.

Steve Guarneri
Belleville, New Jersey

The shortest way would be MIM.

Roger Kares
Marion, Kentucky

The simplest way would be IMM.

Mike Kiehner
Pottsville, Pennsylvania

Dear Readers:

Good grief. I had no idea so many of you cared. My mailbox is full to bursting. I'd still vote for MDCCCCLXXXXVIIII because it's clear, although it sure the heck isn't short, is it? But Roman numerals weren't exactly the most practical number system around, which may be one of the reasons we don't use them any more.

And I'd also vote for scrapping the practice of labeling movies that way. It drives people crazy and has nothing to do with retaining historical accuracy. After all, there aren't any 2,000-year-old movies, are there?!

The most common complaint was that "you can't use Roman numerals more than three times in a row." However, an inscription on the Columna Rostrata, a monument in the Forum, repeats a symbol twenty-three times, routine in those days. And "shorter" isn't synonymous with "correct" or even "better," for that matter. We don't write "kof" instead of "cough" even though it's shorter and easier to see how to pronounce.

◆ ◆ ◆

Dear Marilyn:

When will the twenty-first century begin—January 1, 2000, or January 1, 2001? If it's 2001, will you please explain why?

Grace Antle
Kennesaw, Georgia

Dear Grace:

The first year of the Christian Era was called A.D. 1, so that's when the first century began. Likewise, the second century began with the year A.D. 101. This means that the twenty-first century will begin with the year A.D. 2001.

◆ ◆ ◆

Dear Marilyn:

In the year 2000, how will the year be designated? One can now write 7/14/92, but 7/14/00 would be uncertain.

C. Thomas
Moreno Valley, California

Dear C.:

Why not 7/14/00? It's no more uncertain than 7/14/92. We assume that "92" refers to "1992," not "1892" or "1792," don't we? Likewise, we can assume that "00" refers to "2000" instead of "1900" or "1800." In other words, if the first two digits of the year are absent, we assume the century is "current," so to speak. After all, when we buy tickets to an evening of "fifties" music, we definitely don't expect to hear the Baroque compositions for the harpsichord that were so popular in 1750 or the Verdi operas of the 1850s.

◆ ◆ ◆

Dear Marilyn:

If there is a leap year every four years, how come there was no February 29 in 1900?

Peter D. Bonanno
Mahwah, New Jersey

Dear Peter:

Because adding a day every four years doesn't quite correct our calendar to match the astronomical year (the time taken for the earth to orbit around the sun), and as the centuries go by, we need to adjust it a little more. Therefore, we only add the extra day to century years exactly divisible by 400, of which 1900 is not one, of course. And if you want to get *really* picky, you'll also need to reverse the procedure now and then, making every year evenly divisible by 4,000 a common year, instead.

◆ ◆ ◆

Dear Marilyn:

It is a fact that there are 365 days in a year, and it is also a fact that there are 52 weeks in a year and 7 days in a week. But when you multiply 52 weeks by 7 days, you come up with 364 days instead of 365 days. What happened to the 365th day?

> Larry Adler
> Astoria, New York

Dear Larry:

It's true that there are 7 days in a week, but there aren't 52 weeks in a year. That's only an approximation. Actually, there are about 365.24 days in an average year, and dividing that by 7 gives us the number of weeks—about 52.18.

◆ ◆ ◆

Dear Marilyn:

If "7 to 11" stores are open twenty-four hours a day, seven days a week, 365 days a year, including holidays, why do their doors have locks?

> Greg Larson
> San Diego, California

Dear Greg:

The name itself is a clue. A store that is called "7 to 11" but is open twenty-four hours a day probably got its original locks back when it was still open only from 7:00 in the morning to 11:00 in the evening. But consider the Denny's restaurant chain. Many of them had no locks at all because of the "always open" policy, and at others, the locks were never used. However, locks *have* been installed at about seven hundred of them because over twelve hundred of the restaurants closed for the first time on Christmas day of 1988. But why were those other locks there in the first place? Well, what if an emergency occurred, and everybody had to leave?

◆ ◆ ◆

Dear Marilyn:
    Is the time 12:00 A.M. considered to be midnight or noon?
                                                    Tom Karle
                                                    Syracuse, New York

Dear Tom:
    Our day is considered to begin at midnight, making that 12:00 A.M., and to run through the next twenty-four hours, ending with the last moment of 11:59 P.M. If this doesn't make much sense, and you wonder why the day shouldn't begin with "one" instead of "twelve," consider this. If you're born at a certain moment, you're not a year old until a year later, and then you would call yourself "one." Likewise, if a new day is born at midnight, it's not an hour old until an hour later, and we call it "one in the morning."
    The confusion arises when we call the 12:30 at night or at noon "twelve thirty in the morning or in the afternoon" instead of just "thirty" in the morning or in the afternoon as it might more logically, but ambiguously, be called. After all, if we cleared up that logical point, we'd have to call 12:10 in the afternoon "ten in the afternoon"!

◆ ◆ ◆

Dear Marilyn:
    If a nationwide baby food company offers a prize to the woman who has the first baby of the year, which of the following two women would win—one from New York City who provides proof of birth at 12:02 A.M. on January 1 or one from Los Angeles who submits proof of birth at 12:01 A.M. on the same date?
                                                    Dean F. V. Du Vall
                                                    Williamston, Michigan

Dear Dean:
    I'd give the prize to the woman in Los Angeles even though the baby in New York was born some three hours earlier. Not mentioning a national standard implies that all time zones are in the running according to local standards, and that was probably the intention of the sponsors of the contest.

To make the contest more fair, however, I would begin the race for everyone at the same time—when the new year begins on earth in Greenwich, England, the home of Universal Time, used in astronomy and other sciences. That worldwide event would occur in New York at 7:00 P.M. on December 31 there, in Los Angeles at 4:00 P.M. on the same day, and in Hawaii at 2:00 P.M. That way, it would be a real *nationwide* race, with all time zones on the starting blocks simultaneously.

Some readers voted for the International Date Line, but I don't agree. Philosophically, the date line seems to be determined by the prime meridian, not the other way around.

24.

Sex, Math, and Logic

Dear Marilyn:

I would greatly appreciate your opinion on this. Does one improve the mind by doing crosswords, jigsaws, and other types of games, or are they nothing more than relaxing pastimes?

Nancy Dagen
Evanston, Illinois

Dear Nancy:

I honestly think that the sorts of things you mention rank far closer to entertainment than to enlightenment, with crosswords for the more literate and jigsaws for the more skillful. But who cares, really? We don't have to spend every spare moment improving our minds. Life is too short for such pressure.

◆ ◆ ◆

Dear Marilyn:

I am proficient in my homework, but have trouble finishing the tests. In higher mathematics especially, should time be such an important factor?

Kevin Flaherty
Palm Beach Gardens, Florida

Dear Kevin:

I think it should be less important than it is. For example, it's said that when a top-notch chess player plays a bottom-notch one, the fine player is penalized when a short time is allowed for the players to make their moves. Deep thinking takes longer than superficial thinking and, because such fine things can come of it, should have a greater place in our system of rewards for academic achievement.

◆ ◆ ◆

Dear Marilyn:

Should mathematics students of any level utilize calculators, given the technology exists to solve the problem presented with no thought process necessary?

M. E. D.
Dallas, Texas

Dear Reader:

Sure! While it's important to know how to perform mathematical operations by hand because a calculator may not be available, knowing what information to enter into the calculator is what counts, not the mechanics of how it yields the answer.

For example, let's suppose we know that division is required to solve the next step of a particular problem, and we write it all out like this:

$$
\begin{array}{r}
54321 \\
9876\overline{)536474196} \\
\underline{49380} \\
42674 \\
\underline{39504} \\
31701 \\
\underline{29628} \\
20739 \\
\underline{19752} \\
9876
\end{array}
$$

Now, how many of us can say why the above number pattern produces the correct quotient? In other words, the laborious method is just as mindless as the convenient one!

◆ ◆ ◆

Dear Marilyn:

Is it correct to say that no one can be considered "highly intellectual" without mathematical aptitude?

Thomas R. Jurras
Lake Worth, Florida

Dear Thomas:

I'd say yes, although this aptitude might not evidence itself in the expected ways. Anyone I consider "highly intellectual" has great powers of logic, and logic underlies the whole of mathematical ability. However, they may never have become interested enough in that area of thinking to apply their power to it, even to the point of manifesting ability on an aptitude test.

To put it another way, nearly every fine chess player is extremely bright, but most extremely bright people don't happen to become fine chess players, although many probably could.

◆ ◆ ◆

Dear Marilyn:

Why does matter behave in a way that is describable by mathematics?

Clark Semmes
Bethesda, Maryland

Dear Clark:

The classical Greeks were convinced that nature is mathematically designed, but judging from the burgeoning of mathematical applications, I'm beginning to think simply that mathematics can be invented to describe anything, and matter is no exception.

◆ ◆ ◆

Dear Marilyn:

Which is the biggest, an infinite line, an infinite circle, or an infinite plane?

Anonymous

Dear Reader:

I'd say an infinite plane. When comparing only a line and a circle, no matter how large they grow, the circle would have the greater number of points. (For example, a one-mile-wide circular line "straightened out" would be over three miles long.) If the circle were "filled in" as well, it would have an even greater number of points on its surface. An unbounded plane surface, however, would have even more because it could be said to consist of an infinite number of infinite lines, laid side by side. However bad it would be to mow along an infinite sidewalk, it would be worse to mow the entire lawn it bordered.

◆ ◆ ◆

Dear Marilyn:

If a point is the cross-section of a line, and a line is the cross-section of a plane, and a plane is the cross-section of a cube, then what is a cube the cross-section of?

Max E. Floyd
Kokomo, Indiana

Dear Max:

I don't think a plane is the cross-section of a cube any more than it is the cross-section of a sphere, but have you ever heard of a tesseract? In mathematics, it's the four-dimensional equivalent of a cube, also called a "hypercube."

◆ ◆ ◆

Dear Marilyn:

What is a better way to describe rotation than the movement of hands on a clock? Depending on which side you're on, for example, the rotation of a wheel may be both clockwise and counterclockwise.

Emory C. Walker, Jr.
Denver, Colorado

Dear Emory:

To avoid reference to direction, you could call it "moving compasswise." This is because, of the many sorts of rotation, you could describe it very specifically as the movement of all parts in a circular path with a common angular velocity around 1) a point, or 2) a line. Then again, you could also describe it as the movement of a child on an adjustable stool until a limit is reached by 1) the stool, or 2) his mother.

◆ ◆ ◆

Dear Marilyn:

There are 360 degrees in a circle. Why not 340 or 460 or any other number? Why 360?

Carl Gautreaux
Cumming, Georgia

Dear Carl:

Because Babylonian arithmetic had a base of 60 (called sexagesimal) instead of 10 (called decimal). And brought to us by the same folks are the 60 seconds in a minute and the 60 minutes in an hour. But if we're tempted to complain, we should remind ourselves how nice it is that they didn't pick 17.

◆ ◆ ◆

Dear Marilyn:

I have asked this question of so many people and as yet have had no acceptable answer. A math major told me that it is something "you just have to accept." Can you please explain how a negative times a negative equals a positive?

Anonymous
Pittsburgh, Pennsylvania

Dear Reader:

Well, here's *one* way to look at it.

We say $+1$ times $+1$ equals $+1$, agreed? So $+1$ times -1 would have to equal -1, the "opposite" of the first answer of $+1$, right? Continuing in this way, -1 times -1 would then have to equal $+1$ again, the "opposite" of the second answer of -1!

These equations might illustrate the point a little better:

$$\text{If } +1 \times +1 = +1,$$
$$\text{Then } +1 \times -1 = -1,$$
$$\text{And then } -1 \times -1 = +1.$$

◆ ◆ ◆

Dear Marilyn:

I know how to calculate area, but I fail to believe in the results. It may make sense mathematically, but perceptually, it seems flawed. Let's say I want to fence a small garden, so I buy 20 feet of fence. If I use it to fence a 5-foot by 5-foot square, then I have a garden space of 25 square feet. But if I use it to fence a 2-foot by 8-foot rectangle, I only have garden space of 16 square feet. Isn't this just the hocus-pocus of mathematics? How can my garden be smaller just because I arranged the fence differently?

Dennis Figg
Jefferson City, Missouri

Dear Dennis:

The same way your inner tube can be smaller if you squeeze out the air. The total of the edges imposes an upper limit on the area—your garden would be its biggest if you arranged the fence in a 20-foot circle. But it doesn't define it—you could also lay out the fence in an 11-foot circle around a 9-foot circle, creating a race track for your garden slugs.

◆ ◆ ◆

Dear Marilyn:

I have two apples, and my friend has none. If we *add* them together, we have two apples to share, one for each of us. However, if I have two pears, and my friend has none, and we *multiply* them together, we have no pears at all to share. Where did they go?

Ralph E. Brown
Shelton, Connecticut

Dear Ralph:

They're still in the fruit bowl with the apples. All mathematical operations are not equal. If we want to see how many bananas we have together, we must pile them on top of each other with addition. That is, four bananas plus two bananas equal six bananas.

Multiplication, however, operates on only *one* of the groups: four bananas times one (not one *banana*) equal four bananas; four bananas times two (not two *bananas*) equal eight bananas; four bananas times three (not three *bananas*) equal twelve bananas.

In other words, you can't multiply one group of pears by another group of pears. You can only multiply one group of pears by a number, and if that number is zero, you've ignored your *own* pears. You should have multiplied by *one*.

◆ ◆ ◆

Dear Marilyn:

When I read about certain objects being "inversely proportional" to similar objects, it confuses me. For example, can you simplify the following? "The increase in the number of humans and of domestic plant and animal species is inversely proportional to the number of wild species that can share a limited environment."

John A. Withersty
Muncie, Indiana

Dear John:

Loosely speaking, all it means is that the product of the two quantities is constant. For example, if the number of dogs, let's say 8, varies in inverse proportion to the number of deer, let's say 6, then when the dogs increase to 16, the deer decrease to 3. ($8 \times 6 = 48$, and $16 \times 3 = 48$.)

Your statement could also be phrased, "When the number of humans and of domestic plant and animal species doubles, the number of wild species that can share a limited environment is halved." Or, just as correctly, it could be turned around, as in, "When the number of wild species doubles, the number of humans and of domestic plant and animal species that can share a limited environment is halved."

However, none of this means those statements are true!

◆ ◆ ◆

Dear Marilyn:

If you dropped an object one foot above a table and continually divided the distance it fell in half, wouldn't that prove that the object would never hit the table?

Darrel Harden
Rossville, Kansas

Dear Darrel:

No. The sum of the infinite series $\frac{1}{2} + \frac{1}{4} + \frac{1}{8} + \frac{1}{16}$, and so forth, is 1!

◆ ◆ ◆

Dear Marilyn:

If it is a fact that $\frac{1}{3} = .333$ recurring, why is it true that $\frac{1}{3} + \frac{1}{3} + \frac{1}{3} = 1.000$ and not .999 recurring?

J. Daniel Finn
Mount Clemens, Michigan

Dear Daniel:

I'm afraid this one is going to overwhelm my mailbox again, but here goes, anyway: they *do* equal .999 repeating. The amazing thing is that .999 repeating equals 1.000, and this is why:

No matter how far you extend the .333 repeating, the part you *didn't* write down (the repeating part) totals one-third of the next decimal place. And no matter how far you extend a .666 repeating, the part you didn't write down totals *two*-thirds of the next decimal place. And no matter how far you extend a .999 repeating, the part you didn't write down totals *three*-thirds of the next decimal place. This means that you can stop at any point and add it to what you've already written, and the result will be 1.000.

◆ ◆ ◆

Dear Marilyn:

If one were asked to add each successive number from 1 to 1,000,000, this, of course, would prove to be a monumental task, indeed. Does a formula exist that would simplify the job?

M. F. Kapelanczyk
Baltimore, Maryland

Dear M. F.:

To find the total, we multiply one-half the number of terms by the sum of the first and the last of them, and this is why it works, using the series of numbers from 1 through 10 as an example.

$$
\begin{array}{ccccc}
1 & 2 & 3 & 4 & 5 \\
+10 & +9 & +8 & +7 & +6 \\
\hline
11 & 11 & 11 & 11 & 11
\end{array}
$$

There are ten terms in the series of numbers from 1 through 10. The first and last terms add up to 11, as do the next-to-first and next-to-last terms, and so forth, as seen above. So all ten terms can be added in just five operations. And as all these sums are equal, we can take an additional shortcut by just multiplying one of them by the number of operations performed.

Therefore, the sum of the numbers from 1 through 10 equals one-half the number of terms (5) multiplied by the sum of the first and the last of them (11), which equals 55.

And the sum of the numbers from 1 through 1,000,000 equals one-half the number of terms (500,000) multiplied by the sum of the first and the last of them (1,000,001), which equals 500,000,500,000.

◆ ◆ ◆

Dear Marilyn:

I believe that education has little or nothing to do with whether a person is "logical." What do *you* think?

Don Zukowsky
Clinton, Connecticut

Dear Don:

In a way, I agree. The ability to reason clearly or validly has more to do with intelligence than it does with education. However, I think that nearly all of us possess the ability to a far greater extent than we realize and that education, particularly the study of mathematics, can be of considerable help in realizing our potential.

◆ ◆ ◆

Dear Marilyn:

If a person is killed accidentally while walking along the street, which is the correct statement about what happened?

1) He was in the right place at the right time.
2) He was in the right place at the wrong time.
3) He was in the wrong place at the right time.
4) He was in the wrong place at the wrong time.

Frank Briggs
Topsfield, Massachusetts

Dear Frank:

I'd say he was in the right place at the wrong time, and this is why. Let's say there are four people, two jaywalking across the street and two walking down the sidewalk. One of each pair is hit by a car.

The unhurt person on the sidewalk was in the right place at the right time; the injured person on the sidewalk was in the right place at the wrong time. The unhurt person in the street was in the wrong place at the right time; the injured person in the street was in the wrong place at the wrong time.

◆ ◆ ◆

Dear Marilyn:

Do you think something is really free if you have to buy something else at the regular price in order to receive the "free" item, for example, "buy one/get one free" offers?

Charles Sherwood
Laguna Niguel, California

Dear Charles:

If the item is nearly always on sale for its regular price, and there's a "buy one/get one free" offer for it, then yes, I do think the second item is "free." (It wasn't called simply "get one free.")

But if the item is *often* on sale as a "buy one/get one free" offer, then I consider the regular price to be knowingly inflated in order to take unsporting advantage of an otherwise honest sales technique.

◆ ◆ ◆

Dear Marilyn:

If four single people rent a car for one week at $100 a week, they would each pay $25. But if two persons were single, and the other two were married, would it be the same? Or would the married couple pay a third? It doesn't seem right that the married couple would pay $50 while the other two single persons pay $25 each. I would appreciate your opinion. We're leaving by train to Las Vegas.

Frank Mazzotta
Pittsburgh, Pennsylvania

Dear Frank:

I don't see what being married has to do with it. If a married couple goes out to a movie, they buy two tickets, don't they? And even if they get a reduced rate on a train or a plane, they don't expect the other passengers to pay *more* because of it. Instead, the carrier simply takes less. So if two married people want to pay less than two single people, they should request that discount from the rental car company itself!

25.

Computers

Dear Marilyn:

What will be the best and the worst aspects of computers that will do our thinking for us someday?

Ginny Grabois
Lake Mills, Wisconsin

Dear Ginny:

They have no emotions, and they have no emotions.

◆ ◆ ◆

Dear Marilyn:

I believe the development of artificial intelligence to allow computers to understand vague human communication is detrimental to us because we've not found it to be accurate. What do you think? Also, providing a machine that would attempt to make sense out of nonsense and then make a decision accordingly, could prove to be disastrous. We could believe it, yet it may be *far* from correct because the information on which the reasoning was based was ambiguous and incomplete.

Alexander Muller
Ellisville, Missouri

Dear Alexander:

"Fuzzy logic" is the not-so-common name for this unusual computer theory, now gaining credence and practical use in Japan, although the

reviews from the United States are definitely mixed. Allowing computers to work with terms as indistinct as "cold" or "tall," its advocates
say, gives them more human-like abilities. If that's actually the case,
the question then would be whether that would represent progress or
just a necessary compromise.

◆ ◆ ◆

Dear Marilyn:

Now that libraries let you check out computer disks and videotapes,
I'm wondering about the future of the human race when all of our
information is stored in an electronic warehouse. What would be the
result of a universal power failure, or the finding that we no longer had
the raw material to manufacture batteries?

George A. Gould
Portland, Oregon

Dear George:

The realization that most of our information may someday be beyond
the direct grasp of our senses seems like a precarious situation, all right,
especially to those of us who work with computers and have firsthand
experience with their shortcomings. And the knowledge that human
beings themselves have been more destructive to the system than power
failures doesn't add to our sense of security.

However, this pales in significance when compared to the much
more immediate needs for which technology has now become quietly
essential. If we run out of fuel, for example, our cities could not even
be supplied with goods as basic as food. How's *that* for a worry?

◆ ◆ ◆

Dear Marilyn:

Not long ago, I was fascinated by an article about a concept of
computer information retrieval called "hypermedia." According to its
author, "Flights through info-space" would be made possible by cross-
referencing anything to everything. Can you tell me your best estimate
as to when hypermedia might blossom into full glory, if ever?

Theodore A. Zajac
Dallas, Texas

Dear Theodore:

Data retrieval systems are already growing rapidly, but actually har-
nessing the entire information explosion is unlikely to occur until and

unless there's a market for it. And in this age of increasing specialization, the professional trend is toward knowing more and more about less and less, not necessarily a bad thing, but it's a valid consideration. And so is public interest. For example, how often do you use your encyclopaedia? Several times a day? Once a week? Or has it gathered dust since the kids left home? A "hypermedia" system will be prohibitively expensive for novelty use alone.

◆ ◆ ◆

Dear Marilyn:

Will a computer ever be the world chess champion?

Anonymous

Dear Reader:

Why *should* it be? That is, not unless a race car is allowed to win the New York Marathon. If a computer were called an entrant, it would be no more significant than if a hydraulic lift were allowed to compete in the Olympic weightlifting event. Such contests, in fact, might well cease to exist due to lack of interest. Would anyone really want to watch a rocket launcher throw a fastball past Cecil Fielder? However, if there is ever enough interest in a chess match in which everyone enters his or her own computer, the way cars are entered in the Indianapolis 500, we may have an additional event on the sports agenda.

26.

Choice, Chance, and Lotteries

Dear Marilyn:

Which is safer to play—the stock market or casinos?

Julian Hammer
Carteret, New Jersey

Dear Julian:

It seems safer to invest in stocks than in chips because everybody at the company in which you invest wants your stock to go up and is hard at work to make that happen; on the other hand, everybody at the casino in which you gamble wants your number to *lose* and is hard at work to make *that* happen. Another way of putting it is that when you play Atlantic City, you bet against the house, but when you play Wall Street, you bet *with* the house.

◆ ◆ ◆

Dear Marilyn:

Rolling six dice, what are the chances to roll six of a kind? On May 21, 1989, I rolled six deuces for 10,000 points in a friendly game!

John Huber
Lake Placid, Florida

Dear John:

Well, it's probably not going to happen again for a while! There are 6 different ways to toss one die one time and 36 ways to toss it two times, and that means there are 46,656 ways to toss it six times. As rolling six dice at once is the same as rolling one die six times, and as there are only 6 "six of a kind" possible rolls in all of those, that means your chances of doing it were only 6 out of 46,656, the same as 1 out of 7,776.

◆ ◆ ◆

Dear Marilyn:

A state million-dollar lottery was going off at five-million-to-one odds. I told a friend I bought two tickets and doubled my odds, to two chances in five million or one chance in two-and-a-half million. He told me my odds are still one to five million, no matter how many tickets I buy. If I bought two-and-a-half million tickets, would my odds still be one to five million, or would they be one to two? Please help settle this argument.

John Earl
Linden, New Jersey

Dear John:

Your friend is wrong. While the winning chance of *each ticket alone* that you bought is still only one in five million, *your* chances of winning are doubled because you own both of those tickets. So yes, if you bought two-and-a-half million tickets, your tickets would each have a one in five million chance of winning, but *your* chances of winning would be one in two.

◆ ◆ ◆

Dear Marilyn:

Joe plays a lottery on a regular basis. The odds are 1,000 to 1. He has played 999 times and never won. Moe plays for the first time on Joe's 1,000th try. Are Joe's chances of winning better than Moe's?

Alan Otter
New Boston, Michigan

Dear Alan:

No, they're the same. Each lottery is a separate event, and those odds start fresh with each of Joe's (and Moe's) tries.

◆ ◆ ◆

Dear Marilyn:

A lottery ticket is a winner when its 6 numbers match those drawn from a 40-number pool. A ticket purchaser, basing his selection on family members' birthdates, thus restricted his possible winning combinations to numbers 1 through 31. Did he decrease his chances of winning by his eliminating numbers 32 through 40 from his possible choices? Your answer could quite possibly prevent World War III from breaking out in our family.

Lewis B. Hall
Baltimore, Maryland

Dear Lewis:

I hope I'm not too late. No, there was no change whatsoever in the chances of winning (although the chances of splitting the pot may have increased). No matter which numbers were selected, all the others were eliminated, and the numbers *he* eliminated were no more likely to be chosen than the numbers anyone *else* eliminated. I hope that settles it. And if World War III *does* break out, we'll all going to hold you guys responsible.

◆ ◆ ◆

Dear Marilyn:

This is a lottery question. You said once that a ticket purchaser who based his selection on the birthdates of family members didn't decrease his chances of winning and that the numbers he eliminated were no different from the numbers anyone else eliminated. However, he eliminated these numbers on a systematic basis, and no one else did. This must make some difference. If not, could you please show me the error in my thinking?

Michele A. Leimgruber
Demarest, New Jersey

Dear Michele:

It can make a difference, but not in his chances of winning, and the kind of difference depends on how the lottery is constructed. If the prize is a million dollars, a million different tickets are sold, and the winner is to be drawn from among those, it doesn't matter which ticket he purchases.

But let's say those million people get to *choose* their ticket numbers, the prize to be split among any duplicates. 999,999 people pick #7, and you pick #11. The winner is drawn from the numbers 1 through 1,000,000. While the chances are equal that #7 and #11 will win, you'd have a much better payoff with #11 than all those people sharing #7. In this kind of setup, avoiding "popular" numbers is a wiser bet.

◆ ◆ ◆

Dear Marilyn:

I've been playing Lotto for more than a year and have never won any prize larger than $5. Would you suggest for me to quit or keep playing it until I at least earn back my investment?

Tu Cong Tran
Garden Grove, California

Dear Reader:

Stop! You haven't *invested* your money; you've *spent* it. (And any money you win won't be earned.) I really do dislike gambling and lotteries, too, because if we lose money, and we usually do, it was a bad way to spend it, and even if we *make* money, we don't deserve it.

◆ ◆ ◆

Dear Marilyn:

Is it possible for state lotteries to be won repeatedly using scientific mathematical principles? There are several groups soliciting books claiming this is possible.

Steve Binkoski
Hamden, Connecticut

Dear Steve:

Nope. Remember, if that could be done, and someone knew how to do it, why would he or she write a book about it instead of actually going out and doing it?

Theoretically, however, certain lotteries can be "bought out" by someone with enough resources to spend the millions of dollars required. (Every possible ticket can be purchased, and if the prize is larger than that cost, there will be a profit.)

◆ ◆ ◆

Dear Marilyn:

How come a psychic never wins a lottery?

Julian Hammer
Carteret, New Jersey

Dear Julian:

Good question! Actually, a "psychic" has the same chance as anyone else, so it *can* happen and may already have. A better question would be to ask *them*, "Why don't psychics *always* win lotteries?!"

◆ ◆ ◆

When I innocently printed the following reply, I had no idea that it would provoke a national controversy.

Dear Marilyn:

Suppose you're on a game show, and you're given the choice of three doors. Behind one door is a car, the others, goats. You pick a door, say #1, and the host, who knows what's behind the doors, opens another door, say #3, which has a goat. He says to you, "Do you want to pick door #2?" Is it to your advantage to switch your choice of doors?

Craig F. Whitaker
Columbia, Maryland

Dear Craig:

Yes; you should switch. The first door has a ⅓ chance of winning, but the second door has a ⅔ chance. Here's a good way to visualize what happened. Suppose there are a *million* doors, and you pick door #1. Then the host, who knows what's behind the doors and will always avoid the one with the prize, opens them all except door #777,777. You'd switch to that door pretty fast, wouldn't you?

Sara Brzowsky telephoned me a couple of days after this answer was published and told me that Parade *was getting quite a few telephone calls and letters (from some very credible people), protesting my response.*

So we published the following replies:

Dear Marilyn:

Since you seem to enjoy coming straight to the point, I'll do the same. In the following question and answer, you blew it!

"Suppose you're on a game show, and you're given a choice of three doors. Behind one is a car; behind the others, goats. You pick door #1, and the host, who knows what's behind them, opens #3, which has a goat. He then asks if you want to pick #2. Is it to your advantage to switch?" You answered, "Yes, you should switch. The first door has a ⅓ chance of winning, but the second has a ⅔ chance."

Let me explain. If one door is shown to be a loser, that information changes the probability of either remaining choice, *neither of which has any reason to be more likely*, to ½. As a professional mathematician, I'm very concerned with the general public's lack of mathematical skills. Please help by confessing your error and in the future being more careful.

Robert Sachs, Ph.D.
George Mason University

You blew it, and you blew it big! Since you seem to have difficulty grasping the basic principle at work here, I'll explain. After the host reveals a goat, you now have a one-in-two chance of being correct. Whether you change your selection or not, the odds are the same. There is enough mathematical illiteracy in this country, and we don't need the holder of the world's highest I.Q. propagating more. Shame!

S.S., Ph.D.
University of Florida

Your answer to the question is in error. But if it is any consolation, many of my academic colleagues have also been stumped by this problem.

Barry Pasternack, Ph.D.
California Faculty Association

Dear Readers:

Good heavens! With so much learned opposition, I'll bet this one is going to keep math classes all over the country busy on Monday.

My original answer is correct. But first, let me explain why your answer is wrong. The winning odds of ⅓ on the first choice can't go up to ½ just because the host opens a losing door. To illustrate this, let's say we play a shell game. You look away, and I put a pea under one of three shells. Then I ask you to put your finger on a shell. The odds that your choice contains a pea are ⅓, agreed? Then I simply lift up an empty shell from the remaining other two. As I can (and will) do this regardless of what you've chosen, we've learned nothing to allow us to revise the odds on the shell under your finger.

The benefits of switching are readily proven by playing through the six games that exhaust all the possibilities. For the first three games, you choose #1 and "switch" each time, for the second three games, you choose #1 and "stay" each time, and the host always opens a loser. Here are the results.

	DOOR 1	**DOOR 2**	**DOOR 3**	
Game 1	AUTO	GOAT	GOAT	Switch and you lose.
Game 2	GOAT	AUTO	GOAT	Switch and you win.
Game 3	GOAT	GOAT	AUTO	Switch and you win.
	DOOR 1	**DOOR 2**	**DOOR 3**	
Game 4	AUTO	GOAT	GOAT	Stay and you win.
Game 5	GOAT	AUTO	GOAT	Stay and you lose.
Game 6	GOAT	GOAT	AUTO	Stay and you lose.

When you switch, you win ⅔ of the time and lose ⅓, but when you don't switch, you only win ⅓ of the time and lose ⅔. You can try it yourself and see.

Alternatively, you can actually play the game with another person acting as the host with three playing cards—two jokers for the goat and an ace for the prize. However, doing this a few hundred times to get statistically valid results can get a little tedious, so perhaps you can assign it as extra credit—or for punishment! (*That'll* get their goats!)

I wish we'd had room to include a little more detail, especially to emphasize the game rules I used for the reply, but space constraints prevented that. Still, I expected it to end the debate. Was I ever wrong.

The avalanche began the following day, and Sharon van Ivan, then my personal research assistant, watched in dismay as she found herself disappearing knee-deep into mail. Even my mother called. (But she thought my answer was right!) After reading hundreds of letters (of the thousands we received; a few of which are printed below), I decided to publish the following reply.

Dear Marilyn:
You're in error, but Albert Einstein earned a dearer place in the hearts of people after he admitted his errors.

Frank Rose, Ph.D.
University of Michigan

I have been a faithful reader of your column, and I have not, until now, had any reason to doubt you. However, in this matter (for which I do have expertise), your answer is clearly at odds with the truth.

James Rauff, Ph.D.
Millikin University

May I suggest that you obtain and refer to a standard textbook on probability before you try to answer a question of this type again?

Charles Reid, Ph.D.
University of Florida

I am sure you will receive many letters on this topic from high school and college students. Perhaps you should keep a few addresses for help with future columns.

W. Robert Smith, Ph.D.
Georgia State University

You are utterly incorrect about the game show question, and I hope this controversy will call some public attention to the serious national crisis in mathematical education. If you can admit your error, you will have contributed constructively towards the solution of a deplorable situation. How many irate mathematicians are needed to get you to change your mind?

E. Ray Bobo, Ph.D.
Georgetown University

I am in shock that after being corrected by at least three mathematicians, you still do not see your mistake.

Kent Ford
Dickinson State University

Maybe women look at math problems differently than men.

Don Edwards
Sunriver, Oregon

You are the goat!

Glenn Calkins, Ph.D.
Western State College

You made a mistake, but look at the positive side. If all those Ph.D.'s were wrong, the country would be in some very serious trouble.

Everett Harman, Ph.D.
U.S. Army Research Institute

Dear Readers:

Gasp! If this controversy continues, even the *postman* won't be able to fit into the mailroom. I'm receiving thousands of letters, nearly all insisting that I'm wrong, including the Deputy Director of the Center for Defense Information and a Research Mathematical Statistician from the National Institutes of Health! But math answers aren't determined by votes. For those readers new to all this, here's the original answer, to which the first readers responded.

"Suppose you're on a game show, and you're given the choice of three doors. Behind one is a car; behind the others, goats. You pick a door, say #1, and the host, who knows what's behind them, opens another, say #3, which has a goat. He then says to you, 'Do you want to pick #2?' Should you switch your choice?"

I answered, "Yes; you should switch. The first door has a ⅓ chance of winning, but the second door has a ⅔ chance. Here's a good way to visualize what happened. Suppose there are a *million* doors, and you pick door #1. Then the host, who knows what's behind the doors and will always avoid the one with the prize, opens them all except door #777,777. You'd switch to that door pretty fast, wouldn't you?"

So many readers wrote to say that they thought there was *no* advantage to switching that we published a second explanatory column, affirming the correctness of the original reply and using a shell game and a probability grid as illustrations.

But now we're receiving far *more* mail, and even newspaper columnists are joining in the fray! So let's look at it again, remembering that the original answer defines certain conditions, the most significant of which is that *the host always opens a losing door on purpose.* Anything else is a different question.

The original answer is still correct, and the key to it lies in the question, "*Should you switch?*" Suppose we pause at that point, and a UFO settles down onto the stage. A little green woman emerges, and the host asks her to point to one of the two unopened doors. The chances that *she'll* randomly choose the one with the prize are ½, all right. But that's because she lacks the advantage the *original* contestant had—the help of the host. (Try to forget any particular television show.)

When you first choose door #1 from three, there's a ⅓ chance that the prize is behind that one and a ⅔ chance that it's behind one of the others. *But then the host steps in and gives you a clue.* If the prize is behind #2, the host shows you #3, and if the prize is behind #3, the host shows you #2. So when you switch, you win if the prize is behind #2 OR #3. *YOU WIN EITHER WAY!* But if you *don't* switch, you win only if the prize is behind door #1.

And as this problem is of such intense interest, I'm willing to put my thinking to the test with a nationwide experiment. This is a call to math classes all across the country. Set up a probability trial exactly as outlined below and send me a chart of all the games along with a cover letter repeating just how you did it so we can make sure the methods are consistent.

One student plays the contestant, and another, the host. Label three paper cups #1, #2, and #3. While the contestant looks away, the host randomly hides a penny under a cup by throwing a die until a 1, 2, or 3 comes up. Next, the contestant randomly points to a cup by throwing a die the same way. Then the host purposely lifts up a losing cup from the two unchosen. Lastly, the contestant "stays" and lifts up his original cup to see if it covers the penny. Play "not switching" two hundred times and keep track of how often the contestant wins.

Then test the other strategy. Play the game the same way until the last instruction, at which point the contestant instead "switches" and lifts up the cup *not* chosen by anyone to see if it covers the penny. Play "switching" two hundred times, also.

And here's one last letter.

◆ ◆ ◆

Dear Marilyn:

You are indeed correct. My colleagues at work had a ball with this problem, and I dare say that most of them, including me at first, thought you were wrong!

Seth Kalson, Ph.D.
Massachusetts Institute of Technology

Dear Dr. Kalson:

Thanks, M.I.T. I needed that!

◆ ◆ ◆

Dear Marilyn:

In a recent column, you called on math classes around the country to perform an experiment that would confirm your response to a game show problem. ("Suppose you're on a game show, and you're given the choice of three doors. Behind one door is a car; behind the others, goats. You pick a door, say #1, and the host, who knows what's behind the doors, opens another door, say #3, which has a goat. He then says to you, 'Do you want to pick door #2?' Is it to your advantage to switch your choice?" You answered, "Yes; you should switch. The first door has a ⅓ chance of winning, but the second door has a ⅔ chance. Here's a good way to visualize what happened. Suppose there are a *million* doors, and you pick door #1. Then the host, who knows what's behind the doors and will always avoid the one with the prize, opens them all except door #777,777. You'd switch to that door pretty fast, wouldn't you?" My eighth grade classes tried it, and I don't really understand how to set up an equation for your theory, but it definitely does work! You'll have to help rewrite the chapters on probability.

Pat Gross, Ascension School
Chesterfield, Missouri

Dear Marilyn:

Our class, with unbridled enthusiasm, is proud to announce that our data support your position. Thank you so much for your faith in America's educators to solve this.

Jackie Charles, Henry Grady Elementary
Tampa, Florida

Dear Marilyn:

My class had a great time watching your theory come to life. I wish you could have been here to witness it. Their joy is what makes teaching worthwhile.

Pat Pascoli, Park View School
Wheeling, West Virginia

Dear Marilyn:

Seven groups worked on the probability problem. The numbers were impressive, and the students were astounded.

R. Burrichter, Webster Elementary School
St. Paul, Minnesota

Dear Marilyn:

The best part was seeing the looks on the students' faces as their numbers were tallied. The results were thrilling!

Patricia Robinson, Ridge High School
Basking Ridge, New Jersey

Dear Marilyn:

You could hear the kids gasp one at a time, "Oh my gosh. She was right!"

Jane Griffith, Magnolia School
Oakdale, California

Dear Marilyn:

I must admit I doubted you until my fifth grade math class proved you right. All I can say is, WOW!

John Witt, Westside Elementary
River Falls, Wisconsin

Dear Marilyn:

My classes enjoyed this exercise and look forward to the next project you give America's students. This is the stuff of real science.

Jerome Yeutter, Hebron Public Schools
Hebron, Nebraska

Dear Marilyn:

Thanks for that fun math problem. I really enjoyed it. It got me out of fractions for two days! Have any more?

Andrew Malinoski, Mabelle Avery School
Somers, Connecticut

Dear Marilyn:

I'm a fourth-grade student, and I used your column for a science fair project. My test results showed that you were right. My science fair project won a red ribbon.

Elizabeth Olson, Edgar Road Elementary
Webster Groves, Missouri

Dear Marilyn:

I did your experiment for the Regional Science and Engineering Fair at the University of Evansville, and I won both third place and a special award from the Army called the "Certificate of Excellence"!

Analda House, Evansville Day School
Evansville, Indiana

Dear Marilyn:

I did your experiment on probability as part of a Science Fair project, and after extensive interview with the judges, I was awarded first place.

Adrienne Shelton, Holy Spirit School
Annandale, Virginia

Dear Marilyn:

The teachers in my graduate-level mathematics classes, most of whom thought you were wrong, conducted your experiment as a class project. Each of the twenty-five teachers had students in their middle or high school classes play at least 400 games. In all, we had 14,800 samples of the experiment, and we're convinced that you were correct—the contestant should switch!

> Eloise Rudy, Furman University
> Greenville, South Carolina

Dear Marilyn:

You have taken over our Mathematics and Science Departments! We received a grant to establish a Multimedia Demonstration Project using state-of-the-art technology, and we set up a hypermedia laboratory network of computers, scanners, a CD-ROM player, laser disk players, monitors, and VCRs. Your problem was presented to 240 students, who were introduced to it by their science teachers. They then established the experimental design while the mathematics teachers covered the area of probability.

Most students and teachers initially disagreed with you, but during practice of the procedure, all began to see that the group that switched won more often. We intend to make this activity a permanent fixture in our curriculum.

> Anthony Tamalonis
> Arthur S. Somers Intermediate School 252
> Brooklyn, New York

Dear Marilyn:

I also thought you were wrong, so I did your experiment, and you were exactly correct. (I used three cups to represent the three doors, but instead of a penny, I chose an aspirin tablet because I thought I might need to take it after my experiment.)

> William Hunt, M.D.
> West Palm Beach, Florida

Dear Marilyn:

I put my solution of the problem on the bulletin board in the physics department office at the Naval Academy, following it with a declaration that you were right. All morning I took a lot of criticism and abuse from my colleagues, but by late in the afternoon most of them came around. I even won a free dinner from one overconfident professor.

Eugene Mosca, Ph.D., U.S. Naval Academy
Annapolis, Maryland

Dear Marilyn:

After considerable discussion and vacillation here at the Los Alamos National Laboratory, two of my colleagues independently programmed the problem, and in 1,000,000 trials, switching paid off 66.7 percent of the time. The total running time on the computer was less than one second.

G.P. DeVault, Ph.D.
Los Alamos National Laboratory
Los Alamos, New Mexico

Dear Marilyn:

Now 'fess up. Did you really figure all this out, or did you get help from a mathematician?

Lawrence Bryan
San Jose, California

Dear Readers:

Wow! What a response we received! It's still coming in, but so many of you are so anxious to hear the results that we'll stop tallying for a moment and take stock of the situation so far. We've received thousands of letters, and of the people who performed the experiment by hand as described, the results are close to unanimous: you win twice as often when you change doors. Nearly 100% of those readers now believe it pays to switch. (One is an eighth-grade math teacher who, despite data clearly supporting the position, simply refuses to believe it!)

But many people tried performing similar experiments on computers, fearlessly programming them in hundreds of different ways. Not surprisingly, they fared a little less well. Even so, about 97% of them now believe it pays to switch.

And plenty of people who *didn't* perform the experiment wrote, too. Of the general public, about 56% now believe you should switch compared with only 8% before. And from academic institutions, about 71% now believe you should switch compared with only 35% before. (Many of them wrote to express utter amazement at the whole state of affairs, commenting that it altered their thinking dramatically, especially about the state of mathematical education in this country.) And a very small percentage of readers feel convinced that the furor is resulting from people not realizing that the host is opening a losing door on purpose. (But they haven't read my mail! The great majority of people understand the conditions perfectly.)

And so we've made progress! Half of the readers whose letters were published in the previous columns have written to say they've changed their minds, and only this next one of them wrote to state that his position hadn't changed at all.

Dear Marilyn:
I still think you're wrong. There is such a thing as female logic.
                              Don Edwards
                              Sunriver, Oregon

Dear Don:
Oh hush, now.

◆ ◆ ◆

Dear Marilyn:
A shopkeeper says she has two new baby beagles to show you, but she doesn't know whether they're male, female, or a pair. You tell her that you want only a male, and she telephones the fellow who's giving them a bath. "Is at least one a male?" she asks him. "Yes!" she informs you with a smile. What is the probability that the *other* one is a male?
                              Stephen I. Geller
                              Pasadena, California

Dear Stephen:
One out of three. If we could shake a pair of puppies out of a cup the way we do dice, there are four ways they could land: male/female or female/male or male/male or female/female. So there are three equally probable ways in which at least one of them could be a male: male/female or female/male or male/male. And the partner of a male in those three combinations is a female, a female, or another male. Therefore, the chances of that partner being a male are only one out of three.

I suppose I shouldn't have been surprised when the mail began to arrive. We published the following shortly afterward.

Dear Marilyn:

This is regarding the problem where a shopkeeper has two new baby beagles, but she doesn't know yet whether they're male, female, or a pair. You want only a male, so she telephones the fellow who's giving them a bath. "Is at least one a male?" she asks him. "Yes!" she informs you. What is the probability that the *other* one is a male?

You answered, "One out of three." There are only three possible explanations for this. 1) You are considering the possibility that the second puppy has been neutered, but because you did not make this clear, you leave open the next explanation. 2) You are (still) confused about the difference between game theory and probability. If so, I suggest you brush up on this information. 3) Your incorrect responses are intentional, done as a means to solicit mail. If so, there has to be a better way.

James Larsen, Ph.D.
Wright State University

I disagree with your answer. The observer knows the first dog is a male; the probability that the other is a male is 50-50.

Richard Jones, Ph.D.
University of New Haven

I believe you're wrong! Before you know that one of the baby beagles is male, the chances are one out of three. But once the above fact is known, the chances change to 50-50.

Edward Weiss, Ph.D
Bethel College

Okay. But here's what puzzling to me. If there were only one beagle pup, the probability of it being male would be one out of two. What can explain why the presence of another beagle pup should affect the probability that the pup in question is a male? I know this is cute, but how far away does the second beagle have to be in order for it not to affect the sex of the first beagle?

Steve Marx
Worcester, Massachusetts

Dear Readers:

The original answer is correct. We didn't define a "first beagle" or a "second beagle," and so either beagle can be in a doghouse on the moon, and it would still affect the outcome.

If we could shake a pair of puppies out of a cup the way we do dice, there are four ways they could land: male/female or female/male or male/

male or female/female. So there are three ways in which at least one of them could be a male. And as the partner of a male in those three is a female, a female, or another male, the chances of that partner being a male are only one out of three.

The key is that we didn't specify *which* beagle was a male, so it can be either one. If we'd said instead, "The one nibbling your ankle is a male; what are the chances that the one sleeping is a male?" the chances would be 50-50. But we just specified that "at least one" was a male, so we don't know which it is and whether its partner is awake or asleep. And this means that the chances of that partner being a male are only one out of three.

But letters continued to stream in, so I'll try to put an end to the subject with the following.

Dear Marilyn:

This is regarding the problem where a shopkeeper has two new baby beagles but doesn't yet know their sex. Because you want a male, she phones the fellow who's bathing them. "Is at least one a male?" she asks him. "Yes!" she informs you. What is the probability that the other one is a male? You answered, "One out of three." In a second column on the subject, you stated that your answer was correct and said that "the key is that we didn't specify *which* beagle was a male, so it can be either one."

You are confused about probability. It makes no difference whether you specify which of the two puppies you are talking about; what is crucial is that you are talking about only these two and no others. Exactly the same sort of problems arise in genetic counseling, where the consequences of flawed understanding are very serious.

Steven M. Carr, Ph.D.
Memorial University of Newfoundland

From a geneticist, you unnecessarily attempted to determine probabilities for an individual based on the probabilities of pairwise combinations of two individuals. More parsimonious explanations came from your other readers: the 50% probability of the sex of one pup does not influence that of the other.

H. Glenn Hall, Ph.D.
University of Florida

I'm afraid that you are totally, irrevocably, and unequivocally incorrect in your answer.

> Stephen D. Wolpe, Ph.D.
> Genetics Institute

The fact is that knowing the sex of either puppy leaves only two possible combinations out of the original four possible combinations. To add a modicum of believability to my analysis, I am an analyst for a supercomputing company.

> Bruce Greer
> Hillsboro, Oregon

You are clearly right. I think the reason so many people have disputed your answer is because they are not math teachers. I've been teaching math all my life, and I really get a kick out of your problems.

> Thomas E. Hurst
> Chicopee High School

Dear Readers:

The original answer is correct. We're receiving quite a bit of mail, and most of the critics say a version of the following: "If there's only one puppy left, it's either a male or a female, and therefore the chances are fifty-fifty that it's a male." But that's as flawed as saying that tomorrow morning, the sun is either going to rise or it isn't, and therefore the chances are only fifty-fifty that the sun is going to rise tomorrow.

Here's another way to look at it. The fellow who's bathing the puppies acknowledges, through the shopkeeper, that at least one is a male. That means he's talking about a pair of puppies, not just one. And asking about the probability that the other one is a male is a question about that pair, not a specific dog. In other words, it's the same as asking whether *both* are male.

Here's one last letter, and I think we should all be very thankful that this man got it right!

Dear Marilyn:

You are correct again, and it is all those cocky fellows with an attitude who need a refresher course in math.

> Jonathan P. Dowling, Ph.D.
> Department of the Army
> United States Army Missile Command
> Redstone Arsenal, Alabama

◆ ◆ ◆

Dear Marilyn:

In how many ways is it possible to seat six people at a round table where two are brothers, with the restriction that the two brothers must not sit in adjacent seats?

Keith Byers
Orangeburg, South Carolina

Dear Keith:

Considering different combinations as the only criterion, there appear to be 72 ways, and here's the explanation. If we look at the table as the face of a clock, let's start with one brother seated at 12. The other brother can therefore only be seated at 4, 6, or 8. When he's seated at 4, there are 24 different ways the others can be seated around them, and the same goes for when he's seated at 6 or 8, making a total of 72 seating arrangements.

However, if we want to consider different views from the table as well, we must multiply the result by 6. This means that there are 72 arrangements with the first brother at 12, but 72 more arrangements with him at 2, 72 more at 4, and so forth, a total of as many as 432 ways to seat everyone, depending on whether you tie the first brother to any particular chair. (And if it's a family reunion, maybe you'd better tie them *both*.)

After this appeared, one person wrote and asked me, in all seriousness, to set up the season schedule for his golf foursome!

◆ ◆ ◆

Dear Marilyn:

How many different combinations can you get out of seven numbers? Also, how many more would it be for eight numbers?

Alfred Chacon
San Antonio, Texas

Dear Alfred:

If a hostess wants to seat seven people around a dinner table, there are 5,040 ways in which she can arrange them. And if she joins them herself, there are 40,320 arrangements. (See why we should take Mom out to dinner after planning the seating arrangements for the wedding reception?)

◆ ◆ ◆

Dear Marilyn:

I'm curious to know how many telephone numbers one can get out of the digits 1 through 10, not including long distance numbers. Please tell me how you solved the problem, also.

Denise Kolb
Denver, Colorado

Dear Denise:

About nine million, and here's the explanation.

Let's first assume that you mean the digits 0 through 9 because there is no "10" on the telephone dial. There are 10 different digits, then, that can take the first place in the row of seven places (the number of places in the standard telephone number). Each of these 10 can occur with any one of 10 different digits that can take the second place in the row. Therefore, there are 10×10 ways of filling the two places. And each of these 10×10 can occur with any one of 10 different digits that can take the third place in the row, and so forth. This means that there are $10 \times 10 \times 10 \times 10 \times 10 \times 10 \times 10$, or ten million, ways of filling all seven places.

However, telephone numbers never begin with "0," so let's adjust the mathematics accordingly, putting a "9" in the first place. This means there are $9 \times 10 \times 10 \times 10 \times 10 \times 10 \times 10$, or only nine million, ways of filling all seven places. Of course, there are other restrictions on phone numbers—for example, we never see the number 100-0000—but that's the way it works.

◆ ◆ ◆

Dear Marilyn:

Since there are only twenty-six letters in the English alphabet, are the number of words that can be made limited or limitless?

Orlo E. Hicks
San Diego, California

Dear Orlo:

It's limitless in theory, if not in practice, although with time, we'd be putting up with more words like the twenty-nine–letter *floccipaucini-hilipilification*, the longest "real" word in the Oxford English Dictionary. (It means "the action of estimating as worthless.") Doctors, however, already tolerate more sesquipedalian words than the average person, the worst I've read being a lung disease, the forty-seven-letter plural of which would be called *pneumonoultramicroscopicsilicovolcanoconiosises*.

I've since discovered an error in the above, however, and I want to correct it right now to make sure that none of you will be walking around saying "floccipaucinihilipilification" when you mean "flocciNaucinihilipilification." (I feel much better now.)

27.

Math and Logic Puzzles

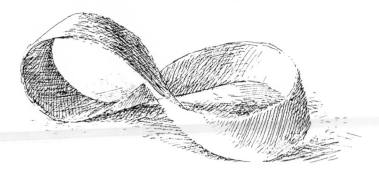

Dear Marilyn:

In the late 1940s, an obituary in the *Philadelphia Evening Bulletin* described the author of the following problem as a professor who had attained international acclaim with the following problem. Some people said it couldn't be done. Here's the problem: Mary is 24 years old. Mary is twice as old as Anne was when Mary was as old as Anne is now. How old is Anne?

Ida Bernkof
Lakeland, Florida

Dear Ida:

Anne is 18. If Mary is 24, and Anne is 18, Mary is 6 years older than Anne. Therefore, when Mary was 18, Anne would have been 12. And that's half of what Mary is now.

◆ ◆ ◆

Times change. Here's a modern problem:

Dear Marilyn:

Please solve this one for me.

A rope over the top of a fence has the same length on each side, and weighs one-third of a pound per foot. On one end hangs a monkey holding a banana, and on the other end a weight equal to the weight of the monkey. The banana weighs two ounces per inch. The length of the rope in feet is the same as the age of the monkey, and the weight of the monkey in ounces is as much as the age of the monkey's mother. The combined ages of the monkey and its mother are thirty years. One-half the weight of the monkey, plus the weight of the banana is one-fourth the sum of the weights of the rope and the weight. The monkey's mother is one-half as old as the monkey will be when it is three times as old as its mother was when she was one-half as old as the monkey will be when it is as old as its mother will be when she is four times as old as the monkey was when it was twice as old as its mother was when she was one-third as old as the monkey was when it was as old as its mother was when she was three times as old as the monkey was when it was one-fourth as old as it is now. How long is the banana?

Eli Esser
Hugo, Colorado

Dear Eli:

Good grief. You aren't the sort of fellow who pulls the wings off flies, are you? Anyway, here are the answers:

1) The monkey's mother is eighteen years old.
2) The monkey is twelve years old and weighs eighteen ounces.
3) The rope weighs four pounds and is twelve feet long.
4) And that means that the banana is 5 ¾ inches long.

And here are *my* questions for *you*:

1) How long can a rope have a monkey and a banana hanging on one end, but only a monkey-size weight on the other?
2) How long can an eighteen-ounce monkey hold an eleven-and-a-half-ounce banana?

And here are my answers:

1) Not long, and
2) Until a bigger monkey comes along.

◆ ◆ ◆

Dear Marilyn:

Three thieves stole a bunch of coconuts and agreed to divide them up evenly the following morning, then retired for the night. After an hour passed, the first thief decided to take his third, and after dividing the nuts evenly, had one left over, which he gave to a monkey. After another hour passed, the second thief did the same thing with the remaining nuts, as did the third thief an hour later. In the morning, the three thieves divided the remaining nuts evenly and had one left over, which they gave to the monkey. What was the least number of coconuts they could have started with and not have to deal with coconut parts?

R. L. Ziers
Bloomfield, New Jersey

Dear R. L.:

If they started with 79 coconuts, the first thief took 26 of those, gave 1 to a monkey, and left 52 for the others. The second thief took 17 of those, gave 1 to the monkey, and left 34 for the others. The third thief took 11 of those, gave 1 to the monkey, and left 22 for the others. Finally, they each took 7 of those and gave 1 to the monkey.

The monkey sounds smarter than they do, however, because this leaves the first thief with 33 coconuts, the second thief with only 24 coconuts, and the third thief with only 18 coconuts, while the monkey gets 4 coconuts just for hanging around.

◆ ◆ ◆

Dear Marilyn:

There were three hungry rabbits. The first hopped into a vegetable garden and found a bunch of carrots that someone had just picked. He ate half of them plus half a carrot and left. The second hopped into the garden and found what the first one had just left. He ate half of them plus half a carrot and left, too. The third then hopped into the garden and found what the second one had left. He ate half of them plus half a carrot and left the last remaining carrot for the owner of the garden. How many carrots were there in the beginning?

William W. Hurley
Princeton, West Virginia

Dear William:

There were 15 carrots. The first rabbit ate 7½ of them, then another ½, for a total of 8, leaving 7 for the second rabbit. The second rabbit ate 3½ of them, then another ½, for a total of 4, leaving 3 for the third rabbit. The third rabbit ate 1½ of them, then another ½, for a total of 2, leaving 1 for the owner of the garden.

◆ ◆ ◆

Dear Marilyn:

A man pays $1 to get into a casino, where he loses half of his money. Then he has to pay $1 to leave. He goes to a second casino, pays another $1 to get in, loses half of his money again, and then pays another $1 to leave. Then he goes to a third casino, pays another $1 to get in, loses half of his money again, then decides to leave and pays another $1 to get out. He's now broke. How much money did he have to begin with?

H. Randall Todd
Riverside, California

Dear Randall:

He started with $21, paid $1 to the first place, taking him down to $20. He lost half of that, taking him down to $10. Then he paid $1 to leave, taking him down to $9. Then he paid $1 to the second place, leaving him with $8, lost half of that, leaving him with $4, and paid $1 to leave, leaving him with $3. Then he paid $1 to the third place, taking him down to $2, lost half of that, taking him down to $1, and paid that final $1 to get out.

You know, I think this guy *deserves* to be broke.

◆ ◆ ◆

Dear Marilyn:

A man had a two-dollar bill and wanted to buy a train ticket that cost $3. He took the two-dollar bill to a pawnshop where he pawned it for $1.50. On the way to the railway station, he met a friend to whom he sold the pawn ticket for $1.50. He then had $3 with which to buy his ticket. Who was out the extra dollar?

Michael Tompkins
Brooklyn, New York

Dear Michael:

The friend. First the poor fellow paid $1.50 just to get the pawn ticket. Then he had to come up with *another* $1.50 to pay back the pawnbroker. After retrieving the two-dollar bill, he'd be left with a loss of $1. But the first fellow might be left with the loss of a friend!

◆ ◆ ◆

Dear Marilyn:

The following problem has been with me since childhood, so far without answer: three people went to a hotel and rented a room for $30, each paying $10 for his share. Later, the clerk discovered that the price of the room was only $25. He handed the bellman five $1 bills and asked him to return them to the three people. The bellman, not knowing how to divide five dollars among three people, instead gave each person one dollar and the rest to charity. Here's the question: the three people originally paid $10 each, but each received $1 back, so they've now paid a total of $27 for the room. Add to that the $2 that the bellman gave away, and you have a total expenditure of $29 instead of $30. What happened to the other dollar?

Robert T. Mann
Austin, Texas

Dear Robert:

There is no missing dollar. The total expenditure is now only $27, accounted for by adding the $25 in the hands of the hotel clerk to the $2 in the hands of charity. In other words, the original $30 now is divided like this: the hotel clerk has $25, the guests have $3, and charity has $2.

The error arose when an asset ($2) was added to an expense ($27) instead of the other asset ($25), thereby mixing "apples and oranges" and giving us fruit salad instead of the correct answer.

◆ ◆ ◆

Dear Marilyn:

Once there was a young fellow with a dollar. He paid 50 cents for a drum, 45 cents for two drumsticks, and 5 cents for a glass of beer. Why did the conductor kick him off the streetcar?

Debbie Jones
Brownsville, Pennsylvania

Dear Debbie:

He didn't have any money left for the fare! (Debbie! How old *is* this? 5 cents for a glass of beer?!)

◆ ◆ ◆

Dear Marilyn:

I thought you might like to ask your readers how to use mathematics to find someone's age without asking directly.

Marguerite Hanna
Jacksonville, Florida

Dear Marguerite:

What a nice little trick! First you ask the person to write down his or her age and then do the following:

Multiply it by 2,
Add 5 to the result,
Then multiply that by 50,

Next, subtract 365,
Then add any change under a dollar in his or her pocket,
And finally, add 115.

The first two digits in the answer is the person's age (or three digits if he or she is 100 or more), and the last two digits is the amount of change!

◆ ◆ ◆

Dear Marilyn:

If I put a penny in a shoebox, add another to double it the next day, and every day continue to double the amount in the shoebox, how long would it take me to have a million dollars?

Donald F. Kochler
Newark, New Jersey

Dear Donald:

Only about a month! (And you'd need about 12,000 shoeboxes, depending on the size of your feet.)

◆ ◆ ◆

Dear Marilyn:

You have fifteen piles of coins, each pile containing twenty coins. The coins appear to be identical in every respect; however, they are not. Fourteen of the piles contain coins that weigh 2 grams each, but one pile is counterfeit, and those coins weight 2.1 grams each. You have at your disposal a single pan scale, such as is used to weigh produce, and your problem is to determine which of the piles contains the counterfeit coins, using the scale once and only once. You may not add or take away coins once they have been placed on the scale.

P. Woods
Newburgh, New York

Dear P.:

You take one coin from the first pile, two coins from the second pile, three coins from the third pile, and so on, taking fifteen coins from the fifteenth pile and placing them on the scale. If all 120 coins now on the scale weighed 2 grams each, the pile would weigh 240 grams. However, it will instead weigh anywhere from 240.1 grams to 241.5 grams, depending on how many counterfeit coins are on it.

If it only weighs 240.1 grams, there's only one counterfeit coin on the scale, so the counterfeit pile is the first one, from which you took one coin. If it instead weighs 240.2 grams, there are two counterfeit coins on the scale, so the counterfeit pile is the second one, from which you took two coins, and so forth.

◆ ◆ ◆

Dear Marilyn:

A farmer had seventeen horses that he wanted to divide among three people. How did he do this if he wished to give one friend one-half of the horses, one friend one-third of the horses, and one friend one-ninth of the horses?

The answer is that he borrowed one horse from a neighbor, giving him a total of eighteen horses to work with. The first friend got one-half, or nine horses; the second friend got one-third, or six horses; the third friend got one-ninth, or two horses. He then returned the remaining horse to his neighbor.

Marguerite Hanna
Jacksonville, Florida

Dear Marguerite:

What a shame that this has been around for a long time. It's all wrong! The question is flawed because you can't give away all of *any* number by giving away one-half, one-third, and one-ninth of it. Those fractions only add up to seventeen-eighteenths of the whole.

And the answer is just as bad. Bringing in extras for the calculation gives the friends more than the farmer originally wanted them to receive. Of the seventeen horses, the first friend (for a one-half share) should have gotten eight and a half horses. The second friend (for a one-third share) should have gotten five and two-thirds horses. And the third friend (for a one-ninth share) should have gotten one and eight-ninths horses. And the farmer would have had seventeen-eighteenths of a horse left over. However, the answer to the riddle gives the friends more than that, leaving the farmer nothing at all. Even so, I think everybody would be happier your way—especially the horses.

◆ ◆ ◆

Dear Marilyn:

If a dozen and a half times a dozen costs a dozen, how much does a half dozen cost?

Newell Peterson
Beldenville, Wisconsin

Dear Newell:

A third.

Sara Brzowsky wouldn't let me get away with publishing the previous answer as cryptic as it originally stood, so we added the following line of explanation: If 18 items (a dozen and a half) × 12 (a dozen)—216 items in all—cost $12 (a dozen), then 6 items (a half dozen) cost $ .33 ⅓ (a third).

◆ ◆ ◆

Dear Marilyn:

Some time ago, a very large section of an iceberg near New Zealand broke off. It was twenty-six miles long, four miles wide, and one mile deep. Could you tell me how many one-inch ice cubes it would make?

Max Travis
Nyack, New York

Dear Max:

The figure is really stunning. A chunk of ice this size could be cut into 26,453,238,349,824,000 cubes. And if you were to put six cubes in a glass, it would fill 4,408,873,058,304,000 glasses, enough for nearly 900,000 glasses of lemonade for every person on earth!

◆ ◆ ◆

Dear Marilyn:

I received this question from my math teacher, and we and other students have tried to figure it out, but none of us can. Can you please help us? An engineer working on the Alaskan pipeline was heard to say, "At the time I said I could finish this section in a week, I expected to get two more bulldozers for the job. If they had left me what machines I had, I'd have been only a day behind schedule. As it is, they have taken away all my machines but one, and I'll be weeks behind schedule." How many weeks was he behind schedule?

Tammy Grimm
Sacramento, California

Dear Tammy:

If his previous number of bulldozers would have finished the job in 8 days, and 2 more would have allowed him to finish in 7, he started with 14. (14 bulldozers working for 8 days would do 112 blocks of work, and 16 working for 7 would do 112 blocks of work.) Therefore, when he was left with only 1 bulldozer to do it all, it would take 112 days. Subtracting the week he still had left on his schedule, this would put him 15 weeks behind.

◆ ◆ ◆

Dear Marilyn:

If painter #1 can paint a house in 15 workdays, and painter #2 can paint the same house in 7½ workdays, how many workdays would it take them to paint the same house working together?

Jack R. Malone
Peoria, Illinois

Dear Jack:

It would take them a total of 5 days. In that amount of time, painter #1 who can paint the whole house in 15 days, would have finished one-third of the house, and painter #2, who can paint the whole house in 7½ days, would have finished the other two-thirds of the house.

◆ ◆ ◆

Dear Marilyn:

One man sells neckties at the price of 2 for $10; another sells them at 3 for $10. They decide to go into business together, and each contributes 30 ties, giving them an inventory of 60 ties, which they will sell at the price of 5 for $20 because that's the same as 2 ties for $10 and 3 ties for $10. After all 60 ties are sold, they find they've earned a total of $240, the price of 5 ties for $20 sold to 12 customers.

Then they went home to their wives, who told them how dumb they were. If the first man had sold his 30 ties separately (at 2 for $10), he would have earned $150, and if the second man had done the same (at 3 for $10), he would have earned $100, a total of $250 instead of $240. Where did the other $10 go?

Anonymous
New York, New York

Dear Reader:

It was divided among the customers. Two ties for $10 and 3 ties for $10 did add up to 5 ties for $20 for a while, but only until the 30 ties contributed by the "3 for $10" man were exhausted, sooner than were the 30 ties contributed by the "2 for $10 man." They then had to dip into the supply contributed by the "2 for $10 man," actually selling some of them as 3 for $10, cheaper than if the "2 for $10 man" had sold them on his own.

◆ ◆ ◆

Dear Marilyn:

Two batters go 31 for 69 during the first month of the season, which means that both have a .449 batting average. In the following week, batter A slumps to 1 for 27. Batter B does somewhat better, hitting 4 for 36 (the same as 1 for 9). However, both batters at that point have the same average! Batter A's 32 for 96 and batter B's 35 for 105 both equal a .333 batting average. How come?

Alvin M. Hattal
Potomac, Maryland

Dear Alvin:

Here's one way to look at it:

Batter A originally has	31 hits out of 69 "at bats."
He now adds these:	1 hit out of 27
For a total of this:	32 hits out of 96 (.333 average)
Batter B originally has	31 hits out of 69 "at bats," too.
HE NOW ADDS THESE:	1 HIT OUT OF 27
Matching A's totals:	32 hits out of 96 (.333 average)
AND THESE:	3 HITS OUT OF 9 (.333 average)
For a total of this:	35 hits out of 105 (still .333)

In other words, regardless of the order in which he actually accomplished it, batter B added a series of "at bats" to equal batter A's final .333 average *and* he added a series of "at bats" equivalent in themselves to another .333, maintaining his new average of .333.

Or, to put it another way, each batter lowered his average, from .449 to .333, but batter A, who recently did worse, lowered it faster (in only 96 "at bats") than batter B (who took 105 "at bats" to do it).

But hey, who's complaining? The Mets would love either one of these guys.

◆ ◆ ◆

Dear Marilyn:

Here's another puzzle for you. I lost the answer years ago, and I go nuts trying to figure it out. Smith and Jones started off together to walk to a nearby town. Smith covered the first half-mile at one mile per hour faster than Jones. He covered the second half-mile at one mile per hour slower than Jones. Jones walked to town at a constant speed all the way. Did they arrive at the same time? And if they didn't, which one got there first?

James LaBella
East Hartford, Connecticut

Dear James:

No matter what his speed is, Jones will always arrive first. This is the reason. When Smith walks one half of the distance one mile slower than Jones, he loses more than he gains when he walks the other half of the distance one mile faster than Jones.

For example, let's say that Smith's "fast" speed is 3 miles per hour, Jones's constant speed is 2 miles per hour, and Smith's "slow" speed is 1 mile per hour. Smith will cover the first half-mile in 10 minutes and the second half-mile in 30 minutes, a total of 40 minutes. However, Jones will cover the whole distance in only 30 minutes. This is because when Smith is traveling fast for half a mile, Jones is traveling ⅔ as fast as he is, but when Smith is traveling slow for half a mile, *he's* only traveling ½ as fast as *Jones* is.

◆ ◆ ◆

Dear Marilyn:

I am driving along the highway at sixty miles per hour when I meet a freight train approaching on a parallel railway. I estimate its speed at sixty miles per hour, also. As I draw even with the locomotive, I check my odometer and wristwatch. When I am even with the back of the caboose, one mile and sixty seconds have gone by. How long is the train?

William G. Brenneman
Denver, Colorado

Dear William:

Two miles long, if you're a better estimator than I am. (I'd have trouble correctly guessing the speed of an object moving toward me, especially if I were moving toward it, also.) But why did you consult your odometer *and* your wristwatch? If you knew you were traveling at sixty miles per hour, either one alone would have been enough.

◆ ◆ ◆

Dear Marilyn:

I have asked the following "mental gymnastic" question many times, but after I give the answer, people still don't believe me. There is a race track one mile around. If you drive around the track the first time at thirty miles per hour, how fast will you have to go around the second time to average sixty miles per hour for both times around?

Kenneth E. Wittman
Fremont, California

Dear Kenneth:

It's impossible to accomplish. To average sixty miles per hour, you'd have to drive around the track twice in two minutes, but you already used up those two minutes when you drove around the track once at thirty miles per hour.

◆ ◆ ◆

Dear Marilyn:

Shame on you! You erred in your answer to the racetrack question: "There's a race track one mile around. If you drive around the track the first time at 30 mph, how fast will you have to go around the second time to average 60 mph for both times around?" You answered, "It's impossible to accomplish. To average 60 mph, you'd have to drive around the track twice in two minutes, but you already used up those two minutes when you drove around the track once at 30 mph."

I don't know what the new math teaches, but the old math taught me that the average of 30 and 90 equals 60.

I. F. Holton
Augusta, Georgia

It should be 90 mph. Race car drivers do this sort of thing quite often. They run two or more laps to qualify. Each lap is timed. Then they are added together and divided by the number of laps.

Gerald Foye
Lemon Grove, California

What does *two minutes* have to do with anything?

John A. Tyburski
Springfield, Virginia

I'll bet you're catching lots of flak over this. Please print a correction. Who knows how many bar bets you've started?

Gil L. Dickau
Floral City, Florida

Dear Readers:

Uh, oh. Here comes the mailman again. The original answer is correct because the length of the track was specified as the determining variable, not the length of time traveled. Envision the track straightened out, and lay the two laps end to end—it's two miles long now, right? If you travel at 30 mph for the first mile, two minutes will have elapsed by the time you reach the halfway point. If you then travel at 90 mph for the second mile, an additional two-thirds of a minute will have elapsed by the time you reach the end, a total of two and two-thirds minutes in all.

And when you travel two miles in two and two-thirds minutes, your average speed is 45 mph, not the 60 mph we were trying to achieve! (And I'm *sure* none of my readers would ever *dream* of taking a bet in a bar, Gil.)

◆ ◆ ◆

Dear Marilyn:

A troop of soldiers half a mile long is marching along at a rate of five miles per hour. A private from the front of the column runs to the rear with a message at the rate of ten miles per hour and returns to the front at the same rate of speed. How long does it take him to complete the trip?

> Chuck Hayworth
> Monte Rio, California

Dear Chuck:

About eight minutes, not counting things like turn-around time, etc. Let's say that the front of the line is at the half-mile mark when the back of the line begins to step away from the armory. If the private runs toward the back of the line for *two* minutes, he'll travel one-third of a mile, ending up at the one-sixth–mile mark just when the *back* of the line does. Then if he turns around and runs toward the front of the line for *six* minutes, he'll travel a mile, ending up at the one and one-sixth–mile mark just when the *front* of the line does. And both trips added together equal eight minutes.

◆ ◆ ◆

Dear Marilyn:

There are 1,000 tenants and 1,000 apartments. The first tenant opens all the doors. The second tenant closes every other door. The third tenant goes to every third door, opening it if it is closed and closing it if it is open. The fourth tenant goes to every fourth door, closing it if it is open and opening it if it is closed. This continues with each tenant until the 1,000th tenant closes the 1,000th door.

How many doors are open?

> Anita Mueller
> Arnold, Maryland

Dear Anita:

There are 31 doors left open, and here are their numbers: #001 #004 #009 #016 #025 #036 #049 #064 #081 #100 #121 #144 #169

#196 #225 #256 #289 #324 #361 #400 #441 #484 #529 #576
#625 #676 #729 #784 #841 #900 #961

Do the first ten numbers look familiar? Yes, these numbers and all
the rest of them are actually the numbers 1 through 31 multiplied by
themselves, most commonly known as the "squares" of those numbers.

A square-numbered door can always be divided by an odd number of
divisors (including 1). This means that if the first tenant opens it, the
last tenant to touch it will also open it. On the other hand, a non–square-numbered door can always be divided by an even number of divisors
(including 1). This means that if the first tenant opens it, the last
tenant to touch it will close it.

In short, all square-numbered doors will be left open at the end,
while all non–square-numbered doors will be left closed. Here are a
couple of examples:

#121 (square)

is opened   by tenant #001,
untouched by tenants #002 through #010,
closed   by tenant #011,
untouched by tenants #012 through #120,
opened   by tenant #121, and
untouched by tenants #122 through #1000.

#122 (non-square)

is opened   by tenant #001,
closed   by tenant #002,
untouched   by tenants #003 through #060,
opened   by tenant #061,
closed   by tenant #122, and
untouched by tenants #123 through #1000.

You can try this yourself with a few numbers. Just choose one from
1 to 1,000 and see how many divisors it has.

◆ ◆ ◆

Dear Marilyn:

Years ago, a young man told a math instructor that he had just
completed a pre-employment test, and he said one of the questions was
to state the value of the following:

SEND + MORE = MONEY

Ever since overhearing this, I have wondered about its solution. Do
you have an answer?

Virginia Huddleston
San Diego, California

Dear Virginia:

In   S   E   N   D
   + M O R E

M O N E Y, let's start by saying S and M cannot be 0, and all the letters must stand for different numerals.

M must be 1 because even if the numbers were 9999 and 9999, and we know they can't be that high, the sum would still only be 19998, so M can't be more than 1.

That makes it   S   E   N   D
     + 1   O   R   E
     1   O   N   E   Y

O must be 0 because even if the numbers were 9999 and 1999, the sum would still only be 11998, so because M is already 1, O must be less than that.

That makes it   S   E   N   D
     + 1   0   R   E
     1   0   N   E   Y

S must be 9 because even if the numbers were 8999 and 1099, the sum would still only be 10098, so because O is already 0, S must be more than 8.

That makes it   9   E   N   D
     + 1   0   R   E
     1   0   N   E   Y

As E cannot be the same as N, there must have been a number carried to that column, which could only be 1. Therefore, E plus 1 is N. And if E is 1 less than N, the only numeral R could be without there having been 1 carried to *that* column would be 9, so because S is already 9, there must have been 1 carried, all right, making R become 8. This way, the carried 1 plus N plus 8 equal E with 1 more to carry to the next column.

That makes it   9   E   N   D
     + 1   0   8   E
     1   0   N   E   Y

And now we're in the home stretch. Following the above, N can't be more than 7, so E can't be more than 6, not to mention less than 2, of course.

Well, E can't be 2 because D would have to be 4, 5, 6, or 7, none of which would bring that column over the 10 required to cause carrying. And E can't be 3 because D would have to be 2, 5, 6, or 7, only the last of which would bring that column over the 10 required to cause carrying, but Y can't be 0 because O already is. And E can't be 4 because D would have to be 2, 3, 6, or 7, only the last two of which would cause carrying, but Y can't be either 0 or 1 because O and M already are. And E can't be 6 because D would have to be 2, 3, 4, or 5, only the last two of which would cause carrying, but Y can't be either 0 or 1, as we now know.

So our last hope for E is 5, which means D would have to be 2, 3, 4, or 7, only the last of which does indeed cause the necessary carrying, making Y equal to 2, and N equal to 6.

That makes it
```
    9 5 6 7
+   1 0 8 5
  ---------
  1 0 6 5 2 !
```
I hope you're not sorry you asked.

◆ ◆ ◆

Dear Marilyn:

You have two identical tumblers before you, one filled within an inch of its top with liquid A, the other filled with an identical volume of liquid B. You take a level tablespoon of A and put it into B, stirring to a perfect mixture. Then you take a level tablespoon of the mixture and put it back into the tumbler containing the A liquid. Is the final result that there is now more A in the B tumbler, or is there more B in the A tumbler?

J. L.
Waldwick, New Jersey

Dear Reader:

They're the same!

But the number of people who wrote to express confusion prompted me to write the following.

Dear Marilyn:

You got one wrong, and I'll bet I'm not the only one to catch you on it. It was the question about the two identical tumblers where you take a tablespoon of one liquid and put it into the other, then take a tablespoon of the mixture and put it back into the first one. Is there now more A in the B tumbler, or is there more B in the A tumbler? You said they're the same.

Say tumbler A is filled with 100% blue dye, and one tablespoon which equals 10% is put into tumbler B, filled with 100% red dye. After mixing, tumbler B contains 110% of 90.1% red and 9.9% blue. A tablespoon of this mixture placed into tumbler A puts almost 10% of the 9.9% blue, or approximately .9% back into tumbler A, giving it a total of 90.9% blue, whereas tumbler B still contains only 90.1% red. I really enjoy your column, but I'm glad you're not mixing prescriptions.

Bill Pearson
Mayer, Arizona

Dear Bill:

The original answer is correct. Here's another way to look at it: Forget the number of spoonfuls and percentages and just look at the two tumblers. If tumbler A contains a certain amount of one liquid, and tumbler B contains the same amount of another liquid, no matter how many times you transfer the liquids back and forth or even whether you mix them well or not at all, as long as each tumbler ends up with an equal volume, there will be as much B liquid in tumbler A as there will be A liquid in tumbler B. This is because however much B liquid is now in tumbler A, it displaces that same amount of A liquid, which we will find (where else?) in tumbler B.

◆ ◆ ◆

Dear Marilyn:

I have given this problem to over 100 people, including people with doctorates in math, and none of them gave me the right answer, even though I repeated it several times. And after I told them the answer, I had to run for my life!

There are two bugs in a gallon jar. Every minute, the number of bugs doubles. If the jar is filled in half an hour, how long is it before the jar is only *half* filled?

Sol Lubitsch
West Palm Beach, Florida

Dear Sol:

As you know, the answer is 29 minutes. If the jar—no matter what its size—is filled in 30 minutes, and if the number of bugs doubles every minute, there would be only half as many bugs one minute before that.

And can you guess how many bugs there would be if two bugs double only thirty times? About two billion!

◆ ◆ ◆

Dear Marilyn:

This is a serious question. Please answer it, if possible. Not long ago, you solved a problem about bugs in a jar. My nineteen-year-old son glanced at the problem and instantly gave the correct answer, also. I said to him, "How can you come up with the answer to a problem many people couldn't answer in a million years, and you cannot pass calculus?" Do *you* know?

Frances W. Cordova
Valdosta, Georgia

Dear Frances:

Despite the fact that your son is bright, did he *choose* to take calculus of his own accord? Or was it a course pressed upon him by such powerful entities as college curriculum requirements or guidance counselors or parents? It's been my own observation that those people who *want* to take courses pass them without undue struggle. Others, however bright they may be, find it much more difficult.

◆ ◆ ◆

Dear Marilyn:

This is one of our family's favorite mind-teasers: You are given a seven-gallon bucket and a five-gallon bucket. With only these buckets to use as measuring devices, you are ordered to bring back exactly four gallons of water. How do you do it?

Benisch Family
Windsor, Wisconsin

Dear Readers:

You fill the seven-gallon bucket and pour it into the five-gallon bucket. This leaves two gallons in the larger bucket. Then empty the smaller bucket, and pour the two gallons into it. Now fill the seven-gallon bucket again and pour it into the five-gallon bucket. As two gallons are already in the smaller bucket, however, it'll only accept three more, leaving four gallons of water in the larger bucket for you to bring back with you.

◆ ◆ ◆

Dear Marilyn:

If you have a set of balances and fifteen balls identical in size, fourteen of which are also identical in weight, the fifteenth being slightly heavier, how do you find the heavy ball in only three uses of the balances?

Jean F. Devine
McAllen, Texas

Dear Jean:

In order to eliminate as many balls as possible, put seven balls on each end for the first weighing. If the scale balances, the heavy ball is the one left over. If it doesn't balance, eight balls—the lighter seven and the extra—are now out of contention. To eliminate more, take the heavier seven and divide it into two groups of three for the second weighing. Again, if the scale balances, the heavy ball is the one left over this time. If not, take the heavier three and put one ball on each side for the third and final weighing. If the scale balances, the heavy ball is the last one left over. If not, the final tip of the scale will be toward the heavy ball.

◆ ◆ ◆

Dear Marilyn:

I'm writing to you for help because I think that the guy who gave me this problem (knowing what type of person he is) has given me something unsolvable. There are three houses and three utilities lined up like this:

GAS	WATER	ELECTRICITY
SMITH	JONES	BROWN

How do you hook each house to each utility by drawing lines without any of them crossing each other? And if it can't be done, why not?

Norman C. Ellis
Baltimore, Maryland

Dear Norman:

It's impossible, all right, and here's the reason, which not only answers your question but also answers the question of why more of us aren't mathematicians. The proof depends on a theorem that states that an uninterrupted closed curve on a surface divides the surface into an inside and an outside area so that any uninterrupted line connecting a point on the inside with a point on the outside must cross over the curve.

And you were right about the kind of guy he is, too!

◆ ◆ ◆

Dear Marilyn:

My son's math teacher gave his class a "brainteaser" and won't reveal the answer until someone gives the correct one and the reasoning behind it. Everyone is stumped. Here's the problem:

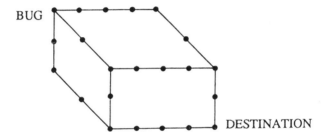

The box is a cube, and the bug must crawl to his destination in the shortest distance possible. My son said the shortest distance between two points is a straight line, so he had the bug go straight along the edge and then across to the destination, but all the teacher said was, "You're getting closer."

What answer is she looking for?

Karen Schweiger
Whittier, California

Dear Karen:

Here's the answer, for which your son has the reasoning.

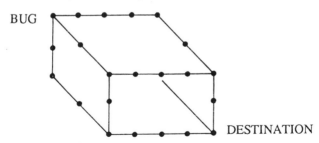

To see this better, unfold the box mentally like this.

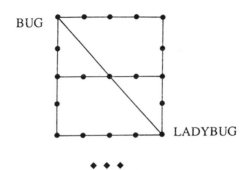

◆ ◆ ◆

Dear Marilyn:

A frog fell into a well thirty-two feet deep. Each day he jumped two feet up the side wall and slid back down one foot each night. How many days did it take him to jump out of the well?

Iris D. Girolamo
South Orange, New Jersey

Dear Iris:

I'm aware that this is going to drive everyone crazy, but I'm going to risk it anyway: it will take him thirty days. Let's suppose instead that the well is only two feet deep. How many days will it take him to jump out? It will take him less than a day because he can land at the bottom, then jump up to the edge and climb right out without sliding back at all. If the well is three feet deep, however, he'll jump up two feet and slide down one during the first twenty-four-hour period, then jump out when the next day arrives, with only one full day behind him. If the well is four feet deep, it'll take him two days, and so on.

◆ ◆ ◆

Dear Marilyn:

I hope there's a response to this problem, which was given at a major university. No one seems to have the answer! Three honor students are seated at a round table and are shown five pieces of tape—three white and two black. Each will be blindfolded, and a piece of tape will be placed on each forehead. When the blindfolds are removed, the first student who knows both what is the color of his tape and why it is that color will receive a lucrative position at a large firm.

A piece of white tape was then placed on each student's forehead, and the black were discarded. Some moments after the blindfolds were removed, a student came up with the right information. How did the student know?

M. J. Lock
Lantana, Florida

Dear M. J.:

Let's call the students Bob, Bill, and Susan. When Susan saw that the two others had white tape on their foreheads, she knew that if she had black tape on hers, both Bob and Bill would either immediately or, after watching each other's reaction, then quickly say they had white tape on their own foreheads.

(There were only two pieces of black tape. If Bob—or Bill—were looking at two pieces of black tape on the others, he'd know his tape was white and would say it immediately. And if he didn't, Bill—or Bob— would know his own tape was white and would then say it quickly.)

But when they didn't, Susan knew that her tape must be white (even though the three pieces of tape were the same, giving all the students an equal chance at the position) because she was the quickest of the three.

◆ ◆ ◆

Dear Marilyn:

This problem has been bugging me for years. A child born in 1980 has 2 parents. Using 30 years as a generation, they were born in 1950. They, in turn, each had 2 parents (4 people) born in 1920. And they, in their turn, each had 2 parents (8 people) born in 1890, and so on. I have figured that, back to the year 960, the child born in the year 1980 would have 21,275,869,184 direct ancestors. Obviously, this cannot be. But why not? No one sees my point. As a matter of fact, they all think I'm crazy, including my husband. Where am I going wrong?

> Eva Lyn Amber
> Cuyahoga Falls, Ohio

Dear Eva:

Your numbers aren't far off (we get 17,179,869,184 for the year 960) but your names are wrong. In other words, the number of ancestral positions is huge, all right, but the same people are occupying more than one of them.

And here's a little diagram to explain why, starting with 8 children:
Jan & John   Joan & Jack   Judy & Jim   Jane & Joe
When grown, they all pair off with each other like this:
Jane & John   Judy & Joe   Joan & Jim   Jan & Jack
And these pairings produce the following 8 people:
Mary & Mike   Marie & Matt   Mindy & Mel   Mona & Marty
When grown, *they* all pair off with each other like *this*:
Mona & Matt   Mindy & Mike   Mary & Marty   Marie & Mel
And *these* pairings produce the *following* 8 people:
Bette & Bob   Bonnie & Bill   Barb & Ben   Beth & Barry
When grown, *they* all pair off with each other like *this*:
Bonnie & Ben   Beth & Bob   Barb & Barry   Bette & Bill
And *these* pairings produce the *following* 8 people:
Sandy & Seth   Sarah & Sam   Sue & Sol   Sheila & Sid
When grown, *they* all pair off with each other like *this*:
Sarah & Sid   Sandy & Sol   Sue & Sam   Sheila & Seth
And *these* pairings produce the *following* 8 people:
Ellen & Ed   Eva & Ernest   Emma & Evan   Eleanor & Ezra
That was four generations. If you're Eva, here's your ancestral tree:

Eva

Sandy Sol

Bonnie Ben | Barb Barry

Mindy Mike | Mary Marty | Mary Marty | Marie Mel

Joan Jim | Jane John | Jane John | Jan Jack | Jane John | Jan Jack | Judy Joe | Joan Jim

In other words, you have 16 ancestral positions, all right, but you have only the same original 8 people filling them.

And if you trace your ancestry back to the first calendar year, you would have 79,029,856,294,838,206,464 roles to fill, all of them occupied by only the approximately 2,500,000 people alive at that time. In addition, you will share these people with a great many others. This is one of the reasons you shouldn't be impressed when you hear that someone is distantly related to famous people of the past. A great many of us are.

28.

Riddles

Dear Marilyn:

A man looks at a portrait on the wall and says, "Brothers and sisters I have none, but this man's father is my father's son." At whose portrait is he looking? I was told this little gem over fifty years ago and am still puzzled as to the answer.

Harold W. Longua
Livingston, New Jersey

Dear Harold:

The man is looking at a portrait of his son.

Publishing that was a mistake. Oh, the answer's *correct, but publishing it without an explanation was certainly a mistake! Within the next two weeks, I received several hundred letters, at which point we stopped counting and started reading.*

Here are a few sample comments: "I know women have poor reasoning power. Book intelligence, yes! But no analytical reasoning ability. As a man once said, 'A woman would make a good president if everything a president needs to know could be written into a book.'"

"Wrong, wrong, wrong! It would be interesting to learn how many below-average I.Q.'s such as myself caught this glaring error."

"You may be a genius according to Guinness, but to me you're a half-note short. . . . It's odds on Parade or you will never acknowledge this egregious error. It's really stupid."

"This was a question in a test given to me as an entrance exam for nursing.

Before someone fails a test because of your answer, please correct it for them.''

"I am a senior at a university. Presently this term, I am taking a class titled 'Thinking.' Our professor gave us the same question to figure out a couple of weeks ago. I was confused, but did figure it out. Our professor also confirmed the answer.''

"I've known the answer for at least fifty years, but to make sure, I've double-checked with twelve professors at San Diego State University. They all agree with me.''

Well, some of the readers were so upset that they wrote to "Dear Abby" about it. She answered it in her column and agreed with me, suggesting the substitution of the names of one's own family members. That didn't pacify them, however, and they persisted, writing to her again. One 73-year-old stated that she'd heard the riddle for "as long as she could remember" and the answer had always been "himself." She even went so far as to complain that I wouldn't admit my error.

Abby took a deep breath and devoted another column to the subject. "Lillian, watch my lips . . ." she began. (Now we know where George Bush gets his material.) She tried to put the matter to rest, but to no avail. The tide of letters continued unabated. Finally, she resorted to a third column on it, printing a similar riddle (with the same answer) that made certain no one could possibly think the answer could be "himself."

It went something like this: A prisoner had a male visitor. After he left, the prisoner's cellmate asked who the visitor was, and the prisoner said, "Brothers and sisters I have none, but that man's father is my father's son." Who was the visitor? And because the visitor is obviously a separate person, the answer can't be "himself."

Here is our own explanation:

We'll call the man speaking "John" and the man in the portrait "Mr. X" and then phrase the sentence in a more normal conversational way without changing the meaning.

John says, "I am an only child, and Mr. X's father is my father's son."

If John were to solve the problem himself, he could go on to say, "And just who is my father's son? As I have no brothers, it can only be me! Then Mr. X's father is me, and Mr. X is my son."

If we solve the problem ourselves, we must say that if John is an only child, and Mr. X's father is John's father's son, then Mr. X's father must be John. And if Mr. X's father is John, Mr. X is John's son.

That means John is looking at a portrait of his son.

◆ ◆ ◆

Dear Marilyn:

Let's say I have two women with me on a journey across the river, my mother and my wife, and only two people can cross in the boat. The other has to be left behind. Whom do I take, my mother or my wife? And why? (I know the answer and reason myself.)

Murphy A. Junaid
Texarkana, Texas

Dear Murphy:

I believe the traditional answer is that you should take your mother because you can get another wife, but you can't get another mother. But I'm not very impressed by it. After all, the same argument could be used to justify all sorts of silly things. For example, let's suppose that instead of your mother, you have your childhood pair of bronzed baby shoes and your wife with you on a journey across the river, and only one of them can cross. Which do you take? According to the above reasoning, you should take your bronzed baby shoes because you can get another wife, but you can't get another pair of bronzed baby shoes!

I expected a few miffed mothers would write to complain, but I didn't expect the following:

"As a mother of two sons, I can tell you if I were given the choice you mentioned, I would take the bronzed baby shoes with me in memory of my wasted life! P.S. I have reopened this letter to add that halfway across the river, I would drop the bronzed baby shoes at the deepest point and continue on my way!"

◆ ◆ ◆

Dear Marilyn:

A man with a fox, a goose, and a bag of corn wants to cross a river, but the boat there will only hold the man himself and one other. He can't leave the fox alone with the goose because the fox would eat the goose, but he also can't leave the goose alone with the corn because the goose would eat the corn. How does he get across?

Anna Willhibe
Springfield, Oregon

Dear Anna:

As you told it to me, he takes the goose across and leaves it on the far shore. Then he goes back and takes the fox across. But instead of leaving the fox alone with the goose over there, he takes the goose back with him and leaves it on the first shore. Then he takes the corn across and leaves it on the far shore with the fox. Finally, he goes back and gets the goose. (Problems like this are solved more easily by those of us who have held family reunions.)

◆ ◆ ◆

Dear Marilyn:

What is the subject of this riddle: you throw away the outside, cook the inside, eat the outside, and throw away the inside?

Cindy Toulou
Fruitland, Wisconsin

Dear Cindy:

Sounds like good, old-fashioned corn on the cob to me, one of my favorites. However, for the sake of our hearts, maybe the answer should be eggs. You would throw away the outer shell, fry what's inside, eat the outer white as you would a delicacy, but throw away the cholesterol-laden yolk.

And this certainly shouldn't diminish anyone's desire to buy eggs. After all, we don't mind if peaches have pits, do we?

Dear Marilyn:

My father-in-law loves to ask this question, which usually ends in an argument. Can you settle it? If a hen and a half can lay an egg and a half in a day and a half, how many hens does it take to lay six eggs in six days?

Kristen Hedberg
Medford, Oregon

Dear Kristen:

My father loved this one, too, but I didn't get it then, and I don't get it now. What's the problem? Is "one hen" too obvious? If a hen and a half can lay an egg and a half, etc., that means a hen can lay an egg in a day. And if just one hen lays one egg a day for six days, we'd have half a dozen right there, wouldn't we? (I'm afraid I'm missing something like a terrible pun about scrambled eggs.)

Well, I missed something, all right—the right answer! What my father actually used to say was, "If a hen and a half can lay an egg and a half in a day and a half, how many days would it take a peg-legged grasshopper to kick the seeds out of a dill pickle?" and I didn't take the question seriously.

The result was that the fax machines at Parade *began grinding on the day the paper arrived on the newsstands, and the postman soon dumped thousands of letters on our doorstep.*

Dear Marilyn:

With regard to the question, "If a hen and a half can lay an egg and a half in a day and a half, how many hens does it take to lay six eggs in six days?"—your answer "one hen" is in fact too obvious, as you say. It should be one and a half hens.

In the puzzle, the production mechanism is one and one-half hens. The fixed rate is one and one-half eggs per one and one-half days. Now, if the above logic is correct, multiplying the time period by four will correspondingly increase the production by four. Therefore, simply let the hen and a half machine run for six days, and the resultant output will be six eggs.

Stephen C. Johnston
St. Louis, Missouri

Dear Stephen:

Good catch, you guys! Your "one and a half hens" is right, and my "one hen" was wrong. I realize some of you said "six hens" or "nine hens," but maybe you're just reluctant to accept the concept of half a chicken the way I was. And here I'd always assumed this was one of those "How much wood would a woodchuck chuck?" kind of tongue-twisters! It's actually a logic puzzle.

◆ ◆ ◆

Dear Marilyn:

There are two men riding horses, and they make a bet of whose horse is the slowest. But then each starts restraining his horse so it can go slower than the other. Finally, they come upon another man and ask him how they might tell whose horse is the slowest. Based upon what they're told, both men start riding the horses as fast as they'll go. What was the solution the other man told them?

Eddie Howell
Tampa, Florida

Dear Eddie:

He told them to ride each other's horses!

◆ ◆ ◆

Dear Marilyn:

Here's a puzzle for you. A man is on his way to Delhi when he comes to a fork in the road. He is wondering which way to go when two men appear. One cannot tell the truth, and the other cannot tell a lie, although he doesn't know which is which. What one question can he ask and learn the right road to Delhi?

> Ralph
> Lexington, Kentucky

Dear Ralph:

He would pick one man, point to the other man, and ask the first man, "Which road would *he* say is the right road to Delhi?" If the man he's asking is the Truthteller, he'll indicate the wrong road, because the Truthteller knows that the Liar would lie about it. If the man he's asking is the Liar, he'll indicate the wrong road too, because the Liar would lie about what the Truthteller would reply. Either way, then, no matter whom he asks, our friend will know which is the wrong road and should therefore take the *other* one on to Delhi.

◆ ◆ ◆

Dear Marilyn:

Here's a riddle:

The person who makes it sells it.

The person who buys it doesn't use it.

The person who uses it doesn't know it.

What is it?

> Rebecca Hawkings
> Bellevue, Washington

Dear Rebecca:

A coffin!

Part Four

Thinking About

Thinking

29.

Intelligence and Common Sense

Dear Marilyn:
If you were asked to name one fault common to all members of the human race, what would it be?

Paul E. Bouchereau
Metairie, Louisiana

Dear Paul:
Wishful thinking.

◆ ◆ ◆

Dear Marilyn:
Is intelligence what a person knows?

Vicki A. Sprout
Lancaster, Pennsylvania

Dear Vicki:
Intelligence isn't what you know; it's what you understand.

◆ ◆ ◆

Dear Marilyn:
Please tell me how you define intelligence.

Tex of Teague
Teague, Texas

Dear Tex:
Dictionaries generally define intelligence as some combination of the

ability to acquire knowledge and the ability to learn. However, I don't think either of these deals adequately with the vast capacity of human intelligence. After all, a computer can acquire knowledge, but certainly isn't intelligent. And the ability to learn implies more of an ability to be instructed, another job we can assign to a computer. Both of these are what I would call "passive" intelligence. To me, human intelligence is "active" intelligence. That is, it's the ability to take action to reach understanding independent of outside sources of "programming."

◆ ◆ ◆

Dear Marilyn:
   What is the essence of intelligence?

Thomas Nenner
Flagstaff, Arizona

Dear Thomas:
   I'd say objectivity. Objectivity makes the difference between a cognitive leap and jumping to a conclusion.

◆ ◆ ◆

Dear Marilyn:
   Please define "objectivity."

Sam Harrod
Eureka, Illinois

Dear Sam:
   Objectivity is a way of thinking that is based on reasons instead of excuses.

◆ ◆ ◆

Dear Marilyn:
   It seems to me your answers to questions are based mainly on logic. Isn't it possible that some things cannot be explained by pure logic?

Marvin Bensend, Sr.
Atkins, Iowa

Dear Marvin:
   Yes, but I'd say that's because language fails us rather than logic.

◆ ◆ ◆

Dear Marilyn:
   Which do you think will help you more in life: intelligence or experience?

Karen Whitlock
South Bound Brook, New Jersey

Dear Karen:

Experience is probably better for making money, but intelligence is better for making progress.

◆ ◆ ◆

Dear Marilyn:

What is the difference between ignorance and innocence?

Cynthia De La Rosa
Harbinger, Texas

Dear Cynthia:

If you're two years old and you overturn your plate of spaghetti onto your head at a fine restaurant, it's innocence. If you're thirty-two years old, it's ignorance. The reverse is the case for the person who took you there each time.

◆ ◆ ◆

Dear Marilyn:

Is there such a thing as common sense?

James R. Koschmeder
Boynton Beach, Florida

Dear James:

Sure, but I wouldn't trust it, if I were you. Common sense is just ordinary thinking. It varies from culture to culture and reflects more the progress of a particular society rather than basic truth. Common sense has been responsible for people thinking that the earth is a flat disk, that the sun and planets revolve around it, and that the stars only come out at night.

◆ ◆ ◆

Dear Marilyn:

When making a decision, should one go by what he feels in his heart or thinks with his head? (Assume the two cannot be compromised.)

Evelyn DeBolt
Ormond Beach, Florida

Dear Evelyn:

If your head tells you one thing and your heart tells you another, before you do anything, you should first decide whether you have a better head or a better heart.

◆ ◆ ◆

Dear Marilyn:

What do you do when your emotions are at war with your intellect?

Anonymous

Dear Reader:

It has been my experience that when my intellect and my emotions disagree, if I act on my intellect, my emotions will follow. With most things in life, what *is* good will eventually *feel* good, but what merely *feels* good eventually feels *bad.*

◆ ◆ ◆

Dear Marilyn:

Does intelligence eliminate emotions?

Gary Merkel
Evansville, Indiana

Dear Gary:

No, but it helps to keep us from relying on them unwisely.

◆ ◆ ◆

Dear Marilyn:

Through the ages, has mankind really gotten any smarter? We can go to the moon and back, split the atom, etc., but we still haven't conquered (to any degree) human emotions (greed, jealousy, anger, etc.) since the stone age. Why?

Herm Jacquez
Buchanan, Michigan

Dear Herm:

I didn't know we were *trying* to conquer emotions. And if we are, I hope we don't succeed. Human life would be about as exciting to lead as plant life.

◆ ◆ ◆

Dear Marilyn:

Do those with a higher intellectual potential have a duty to mankind to develop themselves into the greatest positive influence possible?

Alan Wrober
Fort Hood, Texas

Dear Alan:

You bet they do. And so does everybody else.

◆ ◆ ◆

Dear Marilyn:

I've always thought intelligent people should be doctors. What do *you* think?

Anonymous

Dear Reader:

If you're referring to saving lives, don't you think it would be better for us to have intelligent politicians, instead? The "preventive medicine" practiced by one perceptive politician that would mean one less war would save more lives than all the doctors in the country put together.

◆ ◆ ◆

Dear Marilyn:

Do intellect and imagination operate independently of one another?

Palani Kahala
Honolulu, Hawaii

Dear Palani:

Only at their peril. When intellect operates without imagination, it functions like an automatic pilot; with imagination, it functions like Eddie Rickenbacker singlehandedly attacking seven enemy planes. Likewise, when imagination operates without intellect, it behaves like a child fingerpainting; with intellect, it behaves like Michelangelo frescoing the ceiling of the Sistine Chapel.

◆ ◆ ◆

Dear Marilyn:

Which do you think is more important: imagination or knowledge?

Jason Sloan
Scott County, Virginia

Dear Jason:

For the most part, I think knowledge is more important because it's the way we can make use of the hundreds of years of accumulated experience gained by those who preceded us. For example, if we have no knowledge of how to construct a building and use only our imagination, the building may be attractive, but it probably won't be functional or safe. Or if we have no knowledge of how to operate on a patient and use only our imagination, the operation may be exciting, but we'll probably cause harm. And if we have no knowledge of how to fly a plane and use only our imagination, the flight may be electrifying, but we'll surely kill ourselves.

◆ ◆ ◆

Dear Marilyn:

Please tell me what is the difference between creativity and imagination?

Kristina Reed
Northridge, California

Dear Kristina:

Creativity is imagination that is gainfully employed. Without a job, imagination is inclined to walk around the house in its slippers a lot and not get dressed.

◆ ◆ ◆

Dear Marilyn:

If humans can see only certain colors and hear only certain sounds, can they conceive of only certain dimensions?

Lincoln Doswell
Altoona, Pennsylvania

Dear Lincoln:

Maybe, but not for the reasons you suggested. Seeing colors and hearing sounds are both tied to physical sensation, but conceiving of dimensions leaves the realm of sensory experience. Dimensions are not "felt"; they are conceptualized. The former implies physical limitations; the latter implies mental ones.

◆ ◆ ◆

Dear Marilyn:

Assuming you were responding to some alien entity, how would you describe our thought process?

Robert E. Hintz
Virginia Beach, Virginia

Dear Robert:

I'd show him a computer and tell him that our minds operated with annoying similarity. Even the worst hardware is still excellent, but the software varies tremendously. Some of us are heavily programmed and others lightly, and with information ranging from the fine to the false. And there are glitches in the best of us. What appears on our screens is a result of the mixing of all these factors and more.

◆ ◆ ◆

Dear Marilyn:

If an alien visitor were to land in the Sahara and find an old pocket watch, would he be able to know if it were made by an intelligent being?

Norman Doering
Valparaiso, Indiana

Dear Norman:

I don't think so. We've divided our world into two categories: the living and the nonliving, the latter of which don't have intelligence. Subdivision of the living also has produced two categories: animals and plants, the latter in the same unintelligent shape. Not even all animals have intelligence, however. The difference? Purpose. On the low end of the scale, an amoeba probably doesn't do anything not contained in its genetic programming. On the high end, baseball certainly isn't in our genes (although in the case of one young man I know, I'm willing to consider the possibility). Until and unless your alien knows the object was made on purpose—anywhere from frivolously to seriously—he won't know if an intelligent being made it.

◆ ◆ ◆

Dear Marilyn:

What is the difference between skill and intelligence?

Colleen Kelley
Spokane, Washington

Dear Colleen:

"Skill" is successfully walking a tightrope strung between the twin towers of the World Trade Center. "Intelligence" is not trying.

◆ ◆ ◆

Dear Marilyn:

Is it better to be lucky or to be skillful?

Marie Torgesen
Magnolia, Texas

Dear Marie:

I think it's better to be skillful. I would much rather be operated upon by a surgeon who is skillful than one who is lucky, wouldn't you?

◆ ◆ ◆

Dear Marilyn:

Is there any difference between "luck" and "coincidence"?

Julie Robison
Fort Wayne, Indiana

Dear Julie:

"Luck" is that random occurrence that operates either for or against us. On the other hand, "coincidence" is that random occurrence that brings two or more related circumstances together in time or in space. In other words, "coincidence" is what happens when your two new boyfriends head for your house at the same time. "Luck" is what happens when one of their cars won't start.

◆ ◆ ◆

Dear Marilyn:

What is "bad luck"?

Don Faber
Vero Beach, Florida

Dear Don:

I suspect that what we call "bad luck" is more often like an automobile accident. It may be without purpose and unpredictable, but we probably have more control than we realize. Good driver's education will reduce the accident rate. Even so, you should always wear your seat belt when you drive down the highway of life.

◆ ◆ ◆

Dear Marilyn:

Is the art of winning just being at the right place at the right time?

Loretta Harris
Riverside, California

Dear Loretta:

Neither. A few people will be at the right place at the right time by luck, but more people win by building the right place themselves and spending a heck of a lot of time there.

◆ ◆ ◆

Dear Marilyn:

Which comes first—success or confidence, and why?

N. N.
Honolulu, Hawaii

Dear Reader:

I think confidence usually comes first because success so often requires the cooperation of others, and others seldom believe in us unless we first believe in ourselves. (And this makes more sense than it may seem at first. After all, we should know ourselves better than anyone else does.)

30.

Wisdom and Knowledge

Dear Marilyn:

In as simple language as possible, can you differentiate wisdom from knowledge?

Anthony J. Carbone
New Haven, Connecticut

Dear Anthony:

Knowledge tells you when you're on a one-way street; wisdom tells you to look both ways before you cross it.

◆ ◆ ◆

Dear Marilyn:

If you had the choice between having all-knowledge and having all-wisdom, which would you choose and why?

Dennis E. Sigle
Wichita, Kansas

Dear Dennis:

I'd choose all-wisdom. The best possible libraries would have all-knowledge, but what would they understand? People who have only repositories of data are similarly limited. On the other hand, a person with all-wisdom would know the right course of action to take no matter how few facts were available.

And on the whole, I'd rather know how to handle nuclear power than know how to build the nuclear power plant.

◆ ◆ ◆

Dear Marilyn:

To acquire knowledge, one must study. How does one acquire wisdom?

Donald E. Eggert
Harper Woods, Michigan

Dear Donald:

To acquire knowledge, one must study; to acquire wisdom, one must observe.

◆ ◆ ◆

Dear Marilyn:

Please rank the following characteristics in order of importance: knowledge, wisdom, judgment, intelligence, and ignorance.

Todd A. Hermetz
Cullman, Alabama

Dear Todd:

As far as desirability to our society is concerned, I'd say that wisdom ranks first, followed by intelligence, knowledge, and then judgment, with ignorance trailing in last place. While keeping in mind that people can be a combination of more than one of these types, the wise person knows what is good, and the intelligent person knows what is correct; the knowledgeable person knows the way things are, and the judgmental person knows the way things feel. The ignorant person, however, doesn't know anything at all.

◆ ◆ ◆

Dear Marilyn:

At some point in my life of 68 years, it occurred to me that people having modest intelligence are sometimes possessed of considerable wisdom, whereas others noted for braininess may display appalling foolishness. William F. Buckley, Jr., once remarked that the world's real troubles were not caused by dumb people. My question is, what is the relationship between intelligence and wisdom?

Stuart C. Burdick
Coos Bay, Oregon

Dear Stuart:

All wise people are intelligent—whether they know it or not—but not all intelligent people are wise—whether they know it or not.

◆ ◆ ◆

Dear Marilyn:

Which is more important, the person or his ideas?

Edward J. Kroll, Jr.
Wyandotte, Michigan

Dear Edward:

I'd say the person is more important during his lifetime, but his ideas are more important afterward. After all, the person can make more good ideas, but the ideas can't make more good people.

◆ ◆ ◆

Dear Marilyn:

How do you tell the difference between an ordinary idea and a terrific one?

Stanley Herschenfeld
Boise, Idaho

Dear Stanley:

A good idea will keep you awake during the morning, but a great idea will keep you awake during the night.

◆ ◆ ◆

Dear Marilyn:

Which is worse, being wrong or not being right?

Jose Ontiveros
Naranja, Florida

Dear Jose:

I'll put it this way: people who think they know—and are wrong—are far more dangerous than people who think they *don't* know.

◆ ◆ ◆

Dear Marilyn:

I believe the true definition of genius is being able to adapt to any situation and communicate with another human being on his or her level. What do you think?

Ed Winland
Mantua, Ohio

Dear Ed:

I don't quite agree, but I think you've come up with a nice definition of a good social worker.

◆ ◆ ◆

Dear Marilyn:
Would you please comment on this statement? "Genius is the ability to reduce the complicated to the simple."

Joann S.
Rancho Cordova, California

Dear Joann:
I agree only to a limited extent. Many reductions of the complex to the elementary are not acts of genius; they are acts of hard work. And many problems cannot be reduced without serious loss of steps in the logical order.

◆ ◆ ◆

Dear Marilyn:
Henry Miller is quoted as saying, "The more one penetrates the realm of knowledge, the more puzzling everything becomes." Will you please explain what Mr. Miller meant by the above statement? Is it true?

F. M. R.
Washington, D.C.

Dear Reader:
He may have meant that virtually everything worth knowing about is far more complex than it seems at first, at second, and even at third. This would make it easier to draw conclusions, however mistakenly, when we have fewer facts on which to base them than it would be when we have more. In a way, this may be true if we limit ourselves to knowledge, but the realm of *understanding* is far more comfortable, where deeper penetration makes it *easier* to make judgments instead of the reverse. And the way to live in that domain is simply to make sure that you don't learn more than you understand.

◆ ◆ ◆

Dear Marilyn:
If ignorance is bliss, what is knowledge?

Terry Nagel
Lawrenceville, Georgia

Dear Terry:
If ignorance is bliss, knowledge is sublime.

◆ ◆ ◆

Dear Marilyn:

Can the human mind know more than it has learned?

Anonymous
Baltimore, Maryland

Dear Reader:

Yes. And in the right hands, it's the road to progress. "Insight" is one such avenue, in which man learns separate facts, then puts them together in such a way as to gain new knowledge. It's what occurred when someone realized that the earth revolved around the sun rather than the other way around.

Here's an example of this ability in action: You want to clean the leaves out of the gutter of your new house, but they're out of reach. Then you notice a neighbor painting his house, and you ask him if you can use his ladder to reach your roof. That's insight. After cleaning the gutters, you decide to walk around on the roof to see why the skylight is leaking. The neighbor sees the ladder standing idly against your house and takes it back in annoyance. A couple of hours later, after being forced to break your skylight getting back into your house, you walk over to your neighbor's, wait until he's up on the roof, and resist the temptation to put his ladder away for him. That's *also* insight.

◆ ◆ ◆

Dear Marilyn:

Is it possible for man's mind to reach a breaking point by assimilating "too much" knowledge?

Ken Seibert
Wrightsville, Pennsylvania

Dear Ken:

If you mean an overload point where the mind, like an old-fashioned pinball machine, goes on "TILT," I'd say "yes." There is now so much more information available than we can absorb in our brief lifetimes that the particular mix we *do* absorb is becoming very important to our intellectual lives. In the past, the mix of good and bad to which we were exposed was far more directly related to our actual individual lives and was more readily handled naturally.

Today, however, the same physiological minds are bombarded by the news media with an artificial mix of information gathered selectively from around the world. But the daily news doesn't reflect real life at all. Instead, it emphasizes death and destruction, magnifying it to false proportions in order to attract interest, even at the cost of our mental health, the way salt and sugar are added to food at the cost of our physical health. Thanks to the wonders of modern communication, the experience of the shell-shocked soldier continues to creep a little closer to us all.

◆ ◆ ◆

Dear Marilyn:

Your logical precision reminds me of the late philosopher Ayn Rand. Her own philosophy—objectivism—holds that reality functions objectively, and, therefore, reason is man's one and only means of knowledge. To what extent do you agree or disagree with her?

Donavon Keithley
Salt Lake City, Utah

Dear Donavon:

This is too tall an order for a short column, so let me just comment. Even if *reality* functions objectively, this doesn't mean that *man* does. In other words, the "knowledge" that results from the process is only as good as the reasoning was.

◆ ◆ ◆

Dear Marilyn:

Is there such a thing as true objective reality, or are we a world of individual realities determined by experience, i.e., perception?

Lance Beckwith
Seattle, Washington

Dear Lance:

I believe there is an objective reality, but the person who can perceive it is exceedingly rare. The rest of us live in a world composed of all those individual realities, often our own personal ones. And the greater the extent to which they dominate our intellect, the poorer the thinkers we are.

◆ ◆ ◆

Dear Marilyn:

I believe that whatever happens to me, good or bad, is all my own doing, but I would be interested in your opinion. Simply put, my question is, "Do you think we create our own reality?"

Billy R. Newell
Pasadena, Texas

Dear Billy:

Yes, but with serious reservations—that is, within the limitations imposed upon us from the outside. In other words, I believe the ugly duckling was just lucky.

◆ ◆ ◆

Dear Marilyn:

I'm wondering how you would respond to the idea of solipsism.

Lee D. Hwang
Hanover, New Hampshire

Dear Lee:

The theory that we can only be aware of our own experiences, or that nothing exists outside our minds, is intriguing, but seems egocentric to me. And egocentric views often don't take enough into consideration. One egregious example of egocentric thinking is the theory that the sun revolves around the earth rather than the other way around.

◆ ◆ ◆

Dear Marilyn:

What do you think is mankind's greatest fear?

Alan Ka
Long Island City, New York

Dear Alan:

Not long ago, I would have said it's the fear of the unknown, but I now think there is an even more profound fear—the fear of the unknowable.

◆ ◆ ◆

Dear Marilyn:

Is the difference between "believing" something and "knowing" something a difference of degree or a difference of kind?

A. R. Southergill
Goleta, California

Dear A. R.:

It's a difference in type. When you "believe" something, you accept it on trust; when you "know" something, you accept it on truth.

◆ ◆ ◆

Dear Marilyn:

What is the difference between "truth" and "fact"?

Linda M. Porter
Silver Spring, Maryland

Dear Linda:

Facts are tiny bits of truth that need to be put together like a jigsaw puzzle to see what the whole truth is.

◆ ◆ ◆

Dear Marilyn:

What is the most powerful weapon in the world?

Nicole Moye
Camp Lejeune, North Carolina

Dear Nicole:

I think it's truth. Discovering it has taken us to other planets, eradicated smallpox, and dismantled monarchies.

◆ ◆ ◆

Dear Marilyn:

Is this true? "If the truth hurts, there's nothing wrong with the truth; there's something wrong with you."

Al Dziuk
Hereford, Texas

Dear Al:

Only within a very narrow context. For example, if the truth is that people treat me with less respect because I'm a woman, is there something wrong with *me*, is there something wrong with *women*, or is there something wrong with *them*?

◆ ◆ ◆

Dear Marilyn:

Do you believe in the existence of higher states of consciousness, even though science cannot verify this? And how can one reach these higher states other than through the use of drugs?

Richard Lambert
Watauga, Texas

Dear Richard:

I doubt very much that there are states of consciousness higher than those already known to be reached by humankind, at least on this planet, where we men and women enjoy an awareness completely unknown to roses and robins. If there *are* higher states, perhaps elsewhere, I don't think that we could ever reach them any more than a cat could perform calculus. And drugs commonly produce *lower* states, not *higher* ones. Can you imagine a prescription bearing the words, "Be sure to take this drug while operating a motor vehicle or other dangerous equipment"?

31.

Philosophy

Dear Marilyn:

Do you believe that we are the masters of our own fate?

B. Babcock
Oswego, New York

Dear B.:

Unfortunately, it usually feels more like we're the *mistresses* of it.

◆ ◆ ◆

Dear Marilyn:

What's the easiest way out of this mess we call "life"?

Maurice Copeland
Washington, D.C.

Dear Maurice:

Just stop thinking of it as a mess! This may require a leap of faith at times, such as on the New York City subway system at 9:00 in the morning, but it's much easier than agonizing over it all.

◆ ◆ ◆

Dear Marilyn:

If you could learn either where you are going or how you will *get* there, which would you prefer and why?

Marlow Johnston
Irvine, California

Dear Marlow:

I'd prefer to learn where I'm going because if I don't like the destination, I'd be able to change my course and go somewhere else. Many of us, it seems, pay more attention to what we're doing today or this week or this month than to where those actions will ultimately take us, and that indifference can provide for some nasty surprises as the years go by.

◆ ◆ ◆

Dear Marilyn:

How does one go about finding one's purpose in life, or is this possible?

Cheryl McKay, R.N.
Albuquerque, New Mexico

Dear Cheryl:

I'd suggest *making* one, instead. You'll be happier with it.

◆ ◆ ◆

Dear Marilyn:

At the risk of getting too existential, what is the purpose of our living, if any? I strongly suspect it is to experience love and to spend money. Am I missing anything?

James H. Schmitz
Carrollton, Texas

Dear James:

Yes. You've obviously forgotten to include eating barbecued ribs.

◆ ◆ ◆

Dear Marilyn:

How much is a human life worth?

Jon Brigleb
Las Vegas, Nevada

Dear Jon:

I think a human life is worth whatever happiness it gives minus whatever *unhappiness* it gives.

◆ ◆ ◆

Dear Marilyn:

My philosophy is very simple: "All that has been and all that will be, is *now*." What do *you* think?

A. W. Claybrook
Fort Worth, Texas

Dear A. W.:

I think that maybe the future is just the past getting back at us.

◆ ◆ ◆

Dear Marilyn:

A human being is a member of a global community of living things, but is described as something more. Why are we so drawn to the concept of immortality, when the nature of the world blazes with finitude?

Ric Nix
San Mateo, Florida

Dear Ric:

Maybe it's because we see there are limits to our understanding. After all, a cat can't even master long division, can it? However, this shouldn't be an excuse for taking wild speculation and fanciful explanation seriously, as even the best minds have done throughout the ages.

Then again, maybe it's just wishful thinking.

◆ ◆ ◆

Dear Marilyn:

What is more perfect for living things—to be mortal or immortal?

Arlen Whitaker
Baton Rouge, Louisiana

Dear Arlen:

I believe immortality would be far preferable so that generations of knowledge and wisdom would be accumulated rather than eliminated, resulting in changes of choice instead of chance. We must be very careful not to justify something just because it appears inevitable. Mother Nature and Father Time are indiscriminate killers who cause the death of every living thing.

◆ ◆ ◆

Dear Marilyn:

As a physician, I occasionally get into conflicts with my more physically minded colleagues over the termination of artificial life support. Since I have a hard time conceiving of death being a final end in a universe where nothing is created or destroyed, my reasoning often causes consternation among my peers. What do you think?

Rebecca A. Jessee, M.D.
San Jose, California

Dear Rebecca:

Even if death is not a final end, it is at least an intermission from

which none of us return. As such, I believe that decisions regarding life
support should be based on other criteria. One consideration for your
discussion might be to answer the following question: In this particular
case, how is the support characterized—"artificial life" support or "real
life" support?

◆ ◆ ◆

Dear Marilyn:

If you were the only person in the world who could see, would you
paint your house?

J. W. Dospoly
Pottstown, Pennsylvania

Dear J. W.:

Yes. After all, *I* could see. (And I would finally have an opportunity
to paint it a color *I* like!)

◆ ◆ ◆

Dear Marilyn:

I have a question for you that has psychological "hooks" in it, as it
is very revealing. It was asked of me by an interviewer during a job
screening many years ago. I did not get the job, possibly because my
answer was "redwood tree." The question is, "If you could be anything
in the world except a human being, what would you choose to be?"
Over the years, I've asked this question of many people and have
received some very unusual answers. Most men say a lion or an eagle,
and many women say a flower or a butterfly or even the earth. The most
arrogant reply came from the president of a small company, a self-made
man, who was very successful financially, but obnoxious. He replied,
"That's easy: God."

William J. Borgers
Chula Vista, California

Dear William:

I think I'd like to be the sun, radiant and warm, and a giver of life.
(This has the additional advantage of allowing people to say I'm full of
hot air when they're annoyed with me.)

---

*But a redwood tree? A redwood tree? Good grief. I hope this fellow likes
dogs.*

◆ ◆ ◆

Dear Marilyn:

You, as the person you are now, are being sent back alone in time five hundred years. You will remain the same person with the same knowledge as today. You may bring one item with you. What would that be?

Stacy Kates Miller
Whiteface, Texas

Dear Stacy:

I would take back a book that described how to produce the vaccine for plague, hoping to save the 25,000,000 people who died from the Black Death in the fourteenth century, nearly three-fourths of the population in some areas.

I was shocked to receive dozens and dozens of letters deploring my reply, and I certainly had no intention of letting them go unanswered.

Dear Marilyn:

Regarding the question about being sent back in time to the Middle Ages and being able to bring one item with you, your answer was a vaccine for the Black Death. At first thought, this was a very noble and humane answer. But on second thought, how many people would be added to the present population?

Fred M. Utt
Hazelwood, Missouri

Why would you want to save the 25 million who died from the Black Death? That action would have a devastating effect on today's overpopulation. If you *did* save them, an extra war, disease, or famine might come along later to achieve population control. If I could bring one item back in time, I'd be afraid of making such a large life-and-death decision.

Ruth Lawler
Kasilof, Alaska

Your answer leaves much to be desired, as my wife instantly observed. How could you possibly believe that it would have been beneficial to add 25 generations of reproduction by 25 million people? I believe that this thoughtless response merits some sort of public retraction.

H. White
Portland, Oregon

Dear Readers:

There'll be no retraction here, and I'm not afraid to stand up publicly and say that I'd save those people just the way I'd save the many millions who died under Hitler. You'll just have to count me as one of those folks who prefers family planning to famine, pestilence, and madmen.

◆ ◆ ◆

Dear Marilyn:

Suppose that you could make one change in the physical universe. For example, you could cancel the law of gravity or change the length of day and night. What change would be most useful to mankind?

Clinton Williams
Oxford, Michigan

Dear Clinton:

I'm afraid that a change in just one law in the physical universe will cause the other laws to topple like dominoes, but looking at the situation less strictly, I think I might choose to eliminate the law of entropy, the scientific term for the magnitude of randomness in the cosmos, one of the basic laws of nature, that states that systems move toward greater disorder as time passes and that all processes must operate at less than 100% efficiency. The importance of this cannot be overemphasized, the outcome of which may be the eventual degrading of all useful energy in the universe, with not even enough left to continue to support motion, let alone life itself. But entropy also plays an important part in our everyday lives. For example, every time we copy and recopy a recording of music, the information is degraded until it eventually becomes unintelligible. All this means that without entropy, we might live forever, have a perpetual motion machine to drive, and, yes, at long last, be able to make clean videotape recordings!

◆ ◆ ◆

Dear Marilyn:

Considering the time, work, and energy involved, why does it take longer to create something than it does to destroy it?

Maureen Maus
Erie, Pennsylvania

Dear Maureen:

Because construction typically runs counter to the forces of nature, but destruction typically acts in concert with the forces of nature. In other words, construction is unnatural; destruction is natural.

◆ ◆ ◆

Dear Marilyn:

Is anything impossible?

Anonymous

Dear Reader:

I'd say so, but we may never be in a position to know for certain the full scope of which things they are. Many "impossible dreams" of only a hundred years ago are reality today. In the narrow sense, on the other hand, there appears to be much already known to be impossible, even if not proven as such to the more philosophically sensitive. If, for example, we are unable to "prove" there is no Santa Claus, this says less about the presence of flying reindeer than it does about the absence of adequate methods of proof. The intellectual who can honestly say he or she believes in the possible existence of the Easter Bunny should not be trusted with the car keys.

◆ ◆ ◆

Dear Marilyn:

What, in your opinion, *is* the most important question in the world today?

David E. Moore
Greenfield, Indiana

Dear David:

I believe the most important question in the present is the same as the most important question of the past: *why?* And the next most important question: *how?* The following are two examples: "*Why* should we build more sophisticated weaponry?" and "*How* should we build more sophisticated weaponry?" In general, I believe the former question should be answered before the latter.

◆ ◆ ◆

Dear Marilyn:

When I was in college, I took a philosophy class, and the final exam had one question on it. The entire class spent the full period writing long answers to the question except for one girl, who finished the exam in ten minutes. She turned the paper in to the professor, who told her she got an "A" on the exam. The question was "Why?" What was the answer?

Kathleen Brady
Tucson, Arizona

Dear Kathleen:

I suppose the answer has to be "Why not?", but I'd like to give an "F" to that professor. Philosophy is far too important a subject to be treated with such disrespect. And if I were one of those other students, I'd be plenty angry.

◆ ◆ ◆

Dear Marilyn:

Not long ago, you printed a letter from a girl who said her philosophy teacher gave a test that consisted of one question, "Why?" I liked your disapproving answer, but I'm surprised you didn't mention that the story is an urban myth.

Trister Keane
Brooklyn, New York

Dear Trister:

You haven't seen my mail. While quite a few people wrote to express the same opinion you did, many also wrote to relate their own personal distressing experiences with taking this "test." Some had answered, "Because," and received no credit because the answer was, "Why not?" Others had answered, "Why not?" and received no credit because the answer was, "Because." And one person even answered, "Just because," which earned her only partial credit and a detailed explanation of exactly why her reply fell short of the ideal. But they certainly had one feeling in common: they all hoped their instructors saw my column that week. (And a few were going to have it forwarded to them, "just to be sure.")

◆ ◆ ◆

Dear Marilyn:

Are all the brightest people philosophers?

Anonymous

Dear Reader:

No. I believe there are great specialized intellects, and there are great comprehensive intellects. The specialized intellects belong in a field like physics, and the comprehensive ones belong in a field like philosophy. And either who tries to claim greater understanding of the other's field has overestimated himself or herself. If we consider two equally great minds—given the same twenty-four hours in everyone's day—the comprehensive mind will understand much less about the specifics of one subject than the mind that specialized in it. Likewise, the specialized mind is grossly inadequate in the broader areas. The intellect that searches for a cure for cancer does not belong in politics, and vice versa. And neither should be confident about fixing his or her own plumbing.

◆ ◆ ◆

Dear Marilyn:

If there had been as many women philosophers as men, in what ways do you think western thought might have been different?

Deborah Franzone
Springhill, Florida

Dear Deborah:

Oh, you've touched a nerve here.

I think our entire social fabric would be altered, ranging from political to personal life. I could write a book on this subject, and maybe I will, but let me mention just one difference for now: I think children would carry their mothers' names instead of their fathers', that long-standing tradition in service of the male role of ownership of the female.

Parental behavior in nature is almost exclusively maternal. Only in a very few species are the males likely to be involved even to a minor extent, and whether the young happen to be related to them is incidental. All psychology and no physiology, paternal behavior in humans has far more to do with the woman than with the child.

So if men don't own women, and women are the natural parents, why in the world don't children use their mothers' names? Because women haven't exerted influence appropriate to the reality of the situation.

If I could do one thing for womanhood, it would be to change this situation, one which underlies the entire foundation of the current inequality of the sexes.

◆ ◆ ◆

Dear Marilyn:

If there were a Pandora's box in our time, what do you think it would be?

Dorothy Radke
Joliet, Illinois

Dear Dorothy:

One good candidate would be television. However, instead of unleashing all the evils on the world, the way Pandora did in Greek mythology, it gathers them together and entertains us with them on the daily news, like a conga line in a floor show.

◆ ◆ ◆

Dear Marilyn:

Freedom and virtue, it can be argued, are two ends an enlightened society should seek. Yet when the two come into conflict, as they inevitably will, which should take precedence over the other?

> Piers Spencer
> Alexandria, Virginia

Dear Piers:

We're tempted to choose virtue, of course, but wouldn't it be better to live in a free society where we could decide our own standards of virtue than to live in a controlled society where we had to live by someone *else's* idea of virtue?

◆ ◆ ◆

Dear Marilyn:

I'd like to ask you a question concerning values. Have you developed any lasting values beyond productivity, pleasure, procreation, and preservation?

> John F. Smith
> Wrentham, Massachusetts

Dear John:

Yes. Independence.

Now, what kind of person would I be if I shaped my personal values for the purpose of alliteration?!

◆ ◆ ◆

Dear Marilyn:

Can you make a case for "balance in all things"?

> Ben Nelson
> Dauphin, Pennsylvania

Dear Ben:

I can, but I certainly wouldn't recommend it to everyone. Moderation may be fine for parents and politicians, but science, literature, and art need the bold.

◆ ◆ ◆

Dear Marilyn:
　　Which question has no answer?

Ernest Chapman
Ontario, Canada

Dear Ernest:
　　Here are a few:
　　Why did it all begin?
　　How is it all going to end?
　　and
　　Why didn't you come home last night?

32.

Classic Questions

Dear Marilyn:
Which came first, the chicken or the egg?

Anonymous

Dear Reader:
I think the egg came first. A chicken is not defined by the kind of egg it lays. (A horse is a horse even if it gives birth to a mule.) But an egg is defined by the kind of creature it contains. (An egg that contains a robin is a "robin" egg, no matter what laid it.) Therefore, if you believe in evolution, at some point a creature that was almost a chicken laid an egg that contained a chicken, and as an egg is defined by the kind of creature it contains, the egg came first.

◆ ◆ ◆

Dear Marilyn:
If a genie can do anything, can he create a stone so heavy he can't lift it?

Anonymous

Dear Reader:
Sure. But as soon as he's done it, he can no longer do anything. In other words, if he can so do anything, he can certainly give up his power to do anything. But if this is a disappointment to any genies reading this, don't stop now. At this point, the genie can do anything but lift that special stone he created. His next act, then, could be to

make that stone disappear, restoring himself to his former effectiveness.

◆ ◆ ◆

Dear Marilyn:

What would happen if an irresistible force met an immovable object?

Anonymous

Dear Reader:

Well, if nothing happened, the force was resisted, and if there were any movement, the object was movable. But maybe the force and the object could unite in an intriguing new manner: they could diffuse into each other, creating a new immovable object that would suck all matter into it. The object would not move; it would be invaded. Nor would the force be resisted; it would be transformed.

◆ ◆ ◆

Dear Marilyn:

How many angels can dance upon the head of a pin?

Anonymous

Dear Reader:

I think none can. The size mentioned—that of a pin's head—distracts attention from the real question: can *any* angel dance upon the head of a pin?

As I understand it, angels are beautiful creatures, but they have no physical substance. This means that we can't touch an angel with a pinhead or anything else. And if nothing can touch an angel, angels can't touch anything themselves. Therefore, no angels at all can touch—or dance upon—a pinhead or anything else, no matter how large or small.

◆ ◆ ◆

Dear Marilyn:

If two hands clapping makes a certain sound, and four hands clapping makes a sound twice as loud, does one hand clapping make a sound half as loud?

Jonathan Dize
Fort Wayne, Indiana

Dear Jonathan:

Yours is the best answer I've seen to this silly question, and I hope you'll force it on everyone who asks.

◆ ◆ ◆

Dear Marilyn:

Could you please clear up a question I have? Of these two sayings, which one is true? "The meek shall inherit the earth" or "Only the strong shall survive."

Nicole Hansen
Santa Rosa, California

Dear Nicole:

They may *both* be true. After all, *"weak"* is the opposite of strong, not *"meek."* The first definition of a meek person is one who is gentle, courteous, and kind, someone who shows patience and humility. Sounds like a winner to me.

◆ ◆ ◆

Dear Marilyn:

Which is truer? "Take care of the little things, and the big things will take care of themselves," or "Take care of the big things, and the little things will take care of themselves."

Bob Hitz
Lincoln, Nebraska

Dear Bob:

I'd definitely take care of the big things myself. After all, when things take care of themselves, how often do you like the way they turn out?

◆ ◆ ◆

Dear Marilyn:

Which do you believe is the better choice: the end justifies the means, or the means justifies the end?

Fred Hollman
Skokie, Illinois

Dear Fred:

I believe longer-term thinking is wiser than shorter-term, so I'd pick the first one. Feeling good about where I'm going (even if I feel bad about where I am) makes more sense to me than feeling *bad* about where I'm going (even if I feel *good* about where I am).

◆ ◆ ◆

Dear Marilyn:

I have heard that "time is money" and that "time heals all wounds." Do you think these sayings are true?

Wes Lowdermilk
Council Bluffs, Iowa

Dear Wes:

No, I don't. If time equals money, we should be able to substitute "money" in the other saying, making it read, "Money heals all wounds"!

◆ ◆ ◆

Dear Marilyn:

Which runs the world—love or money?

Anonymous

Dear Reader:

If the struggle is only between those two terms, I'd say that our outer world is run by money, but our inner world is run by love. The romantic wants experience for its own sake; the pragmatic wants experience to get a better job.

◆ ◆ ◆

Dear Marilyn:

Is money the root of all evil?

Edward Jackson
Pasco, Washington

Dear Edward:

I don't think so, but it sure does make a good fertilizer.

◆ ◆ ◆

Dear Marilyn:

If you had to choose between happiness, health, and money, which would you choose, and why?

Wilma Gradwohl
Sunnyvale, California

Dear Wilma:

I'd choose happiness first, then health, with money a distant third. I'd rather live happily for fifty years than unhappily for a hundred. And a rich man would willingly give his money to live, but a poor man would never give his life to be rich.

◆ ◆ ◆

Dear Marilyn:

Who is happier, the wise man or the fool?

Robert E. Wickham
Montville, New Jersey

Dear Robert:

The wise man sees more of reality; the fool sees less of it. If reality is more positive than negative, the wise man will probably be happier; if it's more negative than positive, the fool will probably be happier. And because nearly everyone chooses life over death, life must be overwhelmingly positive. For that reason, the wise man—or woman— is likely to be much happier than the fool.

◆ ◆ ◆

Dear Marilyn:

How can you tell an honest man from a dishonest man?

Anonymous

Dear Reader:

You ask each one of them if he is truly an honest man. The dishonest man will tell you "yes," but the honest man will tell you "no."

◆ ◆ ◆

Dear Marilyn:

I know this is an "old one," but I've never seen anyone who could answer it worth a darn. If we have the right to free speech, do we also have the right to falsely scream "fire" in a crowded theater?

Mike Donadio
Provo, Utah

Dear Mike:

No, we don't, and that doesn't bother me. Rights are just another word for permissions, and the behavior you describe is forbidden. We also have the right to fire a gun, but we don't have the right to fire it into that crowd of people, do we?

◆ ◆ ◆

Dear Marilyn:

In my opinion, there has never been a satisfactory answer to the question, "Why do the good suffer and the wicked prosper?" What do *you* think?

Raidan Trujillo
Pueblo, Colorado

Dear Raidan:

I don't have a satisfactory answer because I doubt the statement is true in any but the narrowest sense. I don't believe that most prosperous people are wicked and most suffering people are good, and I don't believe that most wicked people are prosperous and most good people suffer. Instead, when a wicked person *does* prosper, or when a good person *does* suffer, it draws attention disproportionately because we find it so irritating.

◆ ◆ ◆

Dear Marilyn:
"No good deed goes unpunished." Do you find this "humorous" obser-vation accurate or inaccurate?

Gerald McCall, Ph.D.
San Diego, California

Dear Gerald:
I'm afraid I find it more accurate than inaccurate. There seems to be little we can do in life that someone, somewhere, cannot (and does not) condemn. The courageous criticize the bad; the cowardly criticize the good.

◆ ◆ ◆

Dear Marilyn:
What is the biggest room in the world?

Adrienne Carter
Camp Lejeune, North Carolina

Dear Adrienne:
The room for improvement.

◆ ◆ ◆

Dear Marilyn:
Often the reality of a person or circumstance doesn't match the fantasy we entertained. Given that, is a bird in the hand really worth two in the bush?

Jim Kaslik
Allentown, Pennsylvania

Dear Jim:
Maybe it's that a bird in the hand sings less sweetly than a bird in the bush.

◆ ◆ ◆

Dear Marilyn:
Which is more important, quality or quantity?

Anonymous

Dear Reader:

Painful as it can be to witness, I'd say quantity is more important to our society. In the area of politics, for example, we elect our president not on the quality of the votes he receives, but on the number. Our economy doesn't run on how we earn our money; it runs on the *amount* we earn. Socially, our ideal is "the greatest good for the greatest number," not "the greatest good for the greatest." Even theoretically, quantity appears to win. After all, which would most of us choose, the finest diamond on earth or all the rest of them? And if we're cautious enough to ask which is worth more, we're *still* deciding by quantity—of dollars!

◆ ◆ ◆

Dear Marilyn:

If there's a will, is there a way?

Anonymous

Dear Reader:

I'd say no because it's not always, or even usually, the case. Relatively little of the wealth of human desire can be fulfilled, even in the best of circumstances.

For example, the strongest and most universal desire—the desire to escape death—has not been achieved. And even of those goals known to be possible, satisfaction of ambition is not realized as often as it is frustrated. Most human endeavor requires the cooperation of others, whether it's being elected president or becoming a fine musician, and if we don't get that cooperation for whatever reason, the most dauntless spirit will still not be enough. (And considering what some folks we know want, this may not be all bad.)

◆ ◆ ◆

Dear Marilyn:

They say "an eye for an eye" only leaves both sides blind! What do *you* think and say?

Julian Hammer
Carteret, New Jersey

Dear Julian:

This statement makes more sense for arguments within the law than it does for crimes outside of the law. But it also appears to refer to violence, or at least its equivalent, in forbidden behavior. That being the case, it doesn't make sense to dignify a criminal by calling him one "side" and his victim another "side." If a woman is beaten and robbed of the money in her handbag, does a court fight then ensue whereby both she and the thief take opposing sides to assert claims to the funds?

◆ ◆ ◆

Dear Marilyn:

As I get older and view the world with more experience, I believe, "That which grows slowly, endures." What do you think?

James E. Peters
Springfield, Massachusetts

Dear James:

Leaving nature aside, it may be true. Radical change produces more radicals—who produce more radical change.

◆ ◆ ◆

Dear Marilyn:

Why does time pass faster as we get older?

Carroll Devillier
Maringouin, Louisiana

Dear Carroll:

Maybe we become less egocentric as we mature, gaining a better perspective on the brevity of our lives overall.

Of course, there's the fact that a year represents a much smaller portion of a lifetime to a fifty-year-old than it does to a five-year-old, but maybe there's more than that. Only sixty-one generations—sixty-one $33\frac{1}{3}$-year-olds—stand between us and Julius Caesar. And you probably know three of them personally.

◆ ◆ ◆

Dear Marilyn:

How can you tell if you're dreaming?

Anonymous

Dear Reader:

If you're wondering if you're dreaming, you're dreaming.

◆ ◆ ◆

Dear Marilyn:

Is it possible that everything in the universe happened by chance?

Dennis Wheeler
Savannah, Georgia

Dear Dennis:

If we could somehow prove that the first event happened by chance, then we could say that everything that followed from it was the result of chance. However, I think we'll have a difficult time convincing Jonas Salk of this.

◆ ◆ ◆

Dear Marilyn:

Why do like things tend to cluster together? For example, I mean leaves on a tree, gold crystals in a vein, rich people, etc.

Anonymous
Sacramento, California

Dear Reader:

Perhaps it's because conditions suit their particular needs. For example, leaves won't be found growing on dogs, gold crystals won't be found in roses, and rich people won't be found where there are no good restaurants.

◆ ◆ ◆

Dear Marilyn:

Why do we have to pay extra for an unlisted telephone number that is not in the book?

Julian Hammer
Carteret, New Jersey

Dear Julian:

Don't blame the telephone company. It's because nearly everyone *wants* his or her number listed, thereby establishing the publishing of numbers as the standard operating procedure. This makes removing (and safeguarding) a minority of numbers difficult. It's a little like trying to throw a handful of confetti at a party while holding onto just the red ones.

33.

The Arts

Dear Marilyn:
  What is art?

Susan Martin
Lincoln, California

Dear Susan:
  I think art is the language of the soul. If understood, it is successful.

◆ ◆ ◆

Dear Marilyn:
  What good is art?

Charles D. Williams
San Jose, California

Dear Charles:
  It's as good as beauty.

◆ ◆ ◆

Dear Marilyn:
  Is beauty really in the eye of the beholder?

Anonymous

Dear Reader:
  It would be nice if it were, because then everyone could make that judgment for himself or herself, and much more would probably be considered beautiful as a result. Instead, I think beauty is more likely

to be found in the eye of whoever has the most *influence* on the beholder, and that might range from his or her mother to the most effective advertising agencies. Only the most independent of beholders, if they exist at all, are able to withstand the pressures, both perceived and unperceived, of the outside world. And many of the rest of us have become so accustomed to these circumstances that we very nearly regard the eyes of others as our own.

◆ ◆ ◆

Dear Marilyn:

I can see why painting was so popular before the development of photography. But aren't the master painters now eclipsed by the master photographers?

Joseph Pietro
Collinsville, Illinois

Dear Joseph:

I don't think so. For one thing, an artist can combine the essence of a hundred photographs into one painting. And for another thing, no photographer can capture a unicorn.

◆ ◆ ◆

Dear Marilyn:

Is there a general underlying principle of beauty common to a Mozart sonata, a baseball triple play, and a Rodin sculpture?

Lynn H. Willett
Zanesville, Ohio

Dear Lynn:

I don't think so, at least not with those examples. Mozart sonatas are stirring even to those who've never heard of the man, a baseball triple play is appreciated most by those who are knowledgeable, but a Rodin sculpture is accepted only by those who are believers. In other words, the first is natural, the second acquired, and the third taught.

◆ ◆ ◆

Dear Marilyn:

Today, the serious music listener listens to such composers as Mozart, Beethoven, and Wagner. At the time, however, these composers were writing music to entertain. What will the serious music listener be listening to in 2092? Is it possible that our entertainment music of today, such as musicals and television themes, will be the cherished symphonic pieces of the future? Or will we still be listening to Wolfgang, Ludwig, and Richard?

Dr. Martin Marcus
Morganville, New Jersey

Dear Martin:

Mozart, Beethoven, and Wagner may have written to entertain, but isn't that what all composers do? I think that the works we hear a hundred years from now will come both from the composers of yesterday *and* from the equally serious composers of today and tomorrow, whoever they may be. I doubt, however, that they'll come from outside the ranks of the masters of the music world.

◆ ◆ ◆

Dear Marilyn:

As there is a finite number of musical notes, how can there be, or at least appear to be, an infinite number of songs written with them?

John P. Reilly
Stafford, Virginia

Dear John:

If all other factors were equal, and there were a finite number of notes, there would be a finite number of songs that could be made using them. However, there are probably three main reasons that the variety appears infinite. For one, the number is vast. For another, songs differ in timing, intensity, and in the instruments used, making the number even larger. And for another, when a particular note is repeated from one time to the next, the frequency may be modified significantly for different effects.

Despite all this, I find a great many songs on the radio that certainly *seem* indistinguishable.

◆ ◆ ◆

Dear Marilyn:

Is the voice an instrument?

Thomas Comis
Troy, New York

Dear Thomas:

Yes, of course. But some are violins, some are fountain pens, and some are stethoscopes. And others are just washboards.

34.

Getting Personal

Dear Marilyn:
What was your worst subject in school?

Ben Duncan
Carlsbad, California

Dear Ben:
Art. I consistently underwhelmed everyone around me.

♦ ♦ ♦

Dear Marilyn:
Are you doing what you always wanted to do as a child?

Julian Hammer
Carteret, New Jersey

Dear Julian:
No, thank goodness. At various times in childhood, I've wanted to do things like be a fireman, a poet, and an acrobat, but I eventually abandoned everything chosen before I matured when I finally realized that childhood desires nearly always deserve to be left in childhood. Otherwise, I'd still be with my first real boyfriend, walking on stilts whenever I got the chance, and eating red licorice for lunch.

♦ ♦ ♦

Dear Marilyn:
Do you have a job?

Karen Fleming
Akron, Ohio

Dear Karen:

Yes. I'm also the vice president of a small company that specializes in cardiovascular research. But why don't you think writing for publication is a job? This column reaches nearly seventy million people weekly. Walter Winchell's column had a total circulation of about fifty million people daily back in the 1930s. Don't you think *he* had a job?

◆ ◆ ◆

Dear Marilyn:

I can't imagine anyone ever discriminating against you as a woman. Has it ever happened?

Anonymous Man

Dear Reader:

Good grief. You must have a terrible imagination. It happens every day. One particularly infuriating example occurred when I sold my house in another city not long ago. It was titled in my name alone and purchased before our marriage, but I was required to get my husband's permission before being allowed to sell it. On the other hand, my husband recently sold *his* house, titled in his name alone and purchased before our marriage. He needed no permission at all.

◆ ◆ ◆

Dear Marilyn:

If you're the world's smartest woman, how come you're not married to the world's richest man?

Thomas Littleford
College Park, Maryland

Dear Thomas:

Wow! This question sure says a lot more about *you* than it does about *me*, fella! So marrying a wealthy man is what you think women do with intelligence, huh? Or is it that's what you think they *should* do? Well, either way, if I ever run into the world's *dumbest* woman, I'll be sure to send her *your* way!

◆ ◆ ◆

Dear Marilyn:

Is "vos Savant" actually your family name?

George H. Roberts
San Diego, California

Dear George:

Yes, it is. My grandmother's maiden name was Mary Savant, and my grandfather's name was Joseph vos Savant, so "Savant" appears not just once, but twice.

◆ ◆ ◆

Dear Marilyn:

I've read something of your life in a magazine, and I was impressed with your children's accomplishments. Your daughter was the valedictorian in her high school class of over 500, and your son was a national chess champion, and they're both now in medical school. Have you ever thought of writing a book on raising children?

Tom Jakubowski
Venice, Florida

Dear Tom:

Goodness, no. I don't know enough about it. What they've accomplished is to *their* credit, not to mine. (But I could probably fill a book with what *not* to do!)

◆ ◆ ◆

Dear Marilyn:

Have you learned anything from your experiences being interviewed that you can share with us?

Joseph Fiallo
Sarasota, Florida

Dear Joseph:

Oh, yes. Don't insult the barber until after you've gotten up from the chair.

◆ ◆ ◆

Dear Marilyn:

Would you rather be well liked or well respected?

Charles Hubbard, Jr.
Fort Wayne, Indiana

Dear Charles:

I think I'd rather be well respected. Both are positive qualities, but being highly valued sounds far more productive and substantial than being extremely popular, so I guess you'd have to count me in as one of those few people who would rather be Isaac Newton than Wayne Newton. (Except maybe on the weekends.)

◆ ◆ ◆

Dear Marilyn:

Do you ever get stressed? If so, how do you cope with it?

Anonymous
North Jersey, New Jersey

Dear Reader:

Sure, I get stressed. Who doesn't? My own way of coping with it is to get a massage, and as often as possible. The expensive way can range from hiring a therapist for an hour to buying an armchair with hidden rollers. However, the cheapest way, in this case, is by far the best way, and I highly recommend it: ask a friend. No kidding. The arrangement is, of course, that you will return the favor whenever it's needed. And do it often. That warm human touch, the feel of an old friend's hand on your shoulder, not only provides comfort to the muscles, but consolation to the spirit. Most of us have been so programmed to avoid contact with one another that we've lost touch with the healing properties of simple human affection.

◆ ◆ ◆

Dear Marilyn:

What do you do for fun?

Douglas Roberts
Milpitas, California

Dear Douglas:

I read my mail!

◆ ◆ ◆

Dear Marilyn:

How long does it usually take you to answer these questions?

Raymond Bishop
Springfield, Illinois

Dear Raymond:

It ranges from about five minutes to about five hours. The philosophical ones are the hardest, by far.

◆ ◆ ◆

Dear Marilyn:

What question, if any, would elicit a personal answer from you?

Michael Aaron
San Antonio, Texas

Dear Michael:

There are many, of which the following are only a few:

"Smoking or nonsmoking?"

"Am I late?"

"Would you like general or local anaesthesia?"

◆ ◆ ◆

Dear Marilyn:

Are you ever wrong?

Katherine Taylor
Shrewsbury, Massachusetts

Dear Katherine:

Oh, *gosh* yes. Once a proofreader accidentally inserted a noticeable grammatical error (for which I take responsibility). Another time I oversimplified myself out on a limb so far that a robin couldn't have sat on it, and not long ago, I simply switched formulas in midstream, making the answer dead wrong.

◆ ◆ ◆

Dear Marilyn:

Have you ever done something without thinking and then said to yourself, "Boy, am I dumb"?

Jill Medoff
Atlanta, Georgia

Dear Jill:

No, and I hope no one does. Doing things without thinking is both normal and understandable. If we stopped to think every time we did something, it would probably take us all day just to get through to lunch. The time to feel silly is after you've done something foolish *with* thinking!

◆ ◆ ◆

Dear Marilyn:

I'm beginning to think I *routinely* do irrational things instead of just once in a while, the way I used to think. Do you?

Anonymous

Dear Reader:

I've recently noticed that I do something that defies logic as often as every other day. I actually *pay* for the privilege of leaving my 39th-floor office and taking an elevator to the street only to walk over to the gym and . . . get on the *stair-climbing* machine!

◆ ◆ ◆

Dear Marilyn:

As I know personally that no one has ever asked you this question, and that you've been hoping in vain someone would, I've decided to ask it myself.

What's the worst aspect of writing the "Ask Marilyn" column?
Marilyn vos Savant
New York, New York

Dear Marilyn:

I thought you'd never ask.

Easily the worst aspect is reading the letters of thousands upon thousands of readers and knowing that I have no way of replying to them personally. The column receives some 25,000 letters in one year now, and just *reading* 500 letters a week is as much as my schedule will allow. I couldn't manage even a one-sentence reply to each person, as much as I would like to. This bothers me more than anything else.

I hear from everyone from prisoners to priests, from the famous to the infamous, and from schoolchildren to university professors. And I read them all personally. Richard Romano, my editorial assistant, who first reads, marks, and sorts them for me, often appears in my office to read a special passage aloud. Today, it may be from a young mother in mourning, and tomorrow it may be from an angry old man, hoping there's just one person left in the world who will listen to him. I'm often found waving letters in the air over lunch, poring over a professor's detailed explanation after dinner, or smiling at a compliment over breakfast. But my readers have no way of knowing that they've gotten through to me.

Unless I tell them. And I'm doing that right now. Please don't feel neglected, dear reader, if you don't hear from me. Any columnist who replies to all his or her mail must either use form letters or get very few letters. Anyway, not hearing from me isn't so important. What's important is that *I* hear from *you*. And I do.

Part Five

Questions that Need

No Answer!

35.

The Funniest Questions

Dear Marilyn:

Before you throw this letter away, please, please, give it some serious thought. As yet, no one has been able to answer my question—you are my last hope. I'm dating this really sweet guy. I hope to marry him someday. There is one thing however; sometimes he wears a skirt.

This is okay with me, but he won't shave his legs. I've asked him to either shave or wear tights under his skirt. He insists the idea of the skirt is for lounge and/or comfort. In addition, he says tights are like pants and defeat the purpose of the skirt. He also says that by shaving his legs, he looks less masculine.

As I see it, if he is secure enough to wear a skirt, shaving his legs shouldn't bother him. He has nice legs and casts a nice shape in a skirt if only he would shave his legs.

My question is this: Should men who wear skirts shave their legs? Brian and I have decided to go with your reply. If you say no, I'll stop asking him to shave his legs, but if you say yes, he has agreed to shave his legs and wear pantyhose if I ask him.

C. N.
Toledo, Ohio

◆ ◆ ◆

Dear Marilyn:

What do women want?

H.
Stillwater, Minnesota

◆ ◆ ◆

Dear Marilyn:
Why do some men wear blue bikini underwear?

V. C.
El Cajon, California

(It's because red is sometimes just too bright, of course.)

Dear Marilyn:
Does it really make a difference if a man sits or stands while putting on his pants?

R. C.
New York, New York

◆ ◆ ◆

Dear Marilyn:
Who invented circumcision and how did he or she convince someone to try it?

J. H.
Carteret, New Jersey

◆ ◆ ◆

Dear Marilyn:
Do you believe sex is primarily for recreation or for pleasure?

G. T. T.
Houston, Texas

◆ ◆ ◆

Dear Marilyn:
Why are earlobes the most underrated part of the human body?

S. C.
Brooklyn, New York

◆ ◆ ◆

Dear Marilyn:
Can a human being survive with no nose?

C. D.
Newark, New Jersey

Well, I know plenty of statues who are doing just that!

◆ ◆ ◆

Dear Marilyn:

Why is it that everyone else knows you have bad breath before you do, especially when the nose is only one inch from the mouth?

B. M.

Tempe, Arizona

◆ ◆ ◆

Dear Marilyn:

If you travel a lot, you may want to refill a small toothpaste tube from a more economical large one. How can you do this without any tools, fittings, or attachments, quickly, without spilling, and with one hand held behind the back?

The answer is simple:

1.   Remove caps from both tubes.
2.   Lay large tube on firm seat of chair, opening to left.
3.   Right foot is carefully placed over rear part of tube, and small tube is held in left hand, with opening lined up with large tube opening.
4.   Press openings together, temporarily sealing, as the right foot is rocked gently down on the large tube, forcing toothpaste from large tube into small one.

D. F.

Bethesda, Maryland

◆ ◆ ◆

Dear Marilyn:

I want to pass on a neat tip—used dental floss can be added to soups for healthful fiber reinforcement.

G. M.

Portland, Oregon

◆ ◆ ◆

Dear Marilyn:

Why don't false teeth decay?

Mrs. C. D. L.

Cheraw, South Carolina

◆ ◆ ◆

Dear Marilyn:

What I would like to know about is high-risk contact lenses.

T. B.

Lincoln, Nebraska

◆ ◆ ◆

Dear Marilyn:

Can you please tell us why and how tipping a hairdresser started, and how can it be avoided, if possible, without feeling like a creep? A friend and I are wondering.

Mrs. R. C. J.
East Haven, Connecticut

◆ ◆ ◆

Dear Marilyn:

Is it possible to video-record dreams?

Mrs. S. Z.
Summit, Illinois

◆ ◆ ◆

Dear Marilyn:

Why do people keep buying new novels when books keep getting more expensive, and they're no better than existing novels?

A Reader
Fromberg, Montana

◆ ◆ ◆

It looks as if this next reader has his terminology a little confused.

Dear Marilyn:

Being on the go, I find it difficult to make time to read books. What do you think of people who are tapeworms?

D. P.
Masbury, Ohio

◆ ◆ ◆

Dear Marilyn:

I want to know if the light in the refrigerator goes out or stays on when the door closes.

L. H. K.
Lewiston, Indiana

◆ ◆ ◆

Dear Marilyn:

Is ice cream made to be licked, or eaten like a food?

J. H.
Carteret, New Jersey

◆ ◆ ◆

Dear Marilyn:

Over the years I've eaten in many Chinese restaurants and noticed that none of them had windows. I have asked at many different Chinese restaurants, and no one seems to know why. Is it for privacy, tradition, or some other reason? Can you help me find out?

L. R. S.
Lincoln Park, Michigan

◆ ◆ ◆

Dear Marilyn:

How can a family of three make twenty-seven bags of garbage out of six bags of groceries?

P. S. They do eat.

R. A. K.
Sun Prairie, Wisconsin

◆ ◆ ◆

Dear Marilyn:

What aspirin would you choose if you were stranded on a desert island?

S. S.
Fort Walton Beach, Florida

◆ ◆ ◆

Dear Marilyn:

After death, will human flesh sunburn? I am very curious about this.

D. G. C.
Richmond, Virginia

◆ ◆ ◆

Dear Marilyn:

As we all know, when people are born they are very small and gradually they grow tall to a certain height. How come when they stop growing, they don't start to gradually diminish in size? Think of all the space to be saved in cemeteries!

R. E. K.
Jackson Heights, New York

◆ ◆ ◆

Dear Marilyn:

My husband's question: How do you make a woman happy?

Mr. & Mrs. R. L. S.
Douglasville, Georgia

◆ ◆ ◆

Dear Marilyn:

Are oysters alive? How do they live? Please tell me something about the life of oysters!

> J. H.
> Carteret, New Jersey

◆ ◆ ◆

Dear Marilyn:

Do fish have necks? P.S. Due to legal problems stemming from a divorce, if you must publish the answer, please use a fictitious name and address. Thanks much.

> F. E. B.
> Fort Lewis, Washington

◆ ◆ ◆

Dear Marilyn:

Do fish ever get thirsty?

> B. G.
> Albuquerque, New Mexico

◆ ◆ ◆

Dear Marilyn:

Do insects survive being flushed down the toilet?

> T. D.
> Fargo, North Dakota

◆ ◆ ◆

Dear Marilyn:

This idea has been pestering me off and on for about twenty years. How did the lady bug get its name? It's easy to speculate, but I'd really like to know. Also, is there a bug called the man bug?

> T. C.
> Astoria, New York

◆ ◆ ◆

Dear Marilyn:

Where, I say where, did barn swallows nest 300 years ago?

> D. C.
> Harbor, Oregon

◆ ◆ ◆

Dear Marilyn:
How and why do chickens sing?

H. L. B. S.
Spokane, Washington

◆ ◆ ◆

Dear Marilyn:
I've heard that because rabbits have a high body temperature and that their body heat dissipates very fast through their long ears, they've been used to heat houses. Can you tell me how many rabbits it would take to heat a three-room apartment when the temperature outside is forty-five degrees?

F. K.
Columbus, Maryland

◆ ◆ ◆

Dear Marilyn:
I'm a gifted student. I wanted to know how mice were discovered and when!

J. W.
Camp Lejeune, North Carolina

◆ ◆ ◆

Dear Marilyn:
Do hamsters have individual fingerprints the way humans do?

I. G. A.
El Toro, California

No, but maybe we could just issue them all social security numbers, instead.

◆ ◆ ◆

Dear Marilyn:
I'd like to know why, when you shave an animal for surgery or when you clip cut a few matted tangles on your pet, how does that hair *know* it's been cut, and that it needs to grow back?

M. L. W.
Rio Rancho, New Mexico

◆ ◆ ◆

Dear Marilyn:
Will a ceiling fan cool a dog?

L. B.
Vero Beach, Florida

◆ ◆ ◆

Dear Marilyn:

My dog is an Australian shepherd, and I have sometimes wondered what language she would speak if for some strange reason dogs were able to talk. Would she speak the language from which her breed was derived, or would she speak English like my family? If she spoke English, would she have an Australian accent?

J. P.
Juno Beach, Florida

◆ ◆ ◆

Dear Marilyn:

I have a question for which I cannot find an answer from either books of knowledge or from my most intelligent friends. Why do my dogs show no interest in television?

I have eighteen more questions for which I cannot find answers but if you answer the above, I will respect your intelligence for the rest of my life.

F. E. S.
La Mesa, California

◆ ◆ ◆

Dear Marilyn:

When the second coming of Christ comes, would He be able to "bump off" Sunday afternoon TV football? How would you deal with such a greedy, monied, selfish priority? Pray? Doesn't work.

P. W.
Winfield, Kansas

◆ ◆ ◆

Dear Marilyn:

Why is it that Lois Lane and Jimmie have never been able to figure out that Clark Kent is really "Superman"?

D. C.
Palm Harbor, Florida

◆ ◆ ◆

Dear Marilyn:

What really happened to the members of the lost colony?

B. G.
Asheville, North Carolina

◆ ◆ ◆

Dear Marilyn:

You being the smartest person in the world, could you please explain the ending to the movie *2001*?

R. R. R.
Alameda, California

◆ ◆ ◆

Dear Marilyn:

I would like to know two things: 1) Who played drums on the original Beatles recording of "Love Me Do," and 2) What was the name of the drummer who once made a solo album titled "Blues for Dracula"?

I. G.
East Brunswick, New Jersey

◆ ◆ ◆

Dear Marilyn:

My question is about the song "Hot Sauce," by Thomas Dolby on his album "Aliens Ate My Buick." I realize this is too obscure to interest your readers (or yield a ready answer), but every time I hear the song, I'm reminded of once having heard an older song that had some of the same lyrics—"shag gets in your eyes"—and for a quarter, I can add to your sacks of junk mail by chasing after the impossible chance that you might both recognize his reference *and* have nothing better to write about in an upcoming column.

M. B.
Troy, Missouri

◆ ◆ ◆

Dear Marilyn:

At the end of the song "Since I Don't Have You," by Jimmy Beaumont and the Skyliners, the word "You" is sung thirteen times. I have been told that this song was dedicated to Wilt Chamberlain, and the word "You" that is sung thirteen times stands for the #13 he wore. Is this true?

F. K.
Levittown, Pennsylvania

◆ ◆ ◆

Dear Marilyn:

Why does Larry Bird earn more money than a nurse?

E. B.
Danby, Vermont

◆ ◆ ◆

Dear Marilyn:
What is Zonker Harris's first name, Nate or Edgar?

T. M.
Springfield, Oregon

◆ ◆ ◆

Dear Marilyn:
How old is "Sam Isuzu"? I mean, *honestly*!

T. B.
New Port Richley, Florida

◆ ◆ ◆

Dear Marilyn:
Would you be interested in auditioning? In Pittsburgh?

Reverend S., G. M.
Pittsburgh, Pennsylvania

◆ ◆ ◆

Dear Marilyn:
What kind of a body does the person with the highest I.Q. ever recorded have? Why don't you display a photograph of yourself in a string bikini in the next issue of *Parade* . . . let's get down to basics!

T. P.
Arlington, Virginia

◆ ◆ ◆

Dear Marilyn:
What is the world-famous brand name of lady's underwear? Have you ever had one!?

Father F. J. F.
New Orleans, Louisiana

Don't worry, Father. I know a student wrote that one!

◆ ◆ ◆

Dear Marilyn:
Does a person of your intelligence need help in getting properly dressed in the morning?

J. D.
Cohasset, Massachusetts

I'm pretty good at getting dressed, but I sometimes need a push to get out of bed.

◆ ◆ ◆

Dear Marilyn:

I admire your ability to answer questions. But, so far you have only dealt with easy ones like the meaning of life and the existence of truth. Are you ready for a difficult one?

Why can't anyone manufacture a product that really cleans windows?

R. G. R.
Pasadena, California

◆ ◆ ◆

Dear Marilyn:

If you're so smart, how come you're not the president of a beer company or something?

M. P. W.
Baltimore, Maryland

◆ ◆ ◆

Dear Marilyn:

Why does a smart person like you write in a newspaper instead of doing something for a living?

S. M. S.
Sanford, Maine

◆ ◆ ◆

Dear Marilyn:

Is it possible to make money without polluting the environment?

S. K.
East Falmouth, Massachusetts

◆ ◆ ◆

Dear Marilyn:

When Richard Nixon was put out of office, why did they audit "Fort Knox" in Kentucky? Do they audit Fort Knox every time a president leaves office?

H. C.
North Bay, California

◆ ◆ ◆

Dear Marilyn:

Do you think there will be a World War III or a World War IV? If you do, do you think it will be dangerous?

H. P.
Duluth, Georgia

◆ ◆ ◆

Dear Marilyn:

What would be needed to achieve world peace? If it's not too much trouble, would you mind answering the question on the enclosed post-card. Thank you!!!

W. N.
Honolulu, Hawaii

◆ ◆ ◆

Dear Marilyn:

I often wondered! What is the Pope's salary? Does he get paid by the hour or by the mile?

C. P. G.
Kissimmee, Florida

◆ ◆ ◆

Dear Marilyn:

Are there gravel roads in heaven?

M. K.
Buffalo Center, Iowa

◆ ◆ ◆

Dear Marilyn:

Why do some cars' exhausts smell like chicken noodle soup?

M. L.
Stayton, Oregon

◆ ◆ ◆

Dear Marilyn:

What intelligent use can be found for the hundreds of thousands of "space saver" spare tires and wheels that Americans discard from the trunks of their cars in favor of full-size spare tires and wheels?

C. H. B.
Marblehead, Massachusetts

◆ ◆ ◆

Dear Marilyn:

If you were to get into a rocket, would you go up to explore outer space or would you go down and explore the ground?

S. H.
Tomball, Texas

♦ ♦ ♦

Dear Marilyn:

Many people have seen UFOs with lights on them. My question is, why would a UFO need lights on it?

R. D.
Elmont, New York

♦ ♦ ♦

Dear Marilyn:

Suppose you were sitting with your hands and feet totally immobile and with your jaws wired shut in the center of a frictionless, level plane as large as a baseball diamond. How would you get yourself off without help from the outside?

Blow out your breath fast and jet yourself off seems to be the answer. (Through your nose with your head held back as far as possible.)

W. S. S.
Bethesda, Maryland

♦ ♦ ♦

Dear Marilyn:

Would it be possible to build a telescope powerful enough to enable the viewer to see the back of his head, assuming the earth was completely smooth?

D. C.
San Antonio, Texas

♦ ♦ ♦

Dear Marilyn:

If all the women in the world sprayed their hair at the same time, how would it affect the O Zone?

M. J. W.
Harrisburg, Pennsylvania

♦ ♦ ♦

Dear Marilyn:

In a tornado or severe thunderstorm, why does the sky turn a pukey greenish color?

D. K.

Murrysville, Pennsylvania

♦ ♦ ♦

Here's one that I know would thrill Parade *and excite all of our readers.*

Dear Marilyn:

Please explain in your column *all about water.* It is a real mystery to me. Everything you can tell me about water will be appreciated.

Mrs. J. P.

Pratt, West Virginia

♦ ♦ ♦

Dear Marilyn:

Why is water wet?

C. C.

Albuquerque, New Mexico

♦ ♦ ♦

Dear Marilyn:

If you melt dry ice, can you swim in it without getting wet?

S. R.

Newark, New Jersey

♦ ♦ ♦

Dear Marilyn:

If you empty a swimming pool and fill it with Pepsi, could you swim in it, or would you sink to the bottom of the pool?

M. H.

Fountain Valley, California

♦ ♦ ♦

Dear Marilyn:

Why do people sing in the shower?

E.

Burbank, California

♦ ♦ ♦

Dear Marilyn:
When you plop bleach into water, what splashes up, the bleach or the water?

D. D.
Magnolia, Mississippi

◆ ◆ ◆

Dear Marilyn:
Why do normal, average-tempered women become vicious and hateful when their spouses have affairs?

A. M.
Upper Marlboro, Maryland

◆ ◆ ◆

Dear Marilyn:
How important are trees to us as a nation? Do we need them?

J. H.
Carteret, New Jersey

◆ ◆ ◆

Dear Marilyn:
When making a tree, why is wood the best material?

J. H.
Troy, New York

◆ ◆ ◆

Dear Marilyn:
Where I work, we had a question about which is older: Time or Dirt. I told them that if anyone would know, Marilyn would know.

F. J. D.
Ambridge, Pennsylvania

◆ ◆ ◆

Dear Marilyn:
My question concerns the exact time. I would like to know when— on what date it was started, where—at what location, how—was it determined, and who—was the person or persons involved.

H. T. B.
Baltimore, Maryland

◆ ◆ ◆

Dear Marilyn:
Could you please explain to me the "Riddle of the Universe"? I shall be waiting for your reply in the *Tampa Tribune*.

L. C.
Homosassa, Florida

◆ ◆ ◆

Dear Marilyn:
How does thought occur? Please be architecturally and usefully precise.

J. H. M.
Fort Worth, Texas

◆ ◆ ◆

Dear Marilyn:
What is a simple explanation for everything?

C. W.
Mint Hill, North Carolina

◆ ◆ ◆

Dear Marilyn:
Do the rules of ethics change every ten years? If not, how often?

G. W. S.
Washington, D.C.

◆ ◆ ◆

Dear Marilyn:
What are the new figures for pi? It used to be 3.1416 and then changed to 3.1417, but I understand that it has been changed again.

A. W. M.
Port Matilda, Pennsylvania

◆ ◆ ◆

Dear Marilyn:
Please tell me why "C" is the third letter of the alphabet. I think "D" is a better choice. How about you?

M. R.
Altoona, Pennsylvania

Well, I've always like "E" a lot, myself. But that's just a personal opinion, you know.

◆ ◆ ◆

Dear Marilyn:

I am a foreign-born person trying to learn the English language. Can you please explain to me why Americans would say "tearing a piece of paper *up*"? Whenever I tear paper, it would always seem like I am tearing it *down*, not *up*.

R. T.
Houston, Texas

♦ ♦ ♦

Dear Marilyn:

What does a woman want?

S. M.
South Plainfield, New Jersey

♦ ♦ ♦

Dear Marilyn:

I would like to help with the volume of mail you are not able to answer personally. Please forward them to me. Thanks.

L. R.
Desloge, Missouri

Don't tempt me!

Do you have a question?
Send it to:

ASK MARILYN VOS SAVANT
Ansonia Station
Post Office Box 967
New York, New York 10023

Because of the volume of mail received, we regret that personal replies will not be possible.

A Profile of "Ask Marilyn" Readers

There are two ways to describe the readers who write to "Ask Marilyn." One is to use the demographic data favored by market researchers: 70% are male, and 30% are female. Twenty percent of all correspondents write to voice their thoughts on a previous column, another 20% send a mathematical question or brainteasing puzzle, still another 10% send questions on everyday life, and the remaining 50% write with questions ranging from the philosophical to the mundane, from the frankly emotional to the richly funny.

But I'm not a market researcher, and that's not the way I'd choose to profile my readers. I don't see them as faceless numbers, you see. After reading tens of thousands of letters myself, I see them as individual people, with personal circumstances as colorful and diverse as the questions they ask.

I've been asked to settle disputes among family members, friends, co-workers, professional colleagues, and prisoners, and I've been sent letters, drawings, papers, pamphlets, and entire books of explanation. I've read abstracts and articles from scientists who've written both to and *about* me, and I've read wrinkled letters of anguish from troubled men and women who feel they have nowhere else to turn. And I've read letter after letter from folks who just love to do a little thinking on Sunday morning.

"Ask Marilyn" seems to appeal to the "thinking" American, and there are plenty of them in every state. And even readers who write scathing criticism of an answer seldom fail to add "P.S. I love your column." And then there are the people who write repeatedly. One fellow—a real charmer—was sending us so many letters (nearly every day for a while) that we sent him a rubber stamp with our address to help him avoid writers' cramp!

Although I get my share of grandiose questions, the vast majority of letters illustrate a profile: most of my readers are intelligent and curious and sometimes just a little bewildered about life in late twentieth-century America. Day-to-day living is becoming exponentially complex, and no one can comprehend it all. We can be experts in no more than one or two areas, and usually not even that. It can take all our time just to make a decent living and/or take care of the kids. And some of the questions are amusing in their simplicity, but they have a certain charm that's not lost on me. I have a rare opportunity to view human nature here, and I appreciate it enormously.

There has also been a steady trickle of marriage proposals over the years and suggestions that I run for public office, both of which I take to be the highest compliment. But I'm already married, of course, and I'm already in a position of influence, a position I do not take lightly. After all, I provide millions of readers with the opportunity to know a little more today than they did yesterday, making them think as well as smile on a Sunday morning. What world leader can make that claim? I'm a lucky lady, all right—no doubt about it.

About the Author

———————◆———————

Marilyn vos Savant was born in St. Louis, Missouri, in 1946, the daughter of Mary vos Savant and Joseph Mach, and granddaughter of Mary Savant and Joseph vos Savant and Anna Moravec and Anton Mach. She is married to Robert Jarvik, M.D., inventor of the Jarvik-7 artificial heart, and has a daughter who is a physician and a son in medical school.

Vos Savant was listed in the *Guinness Book of World Records* for five years under "Highest I.Q." and has now been inducted into the Guinness Hall of Fame. She spends much of her time writing and additional time with her husband in artificial heart research. Her special concerns are quality education and quality thinking in America; special interests are humanitarian medicine.

She has published short stories, essays, and political satire in magazines and newspapers, and a stage play called *It Was Poppa's Will* was recently produced. Works in progress include a futuristic political fantasy called *The New Patriot*, a collection of humorous short stories called *Short Shorts,* and a satirical rewriting of a dozen classical civilizations in history called *The Re-Creation.*

Far from the stereotype of the intellectual, vos Savant says she believes that "an ounce of sequins is worth a pound of home cooking," and doesn't engage in the latter "for humanitarian reasons." Her hobby is writing letters to friends around the world.

Modified
Diagram
for
page 238.

Mindy

Jim

Mel

Joan

Barry

Joe

Marie

boy

Judy

Sol

Jack

Marty

Barb

girl

Jan

Eva

John

Ben

Mary

Sandy

Mike

Jane

Bonnie

Mindy

| 1 person | 2 people | 4 people | 6 people | The 8 original people |